AQUINAS ON DIVINE TRUTH

VERITAS DIVINA
Aquinas on Divine Truth

Some Philosophy of Religion

Joseph Bobik

ST. AUGUSTINE'S PRESS
South Bend, Indiana
2001

Library of Congress Cataloging in Publication Data
Bobik, Joseph, 1927–
    Veritas divine : Aquinas on divine truth : some philosophy of religion /
    by Joseph Bobik.
        p. cm.
    Includes bibliographical references and index.
    ISBN 1-890318-93-0 (alk. paper)
    1. Thomas, Aquinas, Saint, 1225?–1274. 2. Theology, Doctrinal.
    I. Title
    B765.T5 B63 2000
    230'.2'092 – dc21   00-045719

∞ *The paper used in this publication meets the minimum requirements of the American National Standard for Information Sciences – Permanence of Paper for Printed Materials, ANSI Z39.48-1984.*

To Teresa

CONTENTS

CHAPTER EIGHT
The Resurrection

CHAPTER NINE
The Eucharist

CHAPTER TEN

The Last Things: Death and Purgatory

CHAPTER ELEVEN

The Last Things: Heaven and Hell

PREFACE

The **plan** of this book -- its arrangement, the ordering of its topics -- is a simple one. The word "religion" can be used to refer to a certain sort of **relation**, a very complex relation, basically intellectual (knowing) and volitional (loving), between man and God. This is explained in the Introduction, the main task of which is to answer the question: **What is philosophy of religion? Revelation,** man's **religious experience** of revelation, and the **religious faith** to which such experience gives rise (considered in Chapter one) are but **three** of the many aspects of this **complex relation**. The word "religion" can also be used to designate a certain sort of **virtue,** a moral virtue which is a kind of justice toward God (as explained in Chapter two). Justice toward God manifests itself in **prayer** (Chapter three), among other things. The God to Whom we pray is a **Trinity** of persons (Chapter four). God loves Himself, and us, with a limitless love; His love for Himself and for us is a kind of **friendship** (Chapter five), which moves Him, in the person of the Son, to the **Incarnation** (Chapter six). This enables Him to undergo **pain and suffering** (Chapter seven), and death, after which comes His **resurrection,** from which comes **our** resurrection (Chapter eight). His love and friendship moves Him, further, to give us the **Eucharist** (Chapter nine), the gift by which He helps us through life, and then through **death and purgatory** (Chapter ten); then brings us to **heaven** and keeps us out of **hell** (Chapter eleven).

The **aim** of this book, like its plan, is also a simple one, i.e., to do some **philosophy of religion**. It takes as its point of departure what Aquinas calls divine truth **(veritas divina),** i.e., the collection of truths revealed to man by God. And it tries **to make as clear as possible** what Aquinas says about **some** of these revealed truths. Then it **agrees or disagrees** with what he says, as needed, for reasons of various sorts, whether philosophical, theological, scientific, historical, etc. -- of whatever sort, just so long as they are relevant and cogent; to do these things as well as possible, **if only in a small way -- pro nostro modulo,** as Aquinas puts it.[1] **Veritas divina** includes not only certain truths which are **attainable** by natural reason, like truths about certain aspects of the virtue of religion, of prayer, of pain and suffering, of friendship, of death; but also certain truths which are **not** attainable by natural reason, like truths about the Trinity, the Incarnation, the Eucharist, Purgatory, Heaven, Hell.

The Introduction is an attempt to answer two questions.   1) How would Aquinas have answered the question: What is philosophy of religion?, **if he had lived in the twentieth century?**   2) How would he have answered that question, **if he had taken it up for explicit consideration when he actually did live,** in the thirteenth?

Chapter one begins with a reflection on three **religious experiences:** 1) that of St. Peter as he responds to Jesus' question, "But who do **you** say that I am?,"   2) that of Moses at the burning bush, and 3) that of Saul on his way to Damascus -- as a kind of background to a consideration of some of the things which Aquinas says about the nature of **revelation,** of **religious experience,** and of the **religious faith** to which religious experience gives rise.

Chapter two takes a look at some of the things which Aquinas says about religion **as a virtue,** as a kind justice, a kind of disposition which inclines us to extol God's excellence and to declare our subjection to Him. This complements what the Introduction has to say about religion **as a relation.**

Chapter three considers some of the things which Aquinas says about **prayer,** one of the interior acts in which the virtue of religion manifests itself. As Aquinas sees it, prayer is an act of the practical intellect; it is a kind of

---

1   Describing what he intends to do as the author of the *Summa Contra Gentiles,* Aquinas writes :   Assumpta igitur ex divina pietate fiducia sapientis officium prosequendi, quamvis proprias vires excedat, propositum nostrae intentionis est veritatem quam fides Catholica profitetur, **pro nostro modulo** manifestare, errores eliminando contrarios, . . . (*C.G.,* I, cap. 2, in medio).

active or efficient cause; it has certain desirable effects, like merit, spiritual refreshment, and impetration. This chapter ends with a brief consideration of Aquinas' reflections on the seven petitions of the Lord's Prayer, which, he notes, is the most perfect of prayers.

Chapter four is concerned with some of the things which Aquinas says about the **Trinity,** about the Triune God, to Whom the virtue of religion inclines us to render His due, and to Whom our prayers are said in order to obtain those things which He has ordained will take place **only** if we pray for them. In this Triune God, there are two processions, four relations, three persons, five notions. Aquinas does a remarkable job of showing that the truths which God has revealed about the Trinity are both **intelligible** and **possible** (or at least **not** impossible).

Chapter five turns to reflect on some of the things which Aquinas says about **friendship:** about man's **friendship** with other men **(amicitia),** and about man's **friendship** with God **(caritas);** with a view to clarifying, if only in a beginning way, God's **friendship** with Himself, and the **friendship** which each divine person has with the other two.

Chapter six focuses on some of the things which Aquinas says about the **Incarnation.** The Triune God, the limitlessly friendly God, Who is His own best friend, and each created person's best friend as well, has taken steps to elevate man to a higher level of life, i.e., to make it possible for man, while remaining man, to become divine -- by the gift of grace. But, not only that. In the person of the Son, God decided to share with man man's humbler level of life. He chose, while remaining God, to become a man. He chose His Incarnation. He wanted thereby to show the depths of His love, to be able to do what He **as God** could **not** do, i.e., to lay down His life (His **human** life) for His friends. Aquinas' reflections on the Incarnation make remarkably clear what it means to say that Christ is truly man and truly God; what it means to say that just as in the mystery of the Trinity there is *more than one* **person** subsisting in *but one* **nature,** so in the mystery of the Incarnation there is *but one* **person** subsisting in *more than one* **nature.**

Chapter seven turns to consider some of the things which Aquinas says about **pain and suffering** -- not only that of man, but that of God as well. God, as Incarnate in the person of the Son, suffered and died in His human nature. But, God suffers in His divine nature as well, infinitely intensely, and eternally; and precisely because God loves. Love and suffering go together. **Infinite** love and **infinite** suffering go together. This chapter concludes with a consideration of Aquinas' view on the compatibility between God's infinite goodness, on the one hand, and the pain and suffering of man, on the other.

Chapter eight is concerned with some of the things which Aquinas says about **resurrection from the dead** -- the resurrection of the Incarnate God, and the resurrection of man. He points out that, although the body perishes because of death, the soul does not; and neither does divinity. Death does not touch the soul. Death does not touch divinity. So that the resurrection of the Incarnate God is the resurrectioon of His **body,** just as the resurrection of man is the resurrection of **his** body -- both, of course, by the power of God.

Chapter nine turns to reflect on some of the things which Aquinas says about the mystery of the **Eucharist,** i.e., about the **change or conversion** in which bread and wine become the body and the blood of Christ. The main task of the philosophy of religion, here, is to show **that,** and **how,** such a change is **both** intelligible **and** possible (or at least **not** impossible). Aquinas does an admirable job with respect to both. He shows that such a change is **intelligible** by reflecting carefully on the fact of change in the **physical** world, and by pointing out wherein it is **like** physcial change, and wherein it is **unlike** physical change. He shows that such a change is **possible,** or at least **not** impossible, by removing the objections which some use to point out what they take to be inner contradictions in claims about the Eucharist. This chapter concludes with some comments on Aquinas' simple, but elegant meditation, the **Adoro te devote,** a poem in which one can see quite clearly certain aspects of his theology of the Eucharist, i.e., of the ever present, but ever hidden God.

Chapter ten turns to some of the things which Aquinas says about **death and purgatory.** The main concern of this chapter is to reflect on the answers which Aquinas gives to the following questions. What exactly is death? Is there a purgatory? What exactly is purgatory? In what does its pain and suffering and cleansing consist?

Chapter eleven, the last chapter, turns to some of the things which Aquinas says about **heaven and hell.** Its main concern is to consider the answers which Aquinas gives to the following questions. What exactly is hell? In what does its pain and suffering and wretchedness consist? Is there a hell? What exactly is heaven? In what does its happiness consist? Is there a heaven?

From **revelation** (through **religious experience,** and the **faith** to which religious experience gives rise) to purgatory, from purgatory to heaven -- by way of prayer, Trinity, friendship, Incarnation, pain and suffering, resurrection, Eucharist, and death; and if not to purgatory and heaven, then to hell. **Philosophical** reflection on these topics (which, taken together, provide a kind of summary of what is most important in the life of a believer) is difficult. But along with, as conjoined to, **theological** and **scientific** reflection (neither of which, however, is to be pursued in this book) on these same topics; philosophical reflection is most desirable, most fulfilling, and above all most human.

*   *   *

For the good things in this book, I thank the **countless** many who touched my thoughts over the years, and thereby made them better.

I thank James Langford, too, retired director of the Notre Dame Press, for suggesting to Bruce Fingerhut, director of St. Augustine's Press, that he publish *Aquinas on Divine Truth;* and Ralph McInerny for encouraging Bruce to act on that suggestion. I thank Bruce for his kindness and encouragement, but especially for his patience in the last weeks before publication. I thank Kirk Besmer, who took time out from work on his doctoral dissertation, to prepare the index; and for doing it so quickly and discerningly. Wendy McMillen, too, for some final page adjustments.

And I thank Teresa, my wife of many years, and my best friend in all the world, for being so selflessly understanding and quietly encouraging. But especially for being so patient in her continuing role as writer's widow.

INTRODUCTION

WHAT IS PHILOSOPHY OF RELIGION ?

IF ST. THOMAS AQUINAS HAD LIVED IN THE TWENTIETH CENTURY --
1925-1974 instead of 1225-1274 -- how would he have replied to the question:
What is philosophy of religion? Very likely as follows. Philosophy of
religion is an attempt to get a certain sort of answer, i.e., a **philosophical** one,
for the question: What is religion?. A philosophical answer, as different from
a **theological** one, on the one hand, and as different from a **scientific** one, on
the other hand.

Having given this brief reply, Aquinas would move on to clarify its
meaning. What this means, he would note, can be made clear by doing two
things: 1) by proposing an initial identifying description of what religion is,
i.e., a beginning way to pick out religion from among other possible objects of
study;   and 2) by showing how a **philosophical** study of religion, once picked
out in a beginning way, differs from a **theological** study of it, on the one hand,
and from a **scientific** study of it, on the other hand.   Thus, Aquinas would
point out, philosophy of religion is one thing, theology of religion is another,
and the sciences of religion -- studies like anthropology of religion, sociology
of religion, psychology of religion -- still another.

What is religion? An initial identifying description,
with some important questions

Before one can study something, whether philosophically or theologically
or scientifically, one must be able to pick it out from among other possible
objects of study. For example, before one can study **trees** in a scientific
biological way, one must be able to identify them in some way, pick them out

in some way. It wouldn't do to apply one's biological methods to bricks or stones, silver or gold, and hope thereby to come up with a scientific biological account of the nature of trees. One has to know in some way, however imperfect it may be, what a tree is. One must be able to identify a tree as, for example, a living thing with roots and trunk and limbs and foliage. That would suffice to pick it out from among other things.

A simple, but useful, initial identifying description of what religion is, Aquinas would suggest, is the following. **Religion is a certain sort of relation, basically intellectual (knowing) and volitional (loving), between man and God.** Both man and God are persons, and as persons they are capable of knowing and loving.

The relation which religion is, is a very complex one, Aquinas would continue, a relation with many aspects. For example, God is said to have revealed Himself to man. Revelation, then, is one aspect of the complex relation which religion is, an aspect originating from the side of God and terminating in man. And so, the question: What is the nature of revelation?, would be, for Aquinas, a very important question about the nature of religion. Not only has God revealed Himself to man, but man (at least certain men, e.g., some of the prophets) has had a religious experience of God revealing Himself. Religious experience, thus, is another aspect of the complex relation which religion is, an aspect originating from the side of man and terminating in God. And so, the question: What is the nature of religious experience?, would be, for Aquinas, another important question about the nature of religion. Having experienced God's revelation, man responds by having faith in God, or by believing in God. And so, another aspect of this complex relation, and another important question about the nature of religion: What is the nature of religious faith or belief? Man also responds by loving God. And by worshipping God, by praying to God, by performing all sorts of religious acts. And so, still other aspects of this complex relation, and still other questions: What is the nature of man's love for God? What is the nature of worship, of prayer, of the other sorts of religious acts which man performs? Further, from the side of God, God is said to love man. What, then, is the nature of God's love for man? Moreover, since friendship is said to be a kind of love, and since man and God love one another; it has been asked whether this reciprocal love is (or can be said to be) a kind of friendship. If it is, or can be, then what kind? From the side of God again, God is said to have performed miracles, for various reasons. What, then, is a miracle? What are the reasons for their having been performed by God?

Quite clearly, Aquinas would note at this point, one cannot understand the nature of a relation (however simple or complex) between two terms, without trying to learn something, however little, about the nature of each of the terms related. And so, two further questions arise immediately, Aquinas would note: 1) What is man?, and 2) What is God?. The question: What is man?, would become, for the philosophy of religion, Aquinas would note, primarily the question: Is man such by nature that he (or some part of him, say his soul or mind) survives death, and is immortal? Coming to know **what God is,** is considerably more difficult and complicated, Aquinas would point out, than coming to know **what man is.** For whereas it is quite obvious that man exists, it is not at all obvious that God exists. And it does not make good sense to ask about a thing: What is it?, unless one knows that the thing exists. For, in asking about a thing: What is it?, one is asking, Aquinas would point out, for an account of those properties or qualitites or ingredients, **intrinsic** to that thing, which account for the thing's existence; one is asking for an account of the **essence** of that thing (the **quid est** of the thing, its **quid rei**). And so, before one can meaningfully ask: What is God?, Aquinas would point out, one must have an **affirmative** answer to the question: Is there a God (the **an est**)?. And this in turn, he would note, raises another question still, namely: What does the word "God" mean (the **quid est quod dicitur**)?. For, until one becomes clear on what the word "God" means, one will not be able to tell what counts as evidence **for,** and what counts as evidence **against,** God's existence.

Philosophy, theology and the sciences

Philosophy, theology and the sciences share the same goal, namely, to decide what's true and what's false about whatever they investigate; and, at times, they might well be investigating the same thing, e.g., man. But each does this in a different way. Theology, in the view of Aquinas, decides what's true and what's false by appealing to a revealing authority. To appeal to an **authority** is to appeal to an **intelligent being other than oneself** for a decision with respect to truth or falsity. To make such an appeal is to admit that one does not know **whether** something is true or false, or **why**; but that he has good reason to believe that the authority does. To appeal to a **revealing authority** is to appeal to an intelligence greater than man's; in the Christian tradition, Aquinas would note, this intelligence is the Divine Intelligence, as manifested in the Bible, the **written** record of revelation, and in Tradition, the **spoken** record of revelation. The special function of God's revealing authority is to tell man things which man (whether **one** man **alone**, or **all** men **in concert**) could **never** come to know **by his own natural knowing powers.** To be sure, God has told man things which man could come to know on his own, though with difficulty and with admixture of error. Theology proceeds in effect as follows. It says that such and such is true or false, because God (or the Bible, or Tradition) has said so, and God ought to know; for God is believed to know everything, and to be absolutely truthful. More correctly put, theology says that such and such is true, or false, because God **is said** to have said so -- **is said,** by certain privileged humans, e.g., Moses, Matthew, Mark, Luke, John.

Philosophy and the sciences, both -- Aquinas would continue -- decide what's true and what's false by appealing only to man's natural knowing capacities (or methods), never to a revealing authority, never to any sort of authority at all. These natural knowing capacities are three in number. There is, first, our **sense-observational** capacity, which is obviously the appropriate one to employ when trying to decide what's true and what's false about things (sense-perceivable individuals) in the public sensible world -- i.e., about MATTER, and its states and activities. To use this capacity requires two things: a) knowing the **meanings** of the words (terms, symbols) in the statement being considered, and b) appealing to the appropriate sense -- sight, hearing, etc. Secondly, there is our **analytic** capacity, which is obviously the appropriate one to use when trying to decide what's true and what's false about things (concepts) in the public intelligible world -- i.e., about IDEAS and their interconnections. To use this capacity requires knowing the **meanings** of the terms in the statement being considered; and **only** that. That is, there is no need (indeed, it would be irrelevant) to appeal to any of the senses. Thirdly, there is our **introspective** capacity, which is obviously the one to use when trying to decide what's true and what's false about things (mental) in the private introspectable world -- i.e., our MINDS, and their states and activites. To use this capacity requires two things: a) knowing the **meanings** of the terms in the statement being considered, and b) appealing to an introspective experience (i.e., to an inward look into our minds, and what is going on in them).

But philosophy and the sciences use man's natural knowing capacities differently. The sciences use our **sense-observational** capacities **as strengthened,** enhanced, refined, sophisticated by controlled experiments, observational instruments, measuring instruments, hypothetico-deductive procedures; in a word, **by scientific method.** -- [Aquinas would have in mind at this point the **physical** sciences, i.e., those which are by intention restricted to investigating the public sensible world, the world of MATTER, in particular **Physics,** the best of our contemporary sciences; and **not** the analytic sciences, i.e., **Mathematics** and **Logic,** which investigate certain parts of the public intelligible world, i.e., certain sorts of IDEAS and their interconnections; **nor** the psychological sciences, which investigate the private introspectable world, the world of MIND]. -- In appealing to hypothetico-decuctive procedures, the sciences use **analysis** to make deductions (predictions) about what else ought to be true about MATTER, but only to return to **sense observation** (strenghtened by scientific method, wherever appropriate and possible) to determine whether the deductions are true or false. And so, the method of the physical sciences begins and ends in **sense observation,** using analysis in between. Philosophy, on the other hand -- as it faces the task of studying the public sensible world, the world of MATTER, though it is **not** restricted to investigating just that world (just as the sciences **in toto** are **not** so restricted) -- does **not** appeal to scientific method. Whereas the physical sciences strive for truths about the world of MATTER which cannot be obtained except by employing scientific method, physical philosophy seeks those truths which can be obtained without using that method. Whereas the intention of the physical sciences is to get **precise quantitative** (i.e., mathematically expressed) knowledge wherever possible (but accepting **precise** qualitative knowledge, when the quantitative sort is not forthcoming); the intention of physical philosophy is to get **precise qualitative** knowledge, and only such as can be obtained without using scientific method. Physical philosophy does, however, use hypothetico-deductive procedures, making deductions (using the method of analysis) from **precise qualitative** hypotheses, then returning to sense observation to determine whether the deductions are true or false.

And so, Aquinas would summarize and clarify, if the revealing authority of God, as this comes to us in the Bible or in Tradition, tells us anything about the nature of revelation, of religious experience, of religious faith, of love, of worship, of prayer, of miracles, of man and immortality, of God, etc., to gather these things together is to produce a **theology** of religion. If controlled experiments, observational instruments, measuring instruments, hypothetico-deduction -- as aids to, as sophistications or extensions of, sense observation (with respect to the world of MATTER) and introspection (with respect to the world of MIND) -- can tell us anything about the nature of revelation, of religious experience, etc., to gather these things together is to give rise to a **science(s)** of religion. And if our natural knowing capacities -- sensory, analytic, and introspective -- without using controlled experiments, observational instruments, measuring instruments; and without appeal to revelation (i.e., God's revealing authority) can tell us anything about the nature of revelation, of religious experience, etc., to gather these things together is to generate a **philosophy** of religion.

Philosophy and pre-philosohical knowledge

At this point, Aquinas might add a few thoughts concerning the difference between philosophy and pre-philosophical knowledge. For this would serve to make a bit clearer what philosophy of religion is.

Human beings, normally functioning human beings, know many things that are true and many things that are false; and very often even know the reasons why the true things are true and the false ones are false, about religion and its many aspects, about man and God, about poetry and novels, about laws and justice, about education and friendship, about presidents and cabinet members, about whatever -- just because they are normally functioning human beings. And **before** they begin to do philosophy; indeed, even before they've heard of the **word** "philosophy." Such knowledge is **pre-**philosophical knowledge, i.e., knowledge acquired **temporally before** acquiring any philosophical knowledge at all.

Having pointed this out, Aquinas would move on to clarify it. Just because a human being has functioning sensory capacities, he learns and knows many things about the world of MATTER. Just beacuse he has a functioning analytic capacity, he learns and knows many things about the world of IDEAS. Just because he has a functioning introspective capacity, he learns and knows many things about the world of MIND. But there is more to being a human being, Aquinas would continue, than having the three natural knowing capacities, by which he learns and knows things **for himself** (as opposed to **by an appeal to authority**). To be a human being is also to be a **social** being, to live in the company of other humans -- one's father, mother, brothers, friends, countrymen, etc., and to accept many things as true and as false on the **authority** of these others. To be a human being is also to be a **temporal** being, to live at some given time in history, and to accept many things as true and as false on the **authority** of those who have lived in an earlier time. Just living at a given time has an important effect on **what** and **how much** a human being knows -- **before** he begins to do philosophy. Those, for example, who came on the scene **after** the writing of the New Testament knew (or know) things about God, e.g., that God is Three in One, and that Jesus Christ is God Incarnate, unknown to those who lived **before**. And those who came on the scene **after** the advent of our modern sciences (say, during the past 350 to 400 years) knew (or know) things about the public sensible world, e.g., the laws of motion from Newton, special and general relativity from Eisnstein, unknown to those who lived **before**. So long as this knowledge remains **unexamined** for a given individual, Aquinas would note, it remains at the pre-philosophical level. As soon as the individual becomes **aware** of it, and begins thereupon to **examine** it (in the special way to be outlined just below), he begins thereby to do philosophy.

What is meant by the examination which raises pre-philosophical knowledge to the philosophical level can be made clear, Aquinas would explain, by considering an example. Two individuals, A and B, are discoursing as follows. A asks B, "Do you think it is true that there is a God?" B replies, "Of couse I do." A asks further, "What is (are) your reason(s) for thinking it's true that there is a God?" B offers, "The obvious orderliness in the world around us requires that there be an Intelligent Orderer, and that's what I take God to be." The discussion so far has proceeded at the pre-philosophical level. Then A asks B, "But what kind of reason is that?" This question is asking, Aquinas would expand, "Is it a reason you discover by looking at the public sensible world, by listening to it, by smelling, tasting, touching it; i.e., is it a reason based on the method of **sense observation**? Or, is it a reason you discover in a way which is like discovering why the Pythagorean Theorem is true, i.e., is it a reason based on the method of **analysis**? Or, is it a reason you discover by looking inwardly into your mental states and activities, i.e., is it a reason based on the method of **introspection**? Or, is it a reason based on some conjunction of methods?" To ask the question: But what kind of reason is that?, is to have become **aware** of, i.e., **to have been struck in a particularly forceful way by**, the fact **that there is a reason**, thereby both giving rise to a desire, and putting oneself into a position, to begin to examine that reason, i.e., to **begin** to do philosophy.

And so, Aquinas would emphasize, one important task for philosophical examination is the **explicit** identification of the method(s) which someone -- you or another -- has used to claim that a given statement is true. And this, in order to determine what **kind** of truth the statement has -- **if** it **is** true (it might be false). The method of sense observation, Aquinas would add, yields one kind of truth, a rather weak kind of truth; the method of introspection yields another kind of truth, a stronger kind, at least at times; and the method of analysis yields still another kind of truth, the strongest kind. But, the statement might be false; humans can make mistakes. And so, Aquinas would add here, philosophical examination turns to devise objections to the **claimed truth** of the statement being considered, and to study objections already in existence. Moreover, Aquinas would continue, a philosophical examination ought to make clear the **meaning** of the ideas in the statement being studied; for without doing this, one could not ask intelligently whether the statement is true or false. How intelligent would it be to say, "I'm going to try to decide whether this statement is true or false, but I have absolutely no understanding of what it means"? At times, it might also be helpful, even necessary, to check the ideas for intelligibility and for possibility. Finally, if there is need for an **argument** in order to come to a decision with respect to the truth or falsity of a statement (sometimes there **is** need, as in the case of the statement: **There is a God**; sometimes there is **not**, as in the case of the statement: **This tomato is green**), philosophy ought to examine the argument for its **logical correctness**. And so, there are three concerns in philosophical examination: 1) a concern with the **truth** of statements, 2) a concern with the **clarity** (and intelligibility, and possibility, when needed) of ideas, and 3) a concern with the **logical correctness** of arguments.

And of course, Aquinas would point out, when philosophy turns to study religion -- that complex knowing and loving relation between man and God, that relation with a multiplicity of aspects some of which originate in God and terminate in man, others of which originate in man and terminate in God -- when philosophy turns to examine what the normally functioning human being already knows about religion at the pre-philosophical level, as well as what such a human knows about the two terms of this relation, i.e., man and God; philosophy has the same three tasks: 1) a concern with the **truth** of statements about man and God, and about the many aspects of the relation, 2) a concern with the **clarity** (and intelligibility and possibility, when needed) of the ideas which function in these statements, and 3) a concern with the **logical correctness** of the arguments which are put forward, if and when they are needed, in support of these statements.

Theological and scientific examination

To ask the question: But what kind of reason is that?, can also initiate a **theological** examination, i.e., an examination in which one appeals to God's revealing authority as an aid to sense observation, introspection and analysis.

What is meant by theological examining can be made clear by an example. Consider two individuals, A and B, discoursing as follows. A asks B, "Do you think it's true that there are three persons in one God: the Father, the Son, and the Holy Spirit?" B replies, "Indeed I do." A asks further, "What is (are) your reason(s) for thinking it's true that there are three persons in one God?" B offers, "God Himself has said that it's true." The discussion so far has been at a level which is both pre-philosophical and pre-theological. Then A asks B, "But what kind of reason is that?" And this question moves the discussion to two other levels: 1) to the philosophical level, where one is concerned to come to understand the nature of the method of theology, and 2) to the theological level, where one is concerned to identify that in Scripture and/or in Tradition which leads one to accept as true the claim that there are three persons in one God.

To ask the question: But what kind of reason is that?, can also initiate a **scientific** examination, i.e., an examination in which one appeals to scientific experiments and/or instruments as aids to sense observation, introspection and analysis. What is meant by scientific examining can also be made clear by an example. Consider two individuals, A and B, discoursing as follows. A asks B, "Do you think it's true that there is a planet, called Neptune, just beyond the planet called Uranus?" B replies, "Indeed I do." A asks further, "What is (are) your reason(s) for thinking it's true that there is a planet, called Neptune, just beyond the planet called Uranus?" B offers, "It was sighted by telescope in 1846, on the basis of mathematical calculations based on certain perturbations in the orbit of Uranus." The discussion so far has been at a level which is both pre-philosophical and pre-scientific. Then A asks B, "But what kind of reason is that?" And this question moves the discussion to two other levels: 1) to the philosophical level, where one is concerned to come to understand the nature of the method of the sciences, and 2) to the scientific level, where one is concerned a) to do for himself the mathematical calculations based on certain perturbations in the orbit of Uranus, and b) to use these calculations as a guide to the sighting of Neptune by telescope for himself.

The man of wisdom

What has preceded in this introduction was an attempt, one will recall, to answer the question: "How would Aquinas have answered the question: What is philosophy of religion?, **if he had lived in the twentieth century?"** What follows is just a bit different. It is an attempt to answer the question: "How would Aquinas have answered the question: What is philosophy of religion?, **if he had taken it up for explicit consideration when he actually did live,** i.e., back there in the thirteenth century?" What follows, it is hoped, will add to, and clarify in a helpful way, what has preceded.

Aquinas would have begun his answer, quite surely, by considering the **man of wisdom,** as he did in the opening chapters of his *Summa Contra Gentiles,* which appears to be, in effect, **a kind (but only a kind)** of treatise in the philosophy of **religion,**[1] i.e., a philosophical treatise which makes **religion** the subject matter of its investigations. The task of the man of wisdom, Aquinas would have said, is to direct things to their appropriate ends. And since there are many sorts of ends, there are also many sorts of men of wisdom. The medical doctor is a wise man of one sort; the military general, a wise man of another sort; the shipbuilder, a wise man of still another sort. But none of these is **simply** a wise man, i.e., a wise man **without qualification;** each is a wise man of a given sort, i.e., with respect to truth in some given limited area. The metaphysician, however, is a wise man without qualification, for his concerns with truth range over **all that there is;** his concerns are not limited to some one given realm of things. Like the metaphysician, **the philosopher of**

---

[1] It becomes quite clear from its opening chapters that the *Summa Contra Gentiles* is about **divine truth,** the truth **revealed** to man by God, the **truth which the Catholic faith professes,** "[veritas] quam fides Catholica profitetur." (*C.G.,* I, cap. 2, in medio). And toward the end of chapter one, Aquinas makes it quite clear that there is some sort of connection between **divine truth** and **religion,** pointing out that the business (task, duty) of the wise man -- **sapientis officium** -- is twofold: 1) to study, to meditate on, to clarify **divine truth,** and thereupon to proclaim it;   2) to assail the **errors** which men have made with respect to divine truth, to assail the falsity which they have accepted, a falsity which, he adds explicitly, "is contrary to **religion,"** (quae **religioni** contraria est), suggesting thereby either 1) that he is taking **religion** here to be the **same thing** as **divine truth,** or 2) that he is referring to his view, expressed elsewhere, that religion, though not the same thing as divine truth, is nonetheless connected with divine truth, inasmuch as **religion** is a **virtue** which inclines one **to accept, and to live by, divine truth.** For some details on religion **as a virtue,** see below, chapter one.

religion, too, Aquinas would have continued, is a wise man without qualification. For, his concerns with truth, like those of the metaphysician, range over **all that there is.** But, unlike the metaphysicain, the philosopher of religion is concerned with truths of a very special sort, i.e., **revealed truths,** truths given to man by God Himself, some of them being truths which men, left to their natural powers, could never have attained; others of them being truths which, though attainable by man, are attainable only by a very few, with great difficulty, with the expenditure of much time and effort, and with a considerable admixture of error.[2]

Now, just as the medical doctor strives **to bring about** health, as well as **to eliminate** its opposite, i.e., sickness; just as the military general strives **to achieve** victory, as well as **to avoid** its opposite, defeat; and the shipbuilder, **to produce** a seaworthy ship, as well as **to avoid** its opposite, i.e., a ship which would sink in the mildest of bad weather; so, too, the philosopher of religion seeks **to gather together** all the truths, both attainable and unattainable by man's natural knowing powers, which God has revealed about all that there is, to clarify their meaning, to defend them against objections; as well as **to eliminate** whatever falsity men may have brought to their interpretation and understanding of these truths.

The task of the philosopher of religion, thus, is twofold: 1) to meditate on the truths which God has revealed about all that there is (on **all** of them -- both the truths which are **attainable** by man's natural knowing powers and those which are **not**), to clarify them, to defend them, to demonstrate those which are demonstrable,[3] and thereupon to proclaim them; 2) to fight against the errors which men, by their natural frailty and weakness, have committed against these truths, especially (though not only) against those which are **not**

---

[2] *S.T.,* I, q.1, a.1, c.; *C.G.,* I, cap. 4.

[3] *C.G.,* I, cap. 9, in princ.: "Ad primae igitur veritatis manifestationem [i.e., truths attainable by human reason, like the **existence** of God, and the **oneness** of God], per rationes demonstrativas quibus adversarius convinci possit, procedendum est." *C.G.,* I, cap. 3, in princ.: "Quaedam . . . [vera] sunt ad quae. . . ratio naturalis pertingere potest, sicut est Deum esse, Deum esse unm, et alia huiusmodi, quae etiam philosophi demonstrative de Deo probaverunt, ducti naturalis lumine rationis."

demonstrable by human reason, by showing wherein their thinking has gone astray.[4]

As an aid in this task, Aquinas would very likely add, the philosopher of religion should take into account the things which he has in common, if any, with those[5] against whose objections and errors he will try to argue. Do they accept the Old Testament, as the Jews do? Then he can argue against their objections and errors by appealing to the authority of the Old Testament, in addtion to appealing to man's natural knowing powers. Do they accept the New Testament, as the heretics do? He can argue against their objections and errors by appealing to the authority of what is written therein, in additon to using man's natural intellectual powers. Do they accept a Tradition, i.e., some orally transmitted revelations from God, as the Jews and the heretics do? He can appeal to that Tradition, in additon to employing the natural powers of the human mind. Do they accept none of these, as is the case with the Mohammadans; with atheists, too, and heathens, and pagans? Here, he must turn to use man's natural knowing and reasoning powers **alone,** though these powers are weak and defective, indeed.[6]

---

[4] *C.G.,* I, cap. 9, in princ.: "Sed quia tales rationes [sc. demonstrativae] ad secundam veritatem [i.e., truths beyond the powers of human reason, like the Trinity and the Incarnation] haberi non possunt, non debet esse ad hoc intentio ut adversarius rationibus convincatur; **sed ut eius rationes quae contra veritatem habet, solvantur;** cum veritati fidei ratio naturalis contraria esse non possit . . ." *C.G.,* I, cap. 3, in princ.: "Quaedam . . . vera sunt de Deo quae omnem facultatem humanae rationis excedunt, ut Deum esse trinum et unum."

[5] These are the Gentiles of the 13-th century, who, for St. Thomas Aquinas in this treatise, are a collection of **errantes,** namely heretics, Jews, Moslems, and pagans -- **errantes** with rspect to the truth which the Catholic faith professes. For an interesting and informative discussion of the Gentiles of the XIII-th century, the Gentiles against whom St. Thomas is writing in his *Summa Contra Gentiles,* see M.-D. Chenu, O.P., *Toward Understanding Saint Thomas* (Translated from the French, with authorized corrections and bibliographical additions, by A.-M. Landry, O.P., and D. Hughes, O.P.), Chicago: Henry Regnery Company, 1964; pp. 288-292.

[6] *C.G.,* I, cap. 2, ad finem: ". . . quidam . . . , ut Mahumetistae et pagani, non conveniunt nobiscum in auctoritate alicuius Scripturae, per quam possint convinci, sicut contra Judaeos disputare possumus per Vetus Testamentum, contra haereticos per Novum. Hi vero neutrum recipiunt. Unde neccesse est ad naturalem rationem reecurere, cui omnes assentire coguntur. Quae tamen in rebus divinis deficiens est."

In whatever way he can, and to the extent that he can (however little that may be),[7] the sort of man of wisdom we find in **the philosopher of religion of the** *Contra Gentiles*[8] strives to direct men's minds **toward what is true**, and **away from what is false**[9] -- by using the Old Testament, the New Testament, a Tradition, the thoughts of theologians, of saints, of philosophers, his own thoughts, whatever works; i.e., by using the thoughts of **God** as well as the thoughts of **man**, with respect to **all the truths** which God has revealed about **all that there is,** as forcefully and convincingly as he can.

---

[7] In his own small way -- **pro nostro modulo.** See above, the Preface, p. 14, footnote 1.

[8] To be sure, the **philosopher of religion of the** *Contra Gentiles*, i.e., the **sapiens** quoad **omnes** veritates **revelatas** a Deo, becomes a **theologian** of religion at certain points in his efforts, i.e., when he appeals to the Old Testament, to the New Testament, or to Tradition (which he often does in arguing against the Jews and the heretics) in his attempts to settle questions about **truth.** Moreover, at certain points he engages in **apologetics** as well, for he does a considerable amount of **defending.** Fr. Chenu points out quite rightly, therefore, that the *Summa Contra Gentiles* "has been considered, in turn, as a **philosophical** *summa*, as an **apologetical** *summa*, as a **theological** treatise." (*Toward Understanding Saint Thomas*, p. 289). It is, in fact, all three -- not throughout, of course, but each at different points.

[9] C.G., I, cap. 2, in medio: ". . . propositum nostrae intentionis est veritatem. . . manifestare, errores eliminando contrarios. . ."

CHAPTER ONE

REVELATION, RELIGIOUS EXPERIENCE, AND FAITH

DIVINE TRUTH (VERITAS DIVINA), as noted above,[1] is the collection of truths revealed to man by God, a collection which includes **both** truths which are attainable by natural reason **and** truths which are **not.** It is God's limitless love for man which moved Him to reveal these truths, so that man's salvation might be brought about more fittingly and more surely, and with much less difficulty.[2]

This chapter is concerned with some of the things which Aquinas says about the nature of **revelation** (which originates **in God**) and the nature of **religious experience** (which takes place **in man**). The two go together. That is, the revelation made **by God** is experienced **by man.** God communicates, reveals, certain truths; man has **a religious experience** of this revealing. Not all men, to be sure. But only certain divinely chosen individuals -- prophets and apostles, like Moses of the Old Testament, and St. Peter and St. Paul of the New Testament[3] -- whose authority as receivers and bearers of His word is established, authenticated, by that same revealing God.[4]

---

1   The Preface, p.13.
2   *S.T.*, I, q. 1, a. 1.
3   *S.T.*, I, q. 1, a. 8, ad 2.
4   *S.T.*, I, q. 1, a. 2, ad 2.

God choosing and authenticating, then establishing the authority
of, the prophets and apostles as receivers and bearers
of His revelation

Flesh and blood hath not revealed it to thee,
but my Father who is in heaven

> 15 Jesus saith to them [i.e., to his disciples]: But who do you say that I am?
>
> 16 Simon Peter answered and said: Thou art Christ, the Son of the Living God.
>
> 17 And Jesus answering, said to him: Blessed art thou, Simon Bar-Jona, because flesh and blood hath not revealed it to thee, but my Father who is in heaven.
>
> 18 And I say to thee: That thou art Peter, and upon this rock I will build my church. And the gates of Hell shall not prevail against it.
>
> 19 And I will give to thee the keys of the kingdom of heaven. And whatsoever thou shalt bind upon earth, it shall be bound also in heaven; and whatsoever thou shalt loose on earth, it shall be loosed also in heaven. (*St. Matthew*, 16: 13-19)

In the gospel account, just above, of this revelation to the apostle Peter, a number of things is to be noticed. First, the revelation is made to **an apostle**, a divinely chosen human individual.   Second, the revelation is **not** made by another human individual (. . . flesh and blood hath not revealed it to thee. . . , 17), and by implication, not by any other material or physical thing either;[5] but by God Himself (. . . but my Father who is in heaven. . . , 17).

---

5   In **nature** religions, the revelation is made **by nature itself,** i.e., by material or physical things (and/or events). In some of these religions, people venerate the powers of nature, or the natural things themselves, things like the "birds or four-legged

Third, Jesus, Who along with the revealing Father is also God, **authenticates** the revelation, by stating explicitly, i.e., by **revealing,** that **a revelation** has been made -- made **by** God, made **to** man, i.e., to **this** man, Peter. Fourth, **further authentication** of the revelation is made as Jesus explicitly establishes Peter's authority as the receiver and bearer of this revelation: Peter is made the rock **(petra),** the foundation, on which the community of the people of God, the church, will be built (verse 18).   A rock which functions **not** as a kind of **passive matter** on which a superstructure rests, but rather as a kind of **active** foundation, in the sense of a founder, a founder divinely chosen and divinely empowered, chosen and empowered to bind and to loose (verses 18-19).

Going beyond this gospel account, it is to be noted, first, that revelation is possible **only if there is a God,** a God Who can do the revealing, and the accompanying authenticating.   Second, revealed propositions can be more easily accepted **as true** if one knows, i.e., **has established by natural reason,** that there is a God,[6] for God is all knowing and all truthful, never intending to

---

animals or snakes," mentioned below by St. Paul, mistakenly taking them to be God; in others, coming closer to the truth, people have reverence for the sacred (holy) which they encounter as somehow present in nature. Nature, made by God, has God's marks on it, and by means of those marks reveals in some way **that He exists,** and something about **what He is,** more clearly to some, less clearly to others. St. Paul himself, speaking about wicked and godless men, points out that they have recognized both that God exists and something about what He is, from the physical things in the midst of which they live: ". . . what can be known about God is evident to them [i.e., to the wicked and godless], because God made it evident to them.   Ever since the creation of the world, his invisible attributes of eternal power and divinity have been able to be understood and perceived in what he has made.   As a result, they have no excuse; for although they knew God, they did not accord him glory as God or give him thanks. Instead, they became vain in their reasoning, and their senseless minds were darkened. While claiming to be wise, they became fools and exchanged the glory of the immortal God for the likeness of an image of mortal man or of birds or of four-legged animals or of snakes. " (*Romans* 1: 19-23.) -- The revelation to Peter as recorded in this gospel account by St. Matthew, however, is **not** of this sort. It is rather a revelation coming **directly from God;** it is **not** a revelation made through His marks in nature.   One should note that even in very primitive times, **before** men "became vain in their resasoning ," and were still **without any thoughts of** "claiming to be wise;" it was known to human beings, more clearly to some than to others, known because of God's marks in nature, both that there is a God and something about what He is.

[6]   Inter ea. . . [per rationem naturalem investigabilia] quae de Deo **secundum se** consideranda sunt [as different from the **processus creaturarum ab ipso,** and from the **ordo creaturarum in ipsum sicut in finem**], praemittendum est, quasi totius operis necessarium fundamentum, consideratio qua demonstratur Deum esse. Quo non habito, omnis conisderatio de rebus divinis necessario tollitur. (*C.G.,* I, cap. 9, in fine).   It is

deceive, indeed incapable of deception by his very nature as God. Third, since there are many propositions which **have been revealed,** and which can also be seen to be true **by natural reason,** there is no reason, in one way of putting it, not to accept as true those **other** propostion which have been reavealed and are **not** attainable by natural reason. Or better, this is **good reason** to accept the latter propositions as true. For, if I can know **by natural reason** that **some** of the propositions revealed by God are true, this argues well for the reasonableness of the claim that **all** the propositions He has revealed are true, whether attainable by natural reason or not.

And so, **revelation** by God, man's religious **experience** of the revelation, **authentication** by God; then religious **faith or belief** in God and in the revelation, i.e., acceptance of the existence of God and of the truth of the revelation, not only by the chosen individual, but also by others, and precisely because of the established authority of the chosen one. Besides being a most precious, and much to be desired, gift from God, **faith** is also something most reasonable. It **can** spring forth (and **in fact does,** for some), at least as a **beginning** bud capable of coming to full blossom, from a knowledge of the existence of God, a knowledge (even of a pre-philosophical sort) achieved by natural and unaided human reason.

Moses at the burning bush

> **2 And the Lord appeared to him [i.e., to Moses] in a flame of fire out of the midst of a bush; and he saw that the bush was on fire and was not burnt. . . .**

> **4 . . . [the Lord] called to him out of the midst of the bush, and said: Moses, Moses. And he answered: Here I am. . . .**

> **6 . . . And he said: I am the God of thy father, the God of Abraham, the God of Isaac, and the God of Jacob. . .**

---

clear that this is why so much effort and energy is devoted, in the doing of philosophy of religion, to the attempt to demonstrate **by natural reason** that there is a God.

12 . . . I will be with thee. And this thou shalt have for a sign that I have sent thee: When thou shalt have brought my people out of Egypt, thou shalt offer sacrifice to God upon this mountain. . .

13 . . . Moses said to God: Lo, I shall go to the children of Israel, and say to them: The God of your fathers hath sent me to you. If they should say to me: What is his name? What shall I say to them?

14 God said to Moses: I AM WHOM AM. He said: Thus shalt thou say to the children of Israel: HE WHO IS hath sent me to you.

15 And God said again to Moses: Thus shalt thou say to the children of Israel: The Lord God of your fathers, the God of Abraham, the God of Isaac, and the God of Jacob, hath sent me to you. . .

1 . . . Moses answered and said: They will not believe me, nor hear my voice. But they will say: The Lord hath not appeared to thee. . .

8 . . . If they will not believe thee, saith he [i.e., the Lord], nor hear the voice of the former sign [i.e., Moses' rod turned into a serpent, then back into the rod], they will believe the word of the latter sign [i.e., Moses' hand turned leprous, then become again as it was before, healthy and whole]. . .

9 But if they will not even believe these two signs, nor hear thy voice, take. . . (*Exodus*, 3: in toto; 4: 1-17)

As in the gospel account which tells of the revelation to the apostle Peter that Jesus is Christ, the Son of the living God (above, p. 17); here, too, in this Old Testament account of Moses at the burning bush, a number of things is to be noticed. First, the revelation is made **to a prophet,** a divinely chosen human individual.   Second, the revelation is **not** made **by a human being;** nor **by nature.** Neither is it made by one person of the Trinity, the Father, and pointed out by another, the Son (which, by way of difference, is what happened in the revelation to Peter). It is made by God, indeed, but without any mention of any of the Divine Persons (quite understandably, to be sure, since this an **Old** Testament revelation). Third, a number of things is revealed: 1) that it is God Himself, the God of Abraham and Isaac and Jacob, Who is speaking out of the midst of the burning bush; 2) that God's special name is HE WHO IS; 3) that as special, this name tells us, in a way in which we humans can come to understand it, something about **what God is.** Fourth, God authenticates the revelation with a number of signs: 1) the bush is burning, but is **not** consumed by the fire (a sign to convince **Moses himself)**; 2) God tells Moses that after he has led the Israelites out of Egypt, he is to offer sacrifice to **this** God, as did his fathers, Abraham and Isaac and Jacob to **their** God (in order to convince **the Israelites** that **this** God, the one who had spoken out of burning bush, was the **same** as the God of their fathers); 3) Moses is given certain powers to use in order to convince **the Egyptians** that the Lord God had appeared and spoken to him: the powers a) to turn his rod into a serpent, and the serpent back again into the rod, b) to turn his hand leprous, and then to restore it to its former whole and healthy self, c) to turn river water into blood.

Thus, again: divine **revelation,** religious **experience** of the revelation, **authentication** of the revelation; then religious **faith** in God and in the truth of the revelation.

Saul's conversion on the way to persecute the Christians in Damascus

1 And Saul as yet breathing out threatenings and slaughter against the disciples of the Lord, went to the high priest.

2 And asked of him letters to Damascus, to the synagogues: that if he found any men and women of this way, he might bring them bound to Jerusalem.

3   And as he went on his journey, it came to pass that he drew nigh to Damascus.   And suddenly a light from heaven shined round about him.

4   And falling on the ground, he heard a voice saying to him: Saul, Saul, why persecutest thou me?

5   Who said: Who art thou, Lord?   And he: I am Jesus whom thou persecutest.   It is hard for thee to kick against the goad.

6   And he, trembling and astonished, said: Lord, what wilt thou have me to do?

7   And the Lord said to him: Arise and go into the city; and there it shall be told thee what thou must do.   Now the men who went in company with him stood amazed, hearing indeed a voice but seeing no man.

8   And Saul arose from the ground; and when his eyes were opened, he saw nothing.   But they, leading him by the hands, brought him to Damsacus.

9   And he was there three days without sight; and he did neither eat nor drink.

15   . . . And the Lord said to him [i.e., to Ananias, whom the Lord had chosen to go to Saul to restore his sight]:   Go thy way [i.e., to Saul]; for this man is to me a vessel of election, to carry my name before the Gentiles and kIngs and the children of Israel.

16   For I will show him how great things he must suffer for my name's sake.

17   And Ananias went his way and entered into the house. And laying his hands upon him, he said: Brother Saul, the Lord Jesus hath sent me, he that appeared to thee in the way as thou camest, that thou mayest receive thy sight and be filled with the Holy Ghost.

18   And immediately there fell from his eyes as it were scales; and he received his sight. And rising up, he was baptized. (*Acts,* 9: 1-18)

Here, too, in this account from the *Acts of the Apostles* -- as in the gospel account of the revelation to St. Peter that **this man,** Jesus, is also Christ, the Messiah, the Son of the living God; and as in the *Exodus* account of the revelation to Moses that the special name of the God of Abraham and Isaac and Jacob is HE WHO IS -- here, too, a number of things should be noticed. First, the revelation is made **to an individual specially chosen by God,** one who was to become an apostle (. . . for this man [Saul] is to me a vessel of election, to carry my name before the Gentiles and kings and the children of Israel. . . , *Acts,* 9: 15).   Second, the revelation is **not** made by a human being, but by God Himself, the God of Abraham and Isaac and Jacob, HE WHO IS, in the person of Jesus Christ (. . . I am Jesus whom thou persecutest . . . , *Acts,* 9: 5).   Third, there is a revelation made **during** Saul's sightlessness, i.e., the revelation **to Ananias** that He, Jesus, had chosen Saul to be His apostle to the Gentiles and their kings, as well as to the children of Israel (*Acts,* 9: 15). Fourth, there were further revelations, made **to Saul,** not here and now during the time of his conversion, but **later on** in his considerable preachings and writings; for example, revelations about the nature of faith, hope, and love, and about the nature of heaven.   Fifth, there was the revelation **to Saul,** shortly **after** his sight had been restored by the instrumentality of Ananias, and while still in Damascus, that Jesus is the Son of God and the Messiah. These things must have been revealed to Saul. Otherwise he could not have proclaimed, while preaching in the synagogues of Damascus, that Jesus was the Son of God (*Acts*, 9: 20); nor could he have confounded the Jews of Damascus with his cogent proofs that Jesus was the Christ, the Messiah (*Acts*, 9: 22). Sixth, God **authenticates** these revelations, all of them -- the revelation to Ananias **during** Saul's blindness, the revelation to Saul **shortly after** his sight had been restored, the many revelations to Saul **later on** in his preachings and writings -- with three miraculous signs: 1) God miraculously struck Saul blind, in his encounter with Jesus, on the way to Damascus, no doubt by the instrumentality of the bright light from heaven which shined round him just before he fell to the ground; 2) God miraculously restored Saul's sight, after three days of blindness, using the hands of Ananias as his instrument; 3) God miraculously filled Saul with the Holy Spirit, thereby **not only** converting him to belief in Jesus as the Son of God, and as Christ the Messiah, **but also** moving him thereby to proclaim these beliefs openly, publicly, fearlessly, in the synogogues of Damascus, and to prove the truth of these beliefs to the Jews who lived in that city, with many cogent scripturally based arguments.

And so, once again, divine **revelations**, religious **experiences** of these revelations, **authentication** by God; then religious **faith** in God and in the truth of the revelations.[7]

---

[7] The **object** of faith, quite clearly, is **twofold,** i.e., both **God** and the **truths** revealed by God. The religious believer is **not** left wondering whether the statements or propositions which express the revealed truths are authored by God or by man. The propositions are perceived as authored somehow by God, and not by man (at least, **not** by man **alone**). For a discusssion of the question whether the **content** of revelation is a body of truths expressed in statements or propositions authored by God (the **propositional** view of revelation), or whether its **content** is God acting in human history, the propositions themselves being authored by man (the **non-propositional** view of revelation), see John H. Hick, *Philosophy of Religion* (3rd edition), Englewood Cliffs, New Jersey: Prentice-Hall, Inc., 1983; pp. 60-66; and pp. 68-72. Religous faith accepts not only that **God exists,** and that **He has revealed certain truths;** but also that the **propositions themselves** which express these truths have been **authored somehow by God**. Religious faith accepts all of this precisely because of, i.e., in and through, the religious experience itself of that revelation, and its attendant authentication.

Aquinas on *St. Matthew*, 16: 13-19

The *Catena Aurea*

The *Catena Aurea*[8] on the gospel according to *St. Matthew*, 16: 13-19, begins with a gloss in which Aquinas notes **where exactly it is** (i.e., the place in which) that Jesus asks his disciples the question, "Who do men say that the **Son of Man** is?,"[9] i.e., What do people, common ordinary people, say about who Christ, the Anointed One, the Messiah, is? He asks this question in the place called the Caesarea **of Philip** (by way of difference from the other Caesarea, that **of Strato**), since that **of Philip** was far out of the way of the Jews, and would therefore free his disciples from any fears they might have about speaking what was in their minds. One should be freed from fear **as one begins** on one's way **to faith.** Moreover, one should **soon thereafter** be freed from the erroneous opinons of others. And this is why Jesus asks about what **men,** i.e., people other than his disciples, common ordinary people, say about who the Christ is. Some say John the Baptist, some say Elias, some say Jeremias, some say one or other of the Prophets of old, come to life again. After they had noted these opinons of the common people, all of them erroneous, Jesus asks another question, ordered toward a revelation of the truth about the Christ, and about Himself. He asks them what **they** say about the Christ, and about Himself[10] -- they who, unlike the multitudes of the

---

[8]   The *Catena Aurea* (or Golden Chain) on the four gospels is an exposition or commentary of an interesting sort, i.e., made up of comments taken from the writings of the Fathers, both Latin and Greek, interspersed with clarifying and connecting glosses. It was undertaken by Aquinas at the request of Pope Urban IV, who died however on 2 October 1264, by which time only the exposition of **one** gospel, that of Matthew, had been finished.

[9]   This question, according to some, is to be understood as asking: "Who do men say that I, Jesus, this Son of man, am?," the expression "Son of Man" being taken to mean simply **a human being,** i.e., someone conceived in, and born of, a woman. Jesus often refers to Himself as a Son of Man to note that He has a human nature, that He is a human being. According to others, "Son of Man" is also a **messianic title,** at least in certain contexts, possibly here as Jesus asks the question, "Who do men say that **the Son of Man** is?," meaning, "Who do men say that **the Messiah** is?" This, according to some, implies in this context the question, "Do any men say that I, Jesus, am the Messiah?" -- For more details on the expression "Son of Man," see *The Oxford Companion to the Bible,* edited by Bruce M. Metzger and Michael D. Coogan, New York, N.Y.: Oxford University Press, Inc., pp. 711-713.

[10]   In *St. Matthew,* 16: 13-19, the two questions, the first asking about what **men** or

common people, were always with Him, and had seen many more, and greater, miracles and signs than the others (the common peopole) had, and had heard from Him many things about His divinity. Peter answers for all the disciples, as he proclaims or confesses (having seen **with the eyes of his soul** the Son of **God** in this Son of **Man,** i.e., in Jesus, **this human being** conceived in and born of a woman, whom he has been seeing all along **with the eyes of his body)** that Thou (Jesus) art not only the Christ, the Anointed One, the Messiah, but also the Son of the Living God. You, Jesus, and not John the Baptist or Elias or Jeremias or one of the Prophets of old, says Peter, are the Christ, the Messiah -- and a **divine** and eternal one at that, not a merely human and temporal, and essentially political one (as the Messiah was understood by many people of Jesus' time); this recognition of divinity being the significant and astonishing part of the Father's revelation to Peter. Jesus points out immediately that what had been revealed to Peter, namely that He, Jesus, was the Messiah, **and that the Messiah was to be divine** (in addition to being human, i.e., a Son of Man), could not have ben revealed to him by anyone but God Himself. That which flesh and blood, i.e., the common people, did not reveal, **indeed could not have revealed,** was revealed to Peter as a gift from God. If one sees the divine in the human, one is either God Himself, or one who has been given God's eyes as a gift, and is therefore a chosen and blessed individual. Then, to authenticate the revelation, Jesus refers to Peter as Barjonas, indicating thereby that Peter has received a revelation from the Holy Spirit (the Spirit of the Father), for Barjonas means: **The son (Bar) of a dove (jonas),** and dove signifies the Holy Spirit.

---

people or the **crowds** say, the second asking about what **you,** i.e., **my disciples,** say: 1) "Who do **people** say that . . . ," and 2) "Who do **you** say that . . . ," may cause some difficulty, since what the first question is asking is not wholly clear, inasmuch as it asks **in a vague way** about **the Son of Man,** i.e., without making clear to whom the expression "Son of Man" refers, "Who do people say that **the Son of Man** is?." The second question does not give rise to such a difficulty, inasmuch as it asks about **Jesus Himself,** "But who do you say that I am?" To be sure, one might say that if one puts the two questions together, they imply that the first question is to be understood as asking , "Who do people say that **I, this Son of Man, i.e., this human being,** the one here speaking to you, am?" -- In *St. Mark,* 8: 27-30, the two questions do not give rise to such a difficulty, for each asks **explicitly** about **Jesus Himself:** 1) "Who do **people** say that I am?," and 2) "But who do **you** say that I am?." -- Similarly, in *St. Luke,* 9: 18-22: 1) "Who do the **crowds** say that I am?," and 2) "But who do **you** say that I am?."

Further authentication follows, as Jesus tells Peter that he is the **rock** (by a kind of participation in the **Rock** which He, Jesus Himself, is) on which He is building His Church, a rock (Peter) so unshakeable (because of the Rock, Jesus), so unbreakable, so solid that the gates of hell -- i.e., vice, sin, the doctrines of heretics, the torments and promises of persecutors, the evil works of unbelievers, all of which are paths to destruction -- shall never prevail against it. Nothing can prevail against God, nor against those whom God has chosen as bearers of His powers.

Even more authentication follows, as Jesus gives Peter, and through Peter to the other apostles as well, though **in a secondary way,** "the keys of the kingdom of heaven," i.e., certain things which belong to God alone, things like the power to forgive sins, and to make the Church secure and immoveable in the midst of many difficulties, arising both from within the Church and from outside of it. These powers were given **in a special way** to Peter, to indicate that Jesus was appointing Peter the head of the apostles, so that the Church might have **one** principal vicar of Christ, to whom all the members of the Church might have recourse, if ever they should have dissensions among themselves. **One** vicar, because there is **one** God with the knowledge and the power to do all things, and to do these things through **many** men, indeed **countlessly many** men, over the **many** years to come.

There are many details of various sorts which Aquinas includes in his *Catena* (his running exposition, the chain of comments collected by him from the works of the Fathers) which were not included above in the immediately preceding paragraphs (pp. 42-44). But the ones which have been included form a chain which is more than sufficient to help clarify the message of *St. Matthew,* 16: 13-19. With respect to how **revelation, religious experience** and **faith** are connected, the following can be seen to be the general message:
1. As one is about to begin moving toward faith (belief), one should be **freed in some way from the fear** of what others might say about him, or think about him, or do to him, because of his beginning to move toward faith.
2. Then, one should be made aware of, and **freed from, the erroneous opinions** of others with respect to what he is about to begin to believe.

3. Then, one should **be told,** should **hear,** things which are not erroneous, things which are **true,** even tough one might not accept them as true when first he hears them.

4. One should be made **to see miracles and signs** which are capable of confirming for him the **truth** of the true things which he has been told, the **meaning** of which he has already understood (in the hearing).

5. One is inspired by God **to proclaim or confess** what has been revealed to him, and thereby make it known **to others.**

6. This implies that a revelation **has been made to him,** and that he has been **chosen by God** to receive the revelation, and then to proclaim it to others.

7. Then **God** in some way **authenticates** the fact that this revelation has been made, and that this person has been chosen to receive it, and to proclaim it to others. This shows not only that something true has been revealed, but also that it is true that something true has been revealed.

The Commentary

Aquinas begins his *Commentary* on *Matthew,* 16: 13-19, by noting that, at this point in the gospel, the Lord Jesus is pointing out the eminence or loftiness of the gospel message **that there are two natures** in the Anointed One, the Christ -- the **divine** nature in addition to the **human** nature (the message about to be revealed to Peter). Then, as he did in the *Catena,* Aquinas notes **where it is** that Jesus asks his disciples, "Who do men say that the Son of Man is?" Jesus asks this question in the Caesarea **of Philip,** to differentiate it from the other Caesarea, the one to which Peter had been sent to Cornelius. And **why** there, i.e., at Philip's Caesarea? Because it was away from the Jews, far enough away, to put His disciples at ease to speak their minds. It is important (one should note again, as noted above, p. 42, p. 44) for minds about to believe or have faith in something new, especially something as astonishing as that divinity is in the Christ in addition to humanity, to be at ease, to be without any of the pressures of **fears** of any kind.

Now, when the wise man asks questions, he uses his questions **to teach,** continues Aquinas citing Jerome. And the question asked by Jesus is being used by Him to teach the truth (about to be revealed to Peter) that there is more in Him, in Jesus, i.e., in the Anointed One, than meets the eye, i.e., more than the visible humanity.   There is more in Me, than the eye can see.   It is also being used to teach the loftiness, the sublimity, of humility.   The question of Jesus refers to the Anointed One as a "Son of **Man,** " i.e., as a human being, someone conceived in and born of a woman. Now, the Anointed One is the Son of **God** (not **a** son of God, but **the** Son of God), and   Jesus Himself is the Anointed One.   Here is God Himself, Who in Jesus has most humbly become a human being, telling us most humbly that He has become a human being. Humility in the becoming, humility in the telling.   What can be more lofty, more sublime, than the humility of a humble God?   It is important, one must note, to be humble when about to begin to believe, or to have faith in, something new -- as humble as a child.   Unless you become as children, you will not enter the kingdom of heaven.[11]   God is Our Father, and that makes us His children. A child-like humility gives rise to faith, and faith is the ticket to heaven.   Being as humble as a child is easier for us humans than being as humble as God. The latter is the ideal for which we should strive, but the former, if achieved, will suffice for faith, and through faith for heaven.   My father has said that such-and-such is so, says the child, and my father knows **just about** everything; besides, my father always tells the truth.   He **can** lie if he wants to, but he never does. God has said that such-and-such is so, says the believer, and God knows **absolutely** everything; besides God always tells the truth.   And God can**not** lie; God is Truth Itself.

After the disciples answered that some preople say the Christ is John the Baptist, some that he is Elias, some that he is Jeremias, some that he is one of the Prophets of old, Jesus asks them, "Who do **you** say that I am?"   This second question is noting, in effect, that His disciples **should know more** about Him than the common ordinary people, since they (the disciples) have been close to Him, and have seen many miracles and signs, and have heard from Him many references to His being divine.   Peter, inspired by the revealing power of the Spirit of the Father, proclaims, or confesses, two wondrous, two sublime, truths: 1) "Thou art the Christ," and 2) "Thou art the Son of the

---

11   *St. Matthew,* 18: 3

living God." Peter has seen **with the eyes of faith** that this human being, this Son of Man, Jesus, has been anointed -- by God. That is, that Jesus was anointed **not** in His divinity, to be sure, since anointing **comes from** divinity; but in His humanity. Further, Peter's eyes of faith have penetrated the outer shell of Jesus' humanity (. . . sed testudine penetrata . . .), and have seen all the way to His divinity, unlike certain of the Jews who did not, and could not for various blinding reasons, see that far, and who had accused Jesus of being a blasphemer,[12] since He considered Himself to be God. For He had said, "My Father and I are one."[13] Peter sees Jesus not as a blasphemer, but as **the** Son of God -- **not** as an **adopted** son of God, i.e., **not** as a Son of Man, and so **not** as a **mere** human being, but as the **natural,** i.e., **divine,** Son of God. And **not** of just **any** god, but of the one and only **living** God; the God who is quite unlike the gods of some, e.g., Jove (Jupiter) who is more mortal than divine; and quite unlike the gods of others, e.g, the elements (earth, water, air, fire) which are **not** living things at all. Thou art truly man, and truly God; truly a **living** man, and truly the **living** God.

Then, notes Aquinas, comes Jesus' twofold approval of Peter's confession: 1) first, by **commending or praising** Peter for having made the confession, and 2) secondly, by **rewarding** him for having made it. Jesus **praises** Peter by calling him blessed (. . . beatus es. . .), and the son of a dove (Barjonas), "bar" meaning **son,** and "jonas" meaning **dove,** which signifies the Holy Spirit, the Spirit of the Father, Who had just revealed to Peter, just **made known** to Peter, that Jesus is both God and man (something which **only** God could have made known to him) and had inspired him to confess or proclaim it. True blessedness consists **in knowing** God, especially those things about God which only God can reveal to us.

Then Jesus **rewards** Peter by giving him the **name** "Petrus, "rock" (his name, recall, was Simon), and by giving him **certain powers.** Simon **is named** the **rock,** as deriving from the Rock, Jesus, and thereby becoming something solid (the rock) on which Jesus is going to build His Church. A rock so solid,

---

12   *St. John,* 10: 33:   The Jews replied, "We are going to stone you **not** for any good deed, but for your blasphemy. You, a mere man, claim to be God."
13   *St. John,* 10: 30.

so unbreakable, so unshakeable that the **gates** leading to Hell, e.g., the doctrines of heretics, sins, and the demons themselves, will not be able to prevail against this Church.   In addition, Peter is given **certain powers,** signified by the keys to the kingdom, the keys which unlock the doors of Heaven, and make it possible for God's grace to flow into the Church and all its members, by the appropriate and worthy use of the sacraments; and beyond that to draw **all others,** not yet members, into the eternal life of that same grace-giving and saving Church.   And these powers are given not only to Peter, but through Peter to the other disciples as well.

Here too, in Aquinas' *Commentary,* as in his *Catena,* there are many interesting details which were not mentioned just above in the immediately preceding paragraphs (pp. 45-48).   But those that were mentioned serve well to deliver again the message of *St. Matthew,* 16: 13-19.   Here too in his *Commentary,* one can see how **revelation, religious experience,** and **faith** are connected:

1. One should be **freed from** as many **fears** as possible, as one begins one's journey toward faith.

2. One should be **taught the truth(s)** about to be revealed, without **then,** at the time of the teaching, being told that it is a truth(s) about to be revealed.

3. One should be **taught to be as humble** in the presence of our **heavenly** Father as a child is in the presence of its **earthly** father.   Such humility is necessary for faith.

4. One should be made aware of what others have said, in order to be **freed from erroneous views.**

5. One should be made to see miracles and signs which are able to confirm the **truth** of the things one has been taught, the **meaning** of which he has already understood, at least in some way understood, in the hearing of them.

6. One is moved by the Spirit of the Father to confess or proclaim what that Spirit has revealed to him, thereby making it known to others -- to those who have not been favored with seeing miracles and signs.

7. This shows that one has been **specially chosen by God** to receive the revelation, and thereupon to proclaim it to others, and through them to others still, and eventually through others still to **all** others.

8. Then, by approving the confession, God is in effect authenticating the revelation. That is, God is showing that a revelation has been made, that what has been reveled is true, and that **this person** has been chosen **to receive** the revelation, and therupon **to proclaim** it, to pass it on, to others.

Aquinas on the nature of faith

The preceding, i.e., Aquinas' exposition of *St. Matthew*, 16: 13-19, in his *Catena* and in his *Commentary*, especially as summarized in the seven points on p. 45 and in the eight points on pp. 48-49, is a **theological,** i.e., scripturally based, **psychology** of faith. To be sure, this **theological** account of how faith can be made to arise, i.e., of how to prepare, to dispose, a human individual for the reception of God's **free gift** of faith to him, makes **philosophical** sense as well. That is, one could with diligent **philosophical** effort come to the same, or at least a very similar, account.

It will be helpful at this point to reflect on Aquinas' view on the nature of faith, to ask with him the question: What exactly is faith?

A **short** answer to the question is given by Aquinas in a context in which he is concerned with the question whether the merit of faith is lessened if it is supported by reasons discovered by the human mind. **Faith,** points out Aquinas, **is belief in the truth of a proposition** *not* **on account of reasons seen by the human mind, but on account of the authority of God, and** *that alone.* One's will assents, one chooses to assent, to truth -- not because one's intellect has been brought by a reasoned demonstration to see the evidence for the truth, but because of God's authority, and that alone, **without** recourse to any **humanly seen** reasons at all.[14]

A **longer** answer to the question is given by Aquinas in a context in which he is concerned **not** with the merit of faith, but with **faith itself.**[15] He begins here, in the first article of question four, by asking whether St. Paul's

---

14   *S.T.*, II-II, q. 2, a. 10
15   *S.T.*, II-II, q. 4.

description of faith in *Hebrews*, 11: 1, is a fitting definition of faith. **Faith, writes St. Paul, is the substance of things to be hoped for, the evidence of things that appear not.** Although St. Paul's description, notes Aquinas, includes all the points needed to define faith, the words themselves are not aranged in the form of a definition. Now faith is a habit, continues Aquinas. And habits are known by their acts, and their acts by their objects. The act of faith is to believe, and this is an act of the intellect; but it is also an act of the will, i.e., of the will as commanding the intellect.

To expand and to clarify. The object of faith, continues Aquinas, is the First Truth -- but **as unseen;** and as unseen, it is an object **hoped for.** One does not hope for what one already has, but only for what one does not have. And so, **as an act of the will,** i.e., of the will as commanding the intellect, faith has as its object things to be hoped for, things not yet seen, and so not yet had. Indeed, faith is the **substance** of things to be hoped for, "substance" in the sense of the **first beginnings** of these things, in the sense of a kind of seed which contains within it in a virtual way **all** the things to be hoped for. This can be likened, observes Aquinas, to the first self-evident principles, which can be said to be the **substance** of science, since these principles are in us the **first beginnings** of science, the **whole** of which is contained in them virtually. **In the beginning** one's hope relates to an object which is like the very small seed of a tree, which however, as the **substance** of the tree, can grow to become the tree itself, something very big indeed, complete and whole in every way.

But, an act of faith is also, and primarily, an act of the intellect. **As an act of the intellect,** faith is described by St. Paul as the "evidence of things that appear not," the word "evidence" being taken to refer to the intellect's **firm adherence** to the truth of these **unseen** things, an adherence motivated by the authority of God, and that alone.

And so, if one were to put St. Paul's description into the form of a defintion, notes Aquinas, one could say the following. **Faith is a habit of the mind, a habit by which eternal life (i.e., knowing God as He is) is begun in us, and which makes the intellect assent to truths which are not seen now (in the present life), but will be seen then (in the next life).** This definition, notes

Aquinas, distinguishes faith from all other things pertaining to the intellect. To describe faith as **evidence** is to distinguisah it from **opinion, suspicion,** and **doubt,** none of which makes the intellect adhere firmly to anything.   To say "of things that appear not" is to distinguish it from **science** a n d **understanding,** the object of each of which is something seen. And to say that it is "the substance of things to be hoped for" is to distinguish the virtue of faith (**religious** faith) from faith in a common sense, which has no reference to the eternal beatitude for which we hope, either in its **present beginnings** or in its **future fullness.**

A brief summary of some important observations made by Aquinas in other articles of this fourth question will be helpful, at this pont, to round out a bit Aquinas' views on the nature of faith:

1.   Faith resides **both** in the intellect **and** in the will, but immediately and properly in the intellect, since **truth** is the object of faith, and **truth** is the object of the intellect.   Faith resides in the intellect **as assenting to truth,** in the will **as commanding the intellect to its assent.**[16]

2.   Faith is related to **love** (the third of the theological virtues), as well as to **hope.** One can**not hope for** the Good not yet had, without being moved by that Good to love It as It should be loved; just as one can**not assent to** the truth not yet seen, without being moved to that assent **by the authority** of that unseen Truth Itself.[17]

3. Faith, by its very nature, **precedes** *all* **other virtues,** whether theological or not. And the theological virtues in turn, precede all non-theological virtues, since the object of the theological virtues is the Last End, God, which precedes all other ends, as that which motivates to action.   Since knowledge of the end (knowledge belongs to the intellect) must precede inclination to the end (inclination belongs to the will), the last end must be in the intellect by faith, **before** it can be in the will (by hope, and by love).   Nonetheless, **some** virtues **can precede** faith -- not by their very nature, but accidentally, e.g., as removing obstacles to belief.   Thus, the virtue of fortitude can remove inordinate fear, the virtue of humility can remove obstinate pride, and the

---

[16]   *S.T.,* II-II, q. 4, a. 2,
[17]   *S.T.,* II-II, q. 4, a. 3.

virtue of obedience can remove determined non-compliance -- all three of which can be serious and burdensome obstacles to belief.[18]

4. Faith, being about **what God has revealed to us** about Himself, is more certain than any other intellectual virtue, like wisdom or science or understanding. For God knows all things, is infinitely truthful, and cannot lie or err. Faith, thus, has a more certain cause, i.e., God, than the other intellectual virtues, the cause of which is mere human reason.[19]

5. From another point of view, however, faith is less certain, since matters of faith are above the human intellect. The more a man's intellect lays hold of a thing, the more certain it is. The objects of the sciences are not above man's intellect, and so the human intellect can lay hold of them in a way in which it cannot lay hold of the Object of faith.[20]

*   *   *

Faith, hope, and love -- these three virtues are our way to life with God. Now, we cannot hope for, nor can we love, what we do not know. Since faith is a kind of knowing, a knowing based on the authoritative word of God, faith is the beginning point, the "substance," as St. Paul puts it, of our life with God. But the authoritative word of God comes to us through revelation, of which certain chosen individuals have a religious experience, which (revelation) they then proclaim to others. And it is God Himself Who does the revealing. Thus, God Himself is the beginning point, the **beginningless** beginning point, of our life with God. God is both the beginning point (**as the revealing cause** which produces faith **in this life**), and the end point (**as the object seen** and possessed in the Beatific Vision **in the life to come**).

---

[18] S.T., II-II, q. 4, a. 7.
[19] S.T., II-II, q. 4, a. 8.
[20] Ibid.

CHAPTER TWO

RELIGION AS A VIRTUE

RELIGION IS NOT ONLY A RELATION, as explained in the introduction; it is also a virtue. Or, to speak more carefully, though the word "religion" can be used to refer to a certain sort of a **relation**, it can also be used to designate a certain sort of **virtue**.

This chapter is concerned with some of the things which Aquinas has to say about religion as a **virtue**.

Religion, as a virtue, is a kind of justice, but a defective kind. As a kind of justice, it can grow into a kind a friendship, though again a defective kind. Religion is neither a theological virtue nor an intellectual virtue. It is a moral virtue. It is a moral virtue which inclines us to render unto God what pertains in a special way to divine worship (or honor or reverence), things like sacrifices and oblations and liturgies, things by which we extoll His excellence and declare our submission to Him, things which ought to be rendered unto God as the First Principle of the creation and governance of all things, rendered because of their usefulness to perfecting us inasmuch as they help make us submissive to God, for to extoll God is also to declare our submission to Him. Religion, as a virtue, can in a sense be equated with sanctity (holiness). Religion is at least the beginning of sanctity.

The words "religious" and "religion"

The comments of St. Thomas Aquinas on the etymology of words are always interesting, often philosophically instructive. A "religious" man is one who frequently reads and re-reads (**qui relegit**) the things which pertain to the worship of God; turns them over, ponders them, in his heart.   And "religion" (**re-lego:** I read again) gets its meaning from that "frequent reading and re-reading" (**a frequenti lectione)** and pondering.   But that is only one suggestion, that of Cicero.   Augustine makes another suggestion, namely that a "religious" man chooses God again and again, after having let Him slip away, after losing Him, through indifference and neglect.   And "religion" (*re-eligo:* I choose again) takes its meaning from "choosing again and again what has been allowed to slip away, to be lost, by lack of concern" (**ex iterata electione eius quod negligenter amissum est**).   There is a third suggestion, also by Augustine, that the "religious" man is one who binds, or ties, himself again and again to God.   And "religion" (**re-ligo:** I bind again) takes its meaning from that "re-binding of oneself" (**a religatione**) to God.

Whether religion be taken as a frequent re-reading, or as a re-choosing,   or as a re-binding, it entails in all three cases, notes Aquinas, an ordering toward God.   For God, continues Aquinas, is that to which we ought to bind ourselves, as to an unfailing and inexhaustible source; that toward which our choices ought continuously to be directed, as to an ultimate end; that, too, which we have lost by being negligently sinful, and which we ought to recover by believing in Him and by protesting our faith in Him.[1]

Religion as a virtue

Religion as a virtue is different from religion as a relation.   As a virtue, religion is but one aspect of religion as a relation.   It is one of the many aspects (of that complex relation) which originate in man and reach out toward, then terminate in, God.   Having either experienced God's revelation, or having become aware of that revelation from those who have experienced it, a man responds by beginning to perform various sorts of religious acts, like worshipping God, praying to God; generally giving honor and praise and thanksgiving to God, along with declaring his subjection to, and need for,

---

[1]   *S.T.*, II-II, q. 81, a. 1, c.

God.[2]   Repeated religious acts give rise to, and perpetuate, the virtue of religion, which inclines a man to continue to perform those acts.

That religion is a virtue is clear. Aquinas argues this point as follows. A virtue is a disposition which makes the one having it, and the actions he performs by means of it, good. Now, the man who renders to another **what ought to be rendered** to the other is a good man; and the act whereby he renders it is a good act, inasmuch as an act of this sort gives him a proper ordering, relates him in a fitting way, to the other. Since it pertains to religion to render to another, i.e., to God, the **honor which ought to be rendered** to God, it is clear that the man who honors God, and his honoring acts as well, are good. Religion, therefore, is a virtue.

Religion is a defective kind of justice

Religion, as a virtue, is a kind of justice, but a defective kind. To be just to another is basically to do two things: 1) to render to the other **what** ought to be rendered, and 2) to render **as much as** ought to be rendered. The religious man renders to God **what** ought to be rendered. This is why the religious man is said to be a just man, just toward God. But, since no one can render to God as much as ought to be rendered to Him, the religious man is at best **defectively** just toward God. It is impossible to do for God what God has done for us. This is very much like the virtue of **piety,** which some children have, and all ought to have, toward their parents. Piety, like religion, is a defective kind of justice. That is, pious children render to their parents **what** ought to be rendered to them, but can never render **as much as** ought to be rendered. A child can never do for a parent what the parent has done for the child.[3]

---

[2]   As Aquinas points out, *S.T.*, II-II, q. 8l, a. 3, ad 2, every religous act either extolls God's excellence or declares man's subjection to God: "...eodem actu homo servit Deo et colit ipsum: nam cultus respicit Dei excellentiam, cui reverentia debetur; servitus autem respicit subjectionem hominis, qui ex sua conditione obligatur ad exhibendum reverentiam Deo. Et ad haec duo pertinent omnes actus qui religioni attribuuntur: quia per omnes homo protestatur divinam excellentiam et subjectionem sui ad Deum..."

[3]   *S.T.*, II-II, q. 80, a. u n. c.

Religion is a defective kind of friendship

Friendship, like justice, is a virtue with respect to our **dealings with others.** Both are **virtutes ad alium (alterum).**   But, whereas justice is **ad alterum** according to the prescriptions of law, friendship is **ad alterum** according to the promptings of a benevolent love.[4] And this benevolent love comes to be motivated by the **goodness** of the other (or, in lesser kinds of friendship, by the **pleasure** which the other affords us, or by his **usefulness** to us). Thus friendship, because prompted by a benevolent love, takes us to points quite beyond where justice takes us.   The religious man will, with growing familiarity with God, move beyond being **just** toward God, to being a **friend** to God.   For, at some point he will become aware of the intensity of God's goodness, and be overwhelmed by it.   The religious man will develop a benevolent love for God, i.e., want for God the same good things he wants for himself, and among these especially an eternal and blessed life. And he will want these good things for God just because God is God, i.e., the Infinitely **Good** One.   Moreover, he will want these same good things for all other persons, just because these others are persons, and just because God wants these same good things for them.   That is, because a friend will love the friends of a friend, even if he hates them, so to speak.   A mother will love the husband of her daughter, even if she hates him.   But, no one can love God with a benevolent love as great as God's benevolent love for us. No one can be God's friend as intensely as He is our friend. The religious man can be at best **defectively** a friend of God; even as, before that, he was at best **defectively** just toward God.

Religion is not a theological virtue

Every virtue is either a theological virtue or an intellectual virtue or a moral virtue.   Clearly, religion is not an intellectual virtue, since religious acts are not acts which are concerned with considering, and discerning, the

---

[4] *S.T.*, II-II, q. 23, a. 3, ad 1.

truth about God. They are, rather, acts some of which extoll God's excellence, others of which declare man's submission to, and need for, God. Nor is religion a theological virtue, since religious acts, unlike acts of faith and hope and charity, are not acts which have God as their object or matter. They are, rather, acts which have God as their end. And so, by elimination, one can conclude that religion is a moral virtue. But, besides elimination, there is a good reason for concluding that religion is a moral virtue, namely that religion is a kind of justice (though a defective kind). And justice is a moral virtue.

That religion is a moral virtue needs no further proof. Neither is further proof required for the claim that religion is not an intellectual virtue. But, it might be helpful to make clearer Aquinas' reason for the claim that religion is not a theological virtue. There are two aspects to religion, notes Aquinas. There is first of all **what** religion renders to God, namely worship, honor, praise, and the like. Secondly, there is **that to which** worship is rendered, namely God himself. Worship is the matter or object of religion, in the sense in which God is the matter or object of the theological virtues. But God is not the matter or object of religion. He is rather its end. Worship and the like **(cultus)** are offered to God not as though the acts by which God is worshipped attain God in the sense in which we attain God by believing (the theological virtue) in God. Rather, the acts by which God is worshipped are done in order to, as a means to, the end of showing reverence to God. And so, religion is not a theological virtue, whose object or matter is God, our ultimate end. It is rather a moral virtue, the acts of which are the means (the object or matter) by which we humans relate reverentially to our ultimate end, God.[5]

Religion is a beginning, sanctity the end

The word "sanctity" ("holiness") carries two meanings. Taken in one way, it means cleanness or purity **(munditia)**. The Greek word "agios" focuses on this meaning, inasmuch as it says "sine terra," i.e., without earth (or ground or

---

[5] "...religio non est virtus theologica, cuius objectum est ultimus finis; sed est virtus moralis, cuius est esse circa ea quae sunt ad finem." (*S.T.*, II-II, q. 81, a. 5, c.).

soil). To mix something with earth or soil is to make it unclean or impure, since earth is the lowliest of the elements. Taken in another way, the word "sanctity" means strength or steadfastness **(firmitas)**. It is with this in mind that the ancients called **holy (sancta)** certain things which were protected, i.e., strengthened, by the law to keep them from being violated. Thus, a thing is said to be **holy (strong)** because it is backed by a law **(lege firmatum)**. But, even in Latin, the word "holy" **("sanctus")** can be used to designate cleanness or purity, understanding "holy" **("sanctus")** as "sanguine tinctus," i.e., sprinkled with blood, because in ancient times those who wanted to be purified were sprinkled with the blood of the sacrificial animal.

In both senses, i.e., in the sense of cleanness and in the sense of strength, **holiness** is attributed to things which are directed toward, used in, divine worship. So that not only men, but the temple as well, and books and vessels and altars, and the like, are said to be sanctified (made holy) because they are directed toward, used in, divine worship.

With respect to men, the mind must be holy **(sancta)** that it might direct itself toward God. That is, the mind must be both **clean** or **pure,** i.e., not submerged into and dragged down by material things, and **strong** or **steadfast,** i.e., unchangeable, because God as ultimate end and first principle is unchangeable (strong and steadfast).

And so, sanctity (holiness) is the virtue by which the mind of man directs itself and its acts toward God. And so is religion. Religion, therefore, is the same as sanctity, at least from the point of view of directing the mind and its acts toward God, i.e., they (religion and sanctity) are the same in essence **(secundum essentiam** or **secundum rem).** There is nonetheless this difference **(differunt ratione).**[6] Whereas religion is concerned with acts which pertain in a special way to divine worship, for example sacrifices, prayers, and the like;

---

[6] "...sanctitas dicitur per quam mens hominis seipsam et suos actus applicat Deo. Unde non differt a religione secundum essentiam, sed solum ratione. Nam religio dicitur secundum quod exhibet Deo debitum famulatum in his quae pertinent specialiter ad cultum divinum, sicut in sacrificiis, oblationibus et aliis huiusmodi: sanctitas autem dicitur secundum quod homo non solum haec, sed aliarum virtutum opera refert in Deum..." (S.T., II-II, q. 81, a. 8, c.).

sanctity is concerned with ordering the acts of **all** of man's virtues toward God, including religion's special acts. Sanctity, therefore, has a broader scope or range than religion. But religion and sanctity are the same in essence.

Thus, the holy man can be said to be even "more" religious than the religious man. The religious man is on his way to becoming a holy man. Religion is a beginning, holiness the end.

CHAPTER THREE

PRAYER

THE VIRTUE OF RELIGION manifests itself in a diversity of acts, some of which are interior acts, namely devotion and prayer; others of which are exterior acts, for example, adoration, sacrifice, oblations, tithes, vows, oaths.

The present chapter is concerned with some of the things Aquinas has to say about the act of prayer.

Prayer is an act of the practical intellect, causing by requesting

Devotion[1]-- which is an act of willigness to be prompt, ready, eager in the service of God -- is not only an act of religion,[2] but an act of religion dictinct from other acts of religion,[3] and an act of the will.[4] Prayer, however, is an act of the intellect (reason).[5]

Aquinas begins his argument by noting an interesting comment on the meaning of the word "oratio" (prayer) made by Cassiodorus: "...oratio dicitur quasi **oris ratio**."[6] That is, Cassiodorus is saying, the word "oratio" has the sound of, and the meaning of, the words "oris ratio," which someone,[7] I note, has translated as **spoken reason;** but which might be better rendered as **the mind of the mouth.** To call a prayer **the mind of the mouth (oris ratio)** is more literal and colorful, and conveys the meaning of "oris ratio" more forcefully. But, perhaps Cassiodorus would have done better to say that

---

[1] *S.T.,* II-II, q. 82.
[2] *Ibid.,* a. 2.
[3] *Ibid., a. 1.*
[4] *Ibid.,* a. 1.
[5] *S.T.,* II-II, q. 83, a. 1, c.
[6] *Ibid.*
[7] Kevin D. O'Rourke, O.P., of the Aquinas Institute, School of Theology, Dubuque. See the Blackfriars' *Summa Theologiae,* vol. 39, p. 49.

"oratio" sounds like "os rationis," and that it means, therefore, **the mouth of the mind,** rather than **the mind of the mouth.** For prayer seems to be better described as **the mind revealing itself** (by means of some sort of mouth it might have) than as the **mouth revealing itself** (i.e., revealing some sort of mind it might have). One wants to ask: Is it better to say that prayer is a **mind with a mouth,** or a **mouth with a mind?** Perhaps one is as good as the other, so long as the **mouth** being mentioned is an **interior** mouth, a **mental** mouth, as opposed to the **bodily** mouth. Prayer, after all, is an **interior** act.

Proceeding to his argument that prayer is an act of the intellect or reason, rather than an act of the will, Aquinas recalls how it is that speculative reason differs from practical reason. Whereas speculative reason simply perceives or apprehends things, practical reason not only apprehends things, but also causes them. Now, continues Aquinas, one thing causes another in two ways: 1) sometimes perfectly, that is, necessarily bringing about the effect, and this occurs when the effect is totally subject to the power of the cause; but 2) sometimes only imperfectly, that is, in a way which only disposes toward bringing about the effect, and this takes place when the effect is not totally subject to the power of the cause. Similarly, reason too causes things in two ways: 1) as a cause imposing necessity, and this belongs to reason **as commanding,** not only the lower parts of the soul, and the members of the body, but subjected human beings as well; 2) as a cause which disposes in some way, by urging or persuading, and this is how reason **requests** that something be done by those who are not subject to it, whether they be equals or superiors. Now, both of these, that is, both commanding **(imperare)** and requesting **(petere sive deprecare),** connote putting things into an orderly sequence, inasmuch as both arrange for something to be done by something else. And so, both belong to reason (as opposed to belonging to the will), since it belongs to reason to put things into an orderly sequence. And this is why Aristotle remarks, observes Aquinas, that **reason requests that we do the things that are the best.** Moreover, this is how we are speaking about prayer in the present context, i.e., as signifying a request or a petition, in the sense which Augustine has in mind when he says that **prayer is a kind of petition;** and Damascene, when he says that **prayer is a petition for fitting things from God.** Aquinas concludes, from the above, that the sort of prayer of which he is now speaking, i.e., a kind of request or petition, is an act of reason. And one can add to this, by way of emphasizing a point made above, that prayer is an act of **requesting practical** reason, as opposed to an act of **commanding practical** reason; and that prayer is an act of reason by which a **superior** is requested to consider doing something, whereas a command is an act of reason by which an **inferior** is **told** that he must do something.[8]

The causality of prayer

One would very likely not think of prayer as being a cause. But that is the view of Aquinas, and a very plausible one, indeed. He brings up the causality of prayer, and makes a brief case for it, in his discussion of the question of the usefulness of prayer.[9]

Three mistakes have been made with respect to prayer, begins Aquinas. **The first mistake.** Some have held, Aquinas points out, that it is utterly **useless** to pray to God, since God does not care about things human, i.e., since things human are not governed by divine providence. The truth is, however, notes Aquinas without argument at this point, that things human **are** governed by divine providence.

The second mistake. Others have held, continues Aquinas, that all things, including things human, come about out of necessity, either because of the immutability of divine providence, or because of a necessity deriving from the stars, or because of a necessity deriving from connections among causes of various sorts. And these reasons led some to deny the usefulness of praying to God. The truth is, however, notes Aquinas without argument at this point, that things human do **not** come about out of necessity.

The third mistake.[10] Others, however, have held the opposite view,

---

[8] "...oratio est actus rationis per quam aliquis superiorem deprecatur; sicut imperium est actus rationis quo inferior ad aliquid ordinatur..." (*S.T.*, II-II, q. 83, a. 10, c.).
[9] *S.T.*, II-II, q. 83, a. 2.
[10] These three views were shown to be unacceptable in the *Prima Pars* of the *Summa Theologiae*. See *S.T.*, II-II, q. 22, a. 2, and a. 4; q. 23, a. 8; q. 115, a. 6; q. 116, a. 3.

Aquinas adds, i.e., the view that prayer **is** useful. According to these, things human are governed by divine providence, but do not come about out of necessity; moreover, the rulings of divine providence are changeable, and can be changed by prayers and by other things which pertain to divine worship. The truth is, however, Aquinas notes without argument at this point, that things human **are** subject to divine providence, and **without** being necessitated; and the rulings of divine providence are **not** changeable.

Now, when thinking about the question of the usefulness of prayer, one must keep in mind, Aquinas urges, that divine providence not only rules or decides which effects will take place, but also by which causes they will take place, and in what order they will take place. Human actions, like other actions, are genuinely causes of certain effects. And so, human beings perform certain actions to bring about certain effects, and in the order ruled or decided by God; but not to change God's rulings. And the same thing is true with respect to the actions of natural causes. It is also true with respect to prayer. We pray to bring about those things which God has ruled would come about by our prayers, and in the order in which He has ruled. We do not pray to change God's rulings.

Thus, the one who prays exerts some sort of causality with respect to bringing about the things for which he prays. And since prayer is an **activity,** its causality is an active or efficient causality. And so, human beings can be said to cause the results of prayer, not as a primary or principal efficient cause (that is God's role), but as a secondary efficient cause working along with, cooperating with, the causality of divine providence. There are in Aquinas' view, one can see, certain things which will take place **only** if we ask for them in prayer, because God has ruled that they will take place **only in that way,** i.e., only by the **requesting efficient causality** of our prayers.

The preceding helps make clear the special meaning of "impetrare," as Aquinas uses this word in talking about prayer. We pray, Aquinas points out, in order to impetrate.[11] Now, to pray is to make a request of a superior, a

---

11   "...propter hoc oramus...ut...impetremus..." (*S.T.* II-II, q. 83, a. 2, c.).

request that the superior do something. And to impetrate, in its ordinary meaning, is to obtain, or to achieve, by requesting. To pray, thus, would seem to mean: to make a request in order to obtain. But, as Aquinas understands it, one prays in order to obtain in a **special** way, i.e., by exercising **the requesting efficient causaltiy** of practical reason with respect to those things which will take place **only** if we pray for them, inasmuch as God has decreed that they will take place **only in that way.** Thus, to impetrate is to obtain by exercising a kind of cooperating causality. This makes clearer what Aquinas is asking when, in another place,[12] he asks whether sinners **impetrate** anything from God when they pray. He is asking: Do sinners, by their prayers, act as secondary efficient causes to bring about certain results which otherwise would not take place? It also makes clearer Aquinas' response to the question. Two things, notes Aquinas in his response, must be taken into account with respect to sinners: 1) their human nature, which God loves; and 2) the sins for which they are responsible, which He hates. Thus, should a sinner pray for something as a sinner, i.e., with a desire for sin in mind, though God will not respond to him out of mercy, He sometimes responds out of motives other than mercy, thereby allowing the sinner to sink more deeply into sin. But, should a sinner pray out of a good desire arising from his human nature, God will respond to him out of mercy -- rather than out of justice, since the sinner does not merit this -- provided the sinner is praying reverently and perseveringly, and for things which are necessary for his salvation.

To whom does it belong to pray?

To consider the question: To whom does it belong to pray?, is an attempt to draw out some of the implications of **what prayer is.**

Since prayer is an act of reason by which a superior **is requested to do something** (just as a command is an act of reason by which an inferior **is told that he must do something**), only those beings can pray, argues Aquinas, which have **both** reason **and** a superior they can pray to.[13] Nothing is superior

---

12 *S.T.*, II-II, q. 83, a. 16.
13 *S.T.*, II-II, q. 83, a. 10, c.

to God, or to any of the Persons in God. And so, it belongs neither to God, nor to any divine Person to pray. And brute animals do not have reason. Thus, it does not belong to them to pray, either.

To the objection that God the Son prays, though He has no superior; Aquinas responds, quite acceptably, that He prays in His assumed nature, i.e., in His human nature, and not in His divine nature. And to the objection that the Holy Spirit, too, prays; Aquinas responds that the Spirit is only **said** to pray, meaning that He prompts or inspires **us humans** to pray.[14]

And what about the angels? Though they have a superior, God; they are not rational beings. Yet they pray. They are purely intellectual beings, i.e., beings with **intuiting** minds, as opposed to rational beings, i.e., beings with **reasoning** minds -- minds which move from premises to conclusions, from effects to causes, or from causes to effects. Aquinas responds as follows, and quite acceptably. In man, intellect (**intuiting** mind) and reason (**concluding** mind) are not different powers, but are related as the perfect to the imperfect.[15] The human mind **intuits** some truths, like two plus two equals four; others it apprehends **only as conclusions,** like the Pythagorean Theorem. And even those truths which it apprehends only as conclusions, it **intuits** in a sense, though imperfectly, inasmuch as the human mind **intuits** some truths in order **by means of them** to be able to conclude others, apprehending the latter in the light of the former. Since purely intellectual creatures, i.e., the angels, do **not** apprehend any truths **as conclusions,** but intuit all the truths they apprehend; it is sometimes said that they are **not** rational creatures. However, since purely intellectual creatures **do** apprehend the truths which human souls apprehend **only as conclusions,** it is sometimes said that they are **rational** creatures. And, it is in this sense that it is said that it belongs to rational creatures to pray. It can be added here that God, too, can be said to be rational in this sense. But, though rational, God is not a creature; and so cannot pray.

---

14   *Ibid.,* ad 1.
15   *Ibid.,* ad 2.

The effects of prayer

Prayer has three effects: 1) merit, which is common to all acts which are performed out of charity, i.e., out of love of God and of neighbor; 2) impetration, which is an effect proper to prayer; and 3) a certain kind of spiritual restoration or refreshment or consolation of the mind.[16] Consolation or refreshment is an effect of prayer which comes about at once, i.e., while one is engaged in the prayer, or in the present. Merit and impetration are effects which come about in the future. Whereas what is consoled or refreshed is the **mind** of the one who is praying, what is merited and impetrated is, in the main, **eternal and blessed life with God.**[17] And whereas prayer has the effect of merit from the **charity** out of which it is performed, it has the effect of impetration from the **faith** on which it is based; for it is by faith that we have knowledge of God's omnipotence and mercy, from which prayer impetrates what it requests.[18]

To be sure, things other than blessed and eternal life with God can be merited and impetrated. Things which are necesary, or at least useful, as means for attaining blessed and eternal life can be merited and impetrated; not so, things which are not. That is, if they are **not contrary** to eternal happiness, one can by such a prayer still merit eternal happiness, though not the things one prays for. But, if one prays for things which **are contrary** to eternal happiness, e.g., if one were to pray for help to go through with some sinful act, one thereby not only does not merit these contrary things, but loses merit with respect to eternal happiness as well.[19]

Impetration is always an effect of prayer when four conditions are met: 1) that the one praying asks for himself, 2) that he asks for things which are necessary for salvation, 3) that he asks piously, and 4) that he asks perseveringly.[20] There is no difficulty in understanding, and thereupon

---

16 *S.T.*, II-II, q. 83, a. 13; a. 15.
17 *S.T.*, II-II, q. 83, a. 15, c.
18 *Ibid.*, ad 3.
19 *Ibid.*, ad 2.
20 "...ponuntur quatuor conditiones, quibus concurrentibus semper aliquis impetrat quod petit: ut scilicet pro se petat, necessaria ad salutem, pie, et perseveranter..." (*Ibid.*).

accepting, the last three conditions. But the first condition seems, at least at first sight, a bit hard to accept; for it seems to make the prayer a **selfish** act. Isn't it better to pray **for another** -- rather than for oneself -- inasmuch as that is something **selfless?**

An initial response one might want to make is that the four conditions noted are conditions **with respect to impetration,** i.e., with respect to **obtaining** what is requested in the prayer, and **not** with respect to **merit.** Merit, unlike impetration, is based on charity. So that, praying for another has merit because of the charity out of which the prayer is said. But even here, charity requires that we love another **as we love ourselves;** so that praying for another is **meritorious** only because we also pray for ourselves.

Moreover, one must also note that the **other,** for whom we pray, has free will, and that God respects the free will He has given to His creatures. Thus, to seek to impetrate from God eternal and blessed life **for another** is to ask God to give eternal life to the other whether that other freely wants it or not. God wants each human to share eternal and blessed life with Him, but each human can actually obtain that eternal and blessed life only if he freely wants it, though not by that free wanting alone. -- But, someone might object, cannot God be said to be the Master Psychologist, capable of **persuading** human beings, in an infinite variety of ways, to **want freely** to share God's eternal and blessed life? Isn't God **our Father in heaven?** Do not our earthly fathers do all in their power **to persuade** us, their children, **to choose freely** to do what is right, though they do not always succeed? Shouldn't **our Father in heaven** do all in His power, which is infinite, **to persuade** us, His children by divine adoption, **to choose freely** to do what is right? And whereas earthly fathers do not always succeed, because their powers of persuasion are of a **finite** sort; shouldn't our heavenly Father always succeed, and with every last human beng, because His powers of persuasion are **infinite?** And so, since God wants us to want freely to share in His eternal and blessed life, and since His powers of persuasion are infinite; it would seem to follow that every last human being will, **as a matter of fact,** be persuaded by God to choose freely what God wants him to choose freely. Thus, if the free will **of another** is an obstacle to **my** impetrating eternal life for that **other,** that obstacle is no match for God's infinite power. From which we may conclude that the **first** of the four conditions for effective impetration should not be restricted to praying **for oneself,** but should be extended to praying **for others** as well. And this seems to be in accord with what Aquinas says elsewhere,[21] where he observes that, since a man in the state of grace is fulfilling God's will, and so is a **friend** of God, it is congruous (or appropriate) that God fulfill the will of that man as he prays for the salvation of another. Friends do for their mutual friends what they request of one another; I do for John, who is my friend and Paul's, what Paul (who is also my friend) asks me to do for John. Indeed, a friend will do for a friend's friend, even if the friend's friend is not his friend; I will do for Joseph, who is Michael's friend, since Michael is my friend, though Joseph is not.

The most perfect prayer

The Lord's Prayer is the most perfect prayer, since prayer is, in one way of putting it, what interprets our desires before God.[22]

Prayer is our interpreter -- Aquinas uses the word "interpres" -- before God. But, what does it mean to say that prayer is our **interpreter?** If we look carefully at the Latin word "interpres," we can see that it comes apart into "inter" and "pretium." When we speak to God in prayer, we can look at the prayer as rising from us to God. And, of course, as rising to God, the prayer is **between** ("inter") us and God, between us and God as telling Him that we desire certain things because those things are of worth or of value ("pretium") to us, i.e., because they are **precious** to us (hence, **orationes** are also called **preces).** Thus, **orationes** are **preces (pretia)** between **(inter)** man and God. **Orationes** are **inter-preces,** i.e., **inter-pres.**

Since prayer discloses our desires to God, it is right to ask for things, if it is right to desire them. Now, in the Lord's Prayer, we not only ask for things

---

[21] "...quia...homo in gratia constitutus implet Dei voluntatem, congruum est, secundum amicitiae proportionem, ut Deus impleat hominis voluntatem in salvatione alterius..." (*S.T.*, I-II, a.114, a. 6, c.).
[22] "...oratio est quodammodo desiderii nostri interpres apud Deum..." (*S.T.*, II-II, q. 83, a. 9, c.).

which it is right to desire, but also in the order in which it is right to desire them.

It is clear, moreover, that the first object of our desire is the end or goal, and then afterwards the things which bring us to the goal. Our goal is God. And we tend toward this goal in two ways: 1) first of all, as wanting God's glory **for God,** and 2) secondarily, as wanting God's glory **for us,** i.e., for us to enjoy it. The first wanting pertains to the love by which we love God in Himself, and the second pretains to the love by which we love ourselves in God. And this is why the first of the seven petitions of the Lord's Prayer is **Hallowed be thy name,** in which we note our desire for God's glory for God Himself; and the second petition is **Thy kingdom come,** in which we note our desire to be brought into His kingdom, that we might enjoy His glory therein.

As regards the things which bring us to our goal, there are two kinds. First, there are those which are useful **of themselves,** or **by their nature itself,** for bringing us to our goal. Secondly, there are those which bring us to our goal **not** of themselves, but accidentally, i.e., by removing obstacles. Of those which are useful of themselves, one is useful directly and principally, namely the one by which we merit eternal happiness, which we do by obeying God. And it is this which we note in the third petition, namely **Thy will be done on earth as it is in heaven.**[23] The other, useful of itself, is such instrumentally, as a kind of help to us in meriting eternal happiness. It is this which we note in the fourth petition, namely **Give us this day our daily bread.** And, "our daily bread" is to be understood **both** as the Sacramental Bread, the daily use of which is of great profit for the life of the soul (and this includes in some way all the other sacraments) **and** as ordinary bread, which is required for the life of the body (and this includes other foods as well, in sufficient amounts); for the Eucharist is our chief sacrament as bread is our chief food.

With respect to being brought to our goal accidentally, i.e., by the removal of obstacles, it is to be pointed out that there are three obstacles which can keep us from achieving eternal happiness. Fist of all, there is **sin,** which directly

---

[23]   The first three petitions will be perfectly fulfilled in the life to come; the last four are concerned with the needs of the present life. (*Ibid.,* ad 1).

excludes us from God's kingdom. This is what we note in the fifth petition, namely **Forgive us our trespasses.** Secondly, there is **temptation** to sin, which can keep us from obeying God's will. This is what we note in the sixth petition, namely **And lead us not into temptation,** in which we do not ask not to be tempted, but rather not to be conquered by the temptation. Thirdly, there are all sorts of **evils in addition to sin** (though lesser evils than sin, which is the greatest of evils), which (along with sin) keep our present life from being a fuller or more abundant enjoyment of the beginnings of eternal happiness. And this is what we note in the seventh petition, namely **Deliver us from evil,** meaning thereby not only, though principally, the evil of sin, but also evils such as the pain and suffering brought on by floods, hurricanes, volcanic eruptions, earthquakes, and the like.[24] -- Luke, unlike Matthew, does not mention the third petition, namely **Thy will be done on earth as it is in heaven,** because it is, in a way, a repetition of the first two petitions, inasmuch as God's will tends chiefly to this, that we humans come to know of His holiness (first petition) and come to reign with Him in His kingdom (second petition). Nor does Luke, unlike Matthew, make mention of the seventh petition, namely **deliver us from evil,** since being delivered from evil means primarily being kept from being overcome by temptation to sin.[25]

---

[24] This ordering of the seven petitions of the Lord's Prayer is set out by Aquinas in *S.T.*, II-II, q. 83, a. 9, c.
[25] *Ibid.*, ad 4.

CHAPTER FOUR

THE TRINITY

THE GOD TO WHOM the virtue of religion inclines us to render His due, and to whom our prayers are said in order to obtain those things which He has ordained will take place **only** if we pray for them -- this God is a triune God.

The present chapter is concerned with some of the things which Aquinas has to say about the Trinity.

That there are three Persons in God cannot be known by natural reason. Aquinas argues for this claim as follows. Man can come to a knowledge of God by natural reason, but only from a knowledge of creatures.[1] To make clearer what this means, one can note that we humans cannot experience God with our natural knowing capacities, which are sense observation, introspection, and analysis. Not by sense observation, because God is not a physical thing. Not by introspection, because God is not a human mind, nor any state or activity of a human mind. Nor by analysis, because the idea of God is not the same as God Himself. If we could experience God by any of our natural knowing capacities, we could know thereby both **that God exists** and all about **what He is,** including the truth that there are three Persons in God.

Now, our knowledge of the creatures we experience, continues Aquinas, leads us to a knowledge of God, Whom we do not experience, as an effect leads to a knowledge of its cause. And so, we can know about God, by natural reason, only those things which must pertain to Him as to the first principle or source of the beings we experience. Now, the creative power of God is

---

[1] "...homo per rationem naturalem in cognitionem Dei pervenire non potest nisi ex creaturis..." (*S.T.,* I, q. 32, a. 1, c.). See also *S.T.,* I, q. 12, a. 4; a. 11, a. 12.

common to all three Persons, to the whole Trinity; whence creative power pertains to the oneness of God's essence, and not to the distinction of Persons. And so, concludes Aquinas, we can know about God, by natural reason, the things which pertain to the oneness of His essence, but not the things which belong to the distinction of Persons.[2]

What, then, can man do with natural reason -- this will be a task for the philosophy of religion -- when he thinks about the Trinity of Persons, or about other truths which are unknowable by natural reason? He can try to defend these truths against obejctions, by showing that what is expressed in these truths is **possible,** or at least **not impossible.**[3] And this, of course, presupposes that what is expressed in them can in some way be made **intelligible,** or understandable, to us humans. Thus, in addition to the task of showing possibility, or at least non-impossibility, philosophy of religion has the prior task of showing intelligibility. And this, of course, will be done by reflecting carefully on the things which we experience. In the case of the Trinity, these experienced things are especially our own intellectual and volitional activities.

Two processions

The Persons of the Trinity are distinguished in the Sacred Scriptures by relations of origin, i.e., of procession. And this makes sense. For, it is easy to see that what has its origin in something is in some way distinct from that in which it has its origin; or that what proceeds from something is in some way distinct from that from which it proceeds. This is why it makes good sense to begin by considering the relevant origins, or processions, and then to consider the relevant relations. In that way one can make suitably clear and intelligible what it means to say that there are Three Persons in one God.

---

[2] *S.T.,* I, q. 32, a. 1, c.
[3] "...sufficit defendere non esse impossibile quod praedicat fides [de Trinitate, et de aliis huiusmodi]..." (*Ibid.*)

Quite naturally, one wants to begin by objecting that to proceed from another, i.e., to have its origin in another, would seem to be excluded by the fact that God is the **first** principle of all things. How can what is first be truly first, and yet proceed from another? Wouldn't that from which the first proceeds be prior even to what is first?[4]

To say that something proceeds from another (or that it originates from, arises out of, another), responds Aquinas, is to say that the other out of which it arises is performing some sort of action or activity. But activity is of two sorts. Some activities terminate in something extrinsic to that in which these activities begin, as in the case of the activity by which fire heats water, or the activity by which something is moved locally. But other activities remain in the things in which these activities begin, as in the case of the activity by which the intellect knows something.[5] Now, activities which terminate in something extrinsic can have no role with respect to the divine processions, since God is not a body, nor is He second to anything. Moreover, since God is above all things, the divine processions are best understood by us by likening them to features of His highest creatures, i.e., intellectual things. And this is why the divine processions should be understood as intelligible or volitional emanations, as emanations of intelligible words or of volitional inclinations, which remain in the one who understands or loves.[6] Clearly, what remains in God can be neither prior to, nor posterior to, God.

One might want to object, further, that there can be no processions in God, because what proceeds from something is diverse from that from which it proceeds. And there is no diversity in God, but utmost simplicity.[7]

In a procession based on activities which terminate in something extrinsic (...id quod procedit secundum processionem quae est ad extra...), responds Aquinas, what proceeds must be diverse from that out of which it proceeds.

---

4 "...procedere ab alio videtur rationi primi principii repugnare. Sed Deus est primum principium..." (S.T., I, q. 27, a. 1, obj. 3).
5 S.T., I, q. 27, a. 1, c.
6 Ibid.
7 "...omne procedens est diversum ab eo a quo procedit. Sed in Deo non est aliqua diversitas, sed summa simplicitas..." (S.T., I, q. 27, a. 1, obj. 2).

Not so, in the case of a procession based on the immanent activities of intellection and volition (...id quod procedit ad intra processu intelligibili, non oportet esse diversum...). Indeed, the more perfect the procession, the more perfectly one are what proceeds and that from which it proceeds. For, it is clear that the better something is understood (and loved), the more deeply is it within the understanding intelligence (and the loving will), and the more thoroughly one are what is understood and what understands (or what is loved and what loves). For the intellect becomes one with what it understands to the extent that it actually understands. Whence, since the divine intellect is the most perfect of intellects, it is necessary that the divine word be perfectly one with that from which it proceeds, without any diversity whatever.[8]

The divine processions, as noted above, are to be understood as based on the **immanent** actions or activites (i.e., actions which remain **within** the agent) which are distinctive of intellectual nature. And these actions are of two sorts.[9] There is, first, the action of the intellect, the action of understanding, on which is based the procession of the concept of the thing which is understood; this is the procession of the **spoken one,** i.e., of the word. And the word remains within that, i.e., the intellect, from which it proceeds. There is, secondly, the action of the will, the action of loving, on which is based the procession of the inclination of the will to want what is good for the thing which is loved; this is the procession of the **loved one,** i.e., of the spirit. And the spirit, too, remains within that, i.e., the will, from which it proceeds. But, whereas the word, the **spoken one,** is **in the** understanding intellect **as a generated likeness** of the thing which is understood; the spirit, the **loved one,** is **in** the loving will **as an inclination** which impels or motivates the will to want what is good for the thing which is loved.

Moreover, there are **only two** immanent activities which pertain to intellectual nature, and so to divine nature, namely understanding **(intelligere)** and loving **(velle).** For sensing, which in a certain way is an

---

8   *S.T.,* I, q. 27, a. 1, ad 2.
9   See *S.T.,* I, q. 27, aa. 3-4.

activity which remains within the sense, is not an intellectual activity. Nor is sensing wholly outside the realm of activities which terminate in something extrinsic to that in which these activities begin; for sensing requires an activity which begins in the sensible object and terminates in the sense itself. From which it is clear that there are **only two** processions in God -- the procession of the **spoken one (processio verbi),** and the procession of the **loved one (processio amoris).** [10]

It is to be noted that the procession of the **spoken one (processio verbi)** in God is called a **generation.** But this is to be properly understood. "Generation" here is **not** taken in the **common sense** it has as used with respect to all generable and corruptible things, i.e., as signifying a movement from non-being to being. Rather, it is taken as used with respect to living things, i.e., in the sense of a birth **(nativitas),** i.e., the origin of a living thing from a living principle joined to it; so that what is generated is **like** what generates with respect to its **species,** as in the case of a man proceeding from a man, or a horse from a horse. In the procession of the word in God, God proceeds from God. This procession is thus a generation; and the word which proceeds is called the begotten **(genitum)** and the Son **(Filius).**[11]

It is to be noted, further, that the procession of the **loved one (processio amoris)** in God is **not** to be called a generation, but rather something else.[12] This is so because of a fundamental difference between the intellect and the will. The intellect is actualized by reason of the fact that the thing understood is in the intellect according to a **likeness** of itself. The will, however, is actualized **not** by the fact that there is in the will a **likeness** of the thing loved, but rather by the fact that there is in the will an **inclination** impelling it toward the thing loved (because of its **likeness** in the intellect). Procession **by likeness** can be called a generation, since **like** generates **like.** Procession **by**

---

10   *S.T.,* I, q. 27, a. 5, c.
11   *S.T.,* I, q. 27, a. 2, c.
12   "...Deum nominare non possumus nisi ex creaturis,... Et quia in creaturis communicatio naturae non est nisi per generationem, processio in divinis non habet proprium vel speciale nomen nisi **generationis.** Unde processio quae non est generatio, remansit sine speciali nomine. Sed potest nominari **spiratio,** quia est processio spiritus..." *(S.T.,* I, a. 27, a. 4, ad 3).

inclination should **not** be called a generation, for an inclination is **not** a likeness (though it is **based** on a likeness). We cannot name God except from creatures; and in the case of creatures, a nature is communicated only by way of generation. Thus, one naturally wants to call the procession in God (by which the divine nature is communicated to divine persons) **generation.** But, since the divine nature is communicated to the **loved one** by way of **inclination** (which is **not** the way of generation) rather than by way of **likeness** (which **is** the way of generation), it ought to have a different name. And this is how the name "spiration" **(spiratio)** came to be suggested.[13]

Four relations

In God, there are, according to Aquinas, **four** relations[14] -- paternity, filiation, spiration and procession -- and **only** four.[15]   These relations are **real** relations,[16] and are **really distinct** from one another;[17] though each relation is **identical** with the divine essence.[18]

These relations are real relations

If paternity and filiation are not really in God, points out Aquinas, it would follow that God is **not really** the Father **nor really** the Son, but only **in our understanding.** But God **is** really the Father and really the Son.[19] Similarly with respect to spiration and procession. If these relations are not really in God, then God is not really the Holy Spirit, but only in our understanding.

---

13   *Ibid.*
14   *S.T.,* I, q. 28, a. 4.
15   *Ibid.*
16   *S.T.,* I, q. 28, a. 1.
17   *S.T.,* I, q. 28, a. 3.
18   *S.T.,* I, q. 28, a. 2.
19   *S.T.,* I, q. 28, a. 1, *sed contra.*

For a fuller grasp of the claim that these relations are real relations, one should note, points out Aquinas, that only relations, among the genera of the accidents, are such that some of them can be things of reason, and in no way real things.[20] For, unlike quantity or quality, relation does **not** signify something which inheres in something else. Relation is a unique accidental category in that it signifies only that something (whatever) is in some way "ordered to" or "ordered toward" something else (whatever). Now, sometimes this "being ordered to or toward" something else **really** belongs to things, i.e., belongs to them as existing in the real world, quite independently of our understanding; as when we say that this person is related to that person as father to son, or as father to daughter. Being a father, being a son, being a daughter -- all of them -- belong to things as they exist in the real world. But sometimes this "being ordered to or toward" belongs to things **only as understood by us,** i.e., with dependence on our understanding; as when we say that animal is related to man as a genus to a species.   Being a genus and being a species do **not** belong to things as they exist in the real world.   They are rather orderings, or relations, which depend **on our understanding.**

Now, when something which proceeds from a source (or principle), and the source from which it proceeds, are **of the same nature** -- it is necessary that both, i.e., what proceeds and the source from which it proceeds, belong to the same order. For example, if one is **real,** so is the other; if one is **of reason,** so is the other; if one is actual, so is the other; if one is a creature, so is the other; if one is divine, so is the other. Moreover, if both are real, the **relations** between them will be real. Since what proceeds, in God, and that from which it proceeds, are identically the divine nature; and since the divine nature is real; it must be that the relations based on these processions are real.[21]

---

20   S.T., I, q. 28, a. 1, c.
21   Ibid.

Each of these relations is identical with the divine essence; yet each is really distinct from the others

If each of these relations is not identical with the divine essence, notes Aquinas, it would be a creature; since every thing which is not the divine essence is a creature. And so, the Father and the Son and the Holy Spirit would be creatures.[22]

The sense of this claim can be made clearer, Aquinas observes, by considering that in each of the nine accidental genera there are two things to take into account: 1) what belongs to each **as an accident,** and this is **common** to them all, namely to exist in a subject; and 2) what belongs to each as the **particular sort** of accident which it is, and this is **proper** to each, that whereby each genus of accident is distinguished from the other eight genera. Now, in genera other than relation, e.g., in quantity and quality, even what is **proper** to each has a **reference to its subject;** quantity is the measure **of substance,** and quality the disposition **of substance.** But what is proper to relation does not have a reference to its subject, but rather to something different from the subject, i.e., to its relative opposite.

Now, there is nothing in God which is an accident inhering in a subject. Rather, whatever is in God is God's essence. And this is why whatever has accidental existence in creatures has substantial existence in God, when transferred to God. For example, God's wisdom is not a divine accident in the divine substance. And so, to the extent that relations in created things have an accidental existence in a subject (relations have this **in common** with the other accidental genera), relations really existing in God have the substantial existence of the divine essence, completely identical with it. But, to the extent that the relation is an "ordering to or toward something" (this is what is **proper** to the genus of relation), it is **not** to or toward the divine essence, but rather to or toward something else, i.e., its relative opposite -- paternity to filiation, and spiration to procession. And so, each of the divine relations is identical with the divine essence; yet each is distinct from the other relations,

---

22   *S.T.,* I, q. 28, a. 2, *sed contra.*

for distinction is included in the nature of relative opposition.[23] Thus, paternity, filiation, spiration and procession -- each of them -- is really identical with the divine essence. But each is really distinct from the others.

There are only four relations in God; neither more than four, nor less than four

Every relation, notes Aquinas citing Aristotle, is based either on quantity, as are **twice as big,** and **half as big;** or on action and passion, as are the maker to the made, and father to son. There is no quantity in God. And so, every real relation in God must be based on action (and passion). But, not on action according to which something extrinsic to God proceeds from God, since God's relations to creatures are not really in God.[24] Thus, the real relations in God must be based on actions according to which what proceeds from God remains within God.

But there are only two such processions,[25] one based on the activity of the intellect, namely the procession of the **spoken one (processio verbi);** the other based on the activity of the will, namely the procession of the **loved one (processio amoris).** Now, there are two relations based on each procession, one being the relation of **what proceeds from a principle (source),** the other being the relation of the **principle (source) itself.** The procession of the **spoken one (processio verbi)** is said to be a generation, in the proper sense which pertains to living things. And the relation of the principle of generation in perfect living things is called **paternity;** whereas the relation of what proceeds from the principle is called **filiation.** The procession of the **loved one,** on the other hand, does not have a proper name, as noted earlier;[26] and hence, neither do the relations based on this procession. The relation of the **principle** of this procession has come to be called **spiration;** and the relation of **what proceeds** has come to be called **procession.** But, it is

---

[23] *S.T.,* I, q. 28, aa. 2-3.
[24] This is shown at some length in *S.T.,* I, q. 13, a. 7, and briefly noted in *S.T.,* I, q. 28, a. 1, ad 3.
[25] *S.T.,* I, q. 27, a. 5.
[26] *S.T.,* I, q. 27, a. 4.

to be noted, both these names, i.e., "spiration" and "procession," are names pertaining to the processions, or to the origins, themselves, and not to the relations.[27]

Three persons

There is a plurality of persons in God,[28] argues Aquinas; but only three.[29]

There is a plurality of persons in God

One might want to begin by objecting that only that is truly one in which there is no number. But plurality implies number. And so, since God is most truly one, we ought to conclude that there is *not* a plurality of persons in God.[30]

Because of God's supreme oneness and simplicity, responds Aquinas, there cannot be a **real** plurality of **absolute** properties in God, i.e., properties like goodness and wisdom; for these are **not** opposed to one another, and so are not really distinct. But, this is not the case with respect to relative properties, i.e., relations. For relations are predicated of a thing as "to or toward another;" and for that reason, though really dictinct because **the others toward which** the relations are predicated are opposed to one another; they do not imply any composition (which would destroy oneness and simplicity) **in that of which** they are predicated.[31]

Moreover, the word "person" in the expression "divine person," quite unlike the word "person" **in common,** signifies a relation as a thing which subsists as having the divine nature.[32] Now, there is a plurality of relations

---

27 *S.T.,* I, q. 28, a. 4, c.
28 *S.T.,* I, q. 30, a. 1.
29 *Ibid.,* a. 2.
30 *S.T.,* I, q. 30, a. 1, obj. 3.
31 *Ibid.,* ad 3.
32 *S.T.,* I, q. 29, a. 4, c.

(four) in God.[33] It folows therefore that there is a plurality of things which subsist as having the divine nature. And this is to say that there is a plutality of persons in God.[34]

To make the immediately preceding clearer and more understandable, one ought to take into account what the word "person" means as said of God. To begin with, it should be noted that there is something in the meaning of a **less** universal word which is **not** included in the meaning of a more universal word. For example, **rational** which is included in the meaning of the word "man" is not of the meaning of "animal." Similarly, there is something in the meaning of "human person" and in that of "divine person" which is **not** of the meaning of "person" **in common.**   "Person," in common, means **an individual substance of a rational nature,** as formulated by Boethius; i.e., a given particular or individual substance which has control or mastery over its own actions, and which is not only acted upon, as are other individual substances, but acts, and of itself, as well.[35] Now, an individual is something undivided in itself, but divided or distinct from others. A person, therefore, of any nature at all, is something, i.e., an individual (of that nature) which is distinct from others. Thus, a **human** person is something with **this** flesh and **these** bones and **this** soul, which are the principles which individuate men. And though such individuating principles are not of the meaning of "person" in common, they are nonetheless of the meaning of "human person." Now, distinction in God comes about **not** by **this** flesh and **these** bones and **this** soul, but only by relations of origin.[36] Moreover, a relation in God is not an accident inhering in a subject, but is the divine essence itself. Whence the relation is subsistent, just as the divine essence is subsistent. Thus, just as deity is God, so too the divine paternity is God the Father, who is a divine person. And so, "divine person" signifies a relation as subsistent. And this is to signify a relation as a substance which is an individual which subsists as having the divine nature; though what subsists as having the divine nature is not something other than the divine nature itself.[37]

---

[33] See above, the section entitled: **Four relations,** pp. 76-80.
[34] *S.T.,* I, q. 30, a. 1, c.
[35] *S.T.,* I, q. 29, a. 1, c.
[36] See above, the section entitled: **Four relations,** pp. 76-80.
[37] *S.T.,* I, q. 29, a. 4, c.

Only three persons in God

There is the person of the Father, which is subsistent paternity. There is, secondly, the person of the Son, which is subsistent filiation. And the Son is really distinct from the Father, because paternity and filiation are opposed to one another as relative opposites. Thirdly, there is the person of the Holy Spirit, which is subsistent procession. For procession is opposed, as a relative, only to spiration; but neither spiration nor procession are opposed either to paternity or to filiation.

To make this clear, one must keep in mind that the plurality of persons in God is a plurality of subsistent relations, really distinct from one another. Now, the real distinction among persons in God obtains only with respect to relative (relational) opposition. Thus, it is necessary that opposed relations belong to different persons; and if there are any relations which are not opposed, they must belong to the same person. Paternity and filiation, therefore, since they are opposed relations, belong necessarily to different persons. And so, subsistent paternity is the person of the Father, and subsistent filiation is the person of the Son. Now, the two remaning relations (i.e., spiration and procession), though opposed neither to paternity nor to filiation, are nonetheless opposed to one another. It is impossible, therefore, that both (spiration and procession) belong to the same person. And so, it must be either that **one** of them belongs to **both** paternity and filiation; or that **one** belongs to paternity, and the **other** to filiation. If **one** belongs to **both** paternity and filiation, which one is it -- spiration or procession? If **one** belongs to paternity, and the **other** to filiation, which one belongs to which?

Can **procession** belong to **both** Father and Son, or to **one** or the **other?** Clearly not. For if procession did belong to both, or to either; then intellectual activity would arise out of volitional activity, which would mean that God **loves** Himself "before" He **knows** Himself; which is unacceptable. Or, perhaps more clearly, it would mean that the **generating** person (by way of **knowing;** this is the Father) and the **generated** person (by way of **being known;** this is the Son) would proceed from the **spirating** person (by way of loving; this would have to be the Holy Spirit); which is unacceptable, inasmuch as **loving** oneself "follows on" **knowing** oneself, just as **being loved** by oneself "follows on" **being known** by oneself. Thus, **spiration** must belong both to the person of the Father and to the person of the Son, inasmuch as spiration is not relatively opposed either to paternity or to filiation. And **procession** must belong to another person, called the Holy Spirit, inasmuch as procession is relatively opposed to spiration. Thus, there are only three persons in God, namely the Father and the Son and the Holy Spirit.[38]

The preceding may become clearer, if one considers that God **as knowing** Himself is the Father, and **as being known** by Himself is the Son. God **as loving** Himself is both the Father and the Son, and **as being loved** by Himself is the Holy Spirit. For **knowing** and **being known** are relative opposites, and so are **loving** and **being loved;** but **knowing** and **loving** are not relative opposites, just as **being known** and **loving** are not relative opposites. Thus, the person of the Father is God **as knowing** and **as loving** God Himself; the person of the Son is God **as known by** and **as loving** God Himself; the person of the Holy Spirit is God **as loved by** God Himself. -- God the Father **does not proceed,** but **is proceeded from;** God the Son both **proceeds** and **is proceeded from;** God the Holy Spirit **proceeds,** but **is not proceeded from.**

A last attempt to make the argument of Aquinas (in *S.T.*, I, q. 30, a. 2, c.) clearer:
1. Paternity and filiation are opposed. Therefore each belongs to a different person.
2. Spiration and procession are opposed. Therefore, each belongs to a different person.
3. Spiration is **not** opposed to paternity. Therefore, both belong to a same person, i.e., to the Father.
4. Spiration is **not** opposed to filiation. Therefore, both belong to a same person, i.e., to the Son.
5. Procession is **not** opposed to paternity. Are we to say, therefore, that both

---

38   *S.T.*, I, q. 30, a. 2, c.

belong to a same person, i.e., to the Father?

6. Procession is **not** opposed to filiation. Are we to say, therefore, that both belong to a same person, i.e., to the Son?

7. But from 3 and 5, in conjunction with 2, **both** spiration and procession cannot belong to the person of the Father, since spiration and procession are opposed.

8. And from 4 and 6, in conjunction with 2, **both** spiration and procession cannot belong to the person of the Son, since spiration and procession are opposed.

9. Thus, either A or B:

A. either spiration belongs to both the Father and the Son; or procession belongs to both Father and Son.

B. spiration belongs to one (either Father or Son), and procession belongs to the other (either Father or Son).

10. Procession cannot belong to both Father and Son, because they (i.e., Father and Son) are opposed on the basis of the **activity of knowing,** and procession is based on the **activity of loving.**

11. Therefore, spiration belongs to both Father and Son (from 9A and 10).

12. Nor can it be that spiration belongs to one, and procession to the other (as in 9B), because Father and Son are opposed on the basis of the **activity of knowing alone,** and in no way on the basis of the activity of loving.

13. Procession must, therefore, belong to a third person, a person distinct from both Father and Son. This person is called the Holy Spirit.

Thus the divine paternity is the person of the Father, the divine filiation is the person of the Son, and the divine procession is the person of the Holy Spirit. Clearly, therefore, there are only three persons in God.

Five notions

There are five notions, according to Aquinas, which pertain to the Trinity of persons in God -- 1) not generated by another **(innascibilitas),** 2) generating another **(paternitas),** 3) generated by another **(filiatio),** 4) jointly spirating another **(spiratio),** 5) spirated by another(s) **(processio).** A notion is a concept **(ratio)** by which we humans come to know or to understand what is distinctive of each of the divine persons;[39] or, a concept (ratio) which "notifies," i.e., makes known to us (notificat) a divine person in its distinction from the other divine persons.[40] It is interesting, and instructive, to "notice" the connection between the noun "notio" and the verb "innotescere." It is by a **notio** (one or more) that what is distinctive of a divine person **comes to be noticed** (known, understood) by us -- **innotescit nobis.**

Aquinas argues for these **five** notions in the following way. The divine persons, he begins, are multiplied in terms of **origin.** Now, origin entails both **"that from which** another (originates)" -- **a quo alius** -- and **"that which** (originates) **from** another" -- **qui ab alio.** And it is in terms of both of these, i.e., 1) **a quo alius,** and 2) **qui ab alio,** that what is distincive of each divine person can be made known **(potest innotescere).** What is distinctive of the person of the Father can**not** be made known by **noticing** that the Father **is from another,** but rather by **noticing** that the Father is **not from another,** not from any other at all. And this is what is conveyed by the notion **innascibilitas** (or **ingenitum** in the sense of **non genitum,** rather than in the sense of **increatum).**[41] But there is more with respect to making known the person of the Father, inasmuch as others are **from the Father;** and this in two ways. First, inasmuch as the **Son** is from the Father, the Father is made known by the notion of **paternity;** secondly, inasmuch as the **Holy Spirit** is from the Father, the Father is made known by the notion of **joint spiration (communis spiratio).** -- The person of the Son can be made known by noticing that the Son **is from another,** i.e., from the Father, by generation **(nascendo);** and this is conveyed by **filiation.** But, because there is another **from the Son,** i.,e., the Holy Spirit, the person of the Son is made known in the same way as the person of the Father, that is by the notion of **joint spiration (communis spiratio).** -- The person of the Holy Spirit, lastly, can be made known by noticing that He (the Holy Spirit) **is from another,** or **from**

---

[39] "...notio dicitur id quod est propria ratio cognoscendi divinam personam..." (S.T., I, q. 32, a. 3, c.).

[40] "...notiones significantur ut rationes **notificantes** personas..." (S.T., I, q. 32, a.3, ad 2).

[41] See S.T., I, q. 33, a. 4, ad 3. But the Father **is not from another,** it ought to be pointed out, not only as from a father, and so **ingenitus** or **non genitus;** but also **not from another** as from a spiration.

others; and this is conveyed by the notion of **procession**. But, the person of the Holy Spirit can**not** be made known by noticing that **another is from Him;** for there is **no** divine person who proceeds from the Holy Spirit. -- Aquinas concludes, from the immediately preceding, that there are five notions which pertain to the Trinity of persons in God, namely: **innascibilitas, paternitas, filiatio, communis spiratio, processio.** Three of these function to identify the person of the Father, namely: **innascibilitas, paternitas,** and **communis spiratio.** Two function to identify the person of the Son, namely: **filiatio,** and **communis spiratio.** One functions to identify the person of the Holy Spirit, namely **processio.** There is no reason, as I see it, why there should not be a sixth notion, a **negative** one, namely: another does **not** proceed from the Holy Spirit (neither as from a father, nor as from a joint spiration), which was noted by Aquinas himself in the **sed contra.** [42] This would correspond, in a way, to the **negative** notion of **innascibilitas,** which is one of the three which function to identify the person of the Father.[43]

Aquinas brings the **corpus** of this article to a clarifying end by noting that of the **five names** used to designate the **five divine notions,** only four are used to designate the divine **relations;** for **innascibilitas** is not a relation, except reductively.[44] Furthermore, only four of the five are used to designate **properties** of the divine persons; joint spiration **(communis spiratio)** is **not** a property, because it belongs to **two** persons. Three function as **personal notions (notiones personales),** i.e., as indicating what **constitutes** a given person, namely: **paternitas** (constitutive of the Father), **filiatio** (constitutive of the Son), and **processio** (constitutive of the Holy Spirit). **Communis**

---

[42] "Sed contra, videtur quod [notiones] sunt plures. Quia sicut Pater **a nullo est,** et secundum hoc accipitur notio quae dicitur **innascibilitas,** ita a Spiritu Sancto **non est alia persona.** Et secundum hoc oportebit accipere **sextam** notionem..." (*S.T.,* I, q. 32, a. 3, *sed contra.*).

[43] See just above, footnote 41.

[44] Aquinas explains what he means by this **reductive** sense: "...ingenitum uno modo significat idem quod **increatum:** et sic [ingenitum] secundum substantiam dicitur; per hoc enim differt substantia creata ab increata. Alio modo significat id quod non est genitum. Et sic relative dicitur, eo modo quo negatio reducitur ad genus affirmationis, sicut **non homo** ad genus substantiae, et **non album** ad genus qualitatis. Unde, cum **genitum** in divinis relationem importet, **ingenitum** etiam ad relationem pertinet. Et sic non sequitur quod Pater ingenitus distinguitur a Filio genito secundum substantiam; sed solum secundum relationem, inquantum scilicet relatio Filii negatur de Patre..." (*S.T.,* I, q. 33, a. 4, *ad 3*).

spiratio and **innascibilitas,** lastly -- though **not** personal notions, inasmuch as **communis spiratio** does **not** constitute a person (being **common to two**), and neither does **innascibilitas** (being something **negative**) -- are nonetheless **notions of a person (notiones personarum,** as distinct from **notiones personales),** inasmuch as they serve to identify **in some way** what belongs to certain divine persons.

CHAPTER FIVE

FRIENDSHIP

THE TRIUNE GOD, about whom the religious man reads again and again (**re-lego:** I read again), whom the religious man chooses again and again after having let Him slip away through indifference and neglect (**re-eligo:** I choose again), and to whom the religious man binds himself again and again (**re-ligo:** I bind again)[1] -- this triune God is a friendly God, an unimaginably, superabundantly, limitlessly friendly God. He offers His friendship to every created person, human and angelic, even though He is infinitely above them all; even though friendship seems difficult, if not impossible, among unequals. He is each such person's best friend, inasmuch as He is both unlimitedly lovable and unlimitedly loving. Moreover, He is His own best friend. That is, each divine person loves the other two as he loves himself. Each divine person loves the unlimited lovableness of the other two with the unlimited love with which he loves his own.

The present chapter is concerned with some of the things which Aquinas has to say about man's friendship with man (**amicitia**), and about man's friendship with God (**caritas**), in order to help illuminate, if only in a beginning way, God's friendship with Himself, and the friendship which each divine person has for the other two.

---

[1] See above pp. 53-54.

Friendship between man and man

As Aquinas sees it, friendship is a certain kind of love, and love is the wanting of good things, either for oneself or for another.[2] Friendship is **benevolent** love, i.e., wanting good things for another **for the other's sake,** rather than for one's own sake (or, at least **not wholly** for one's own sake).[3] Friendship is, secondly, a **mutual** love, love with a return of love.[4] A friend is friend to a friend.[5] It would be odd to say that we are friends, but that our friendship is **not** mutual -- that I love my friend, but he does not love me; or that he loves me, and I do not love him. Thirdly, friendship is a love which is **not hidden** from,[6] a love which is recognized by, known by, each of the friends. I love another, and the other **knows** about it; just as the other loves me, and I **know** about it. It would be odd to say that we are friends, but that we (one, or the other, or both) do **not** know about it. Friendship is, fourthly, a love which is motivated by virtue, or by pleasure, or by usefulness.[7] We love one another because of the virtue we see in one another, or because of the pleasure we get from one another, or because we are useful to one another (or all three). It would be odd to say that we are friends, but we have **nothing** which motivates us. Fifthly, friendship is a love which is based on, in the

---

2   "...sicut Philosophus dicit in *II Rhetoric.,* amare est velle alicui bonum,... vel sibi vel alio..." (S.T., II, q. 26, a. 4, c.).

3   "...oportet amico velle bonum gratia illius et non propter bonum amantis..." (*In VIII Ethic.,* lect. 2, n. 1558). "...non quilibet amor habet rationem amicitiae, sed amor qui est cum benevolentia: quando scilicet sic amamus aliquem ut ei bonum velimus. Si autem rebus amatis non velimus bonum, sed ipsum eorum bonum velimus nobis, sicut dicimur amare vinum aut equum aut aliquid huiusmodi, non est amor amicitiae..." (*S.T.,* II-II, q. 23, a. 1, c.).

4   "...amicitiam dicimus esse benevolentiam in contrapassis, ut scilicet amans ametur..." (*In VIII Ethic.,* lect. 2, n. 1559).

5   "...nec benevolentia sufficit ad rationem amicitiae, sed requiritur quaedam mutua amatio: quia amicus est amico amicus..." (*S.T.,* II-II, q. 23, a. 1, c.).

6   '...apponendum est ad complendam rationem amicitiae, quod sit...non latens: multi enim sunt benevoli, quos nunquam viderunt, inquantum ex auditis existimant eos esse...virtuosos, vel utiles sibi. Et potest esse quod idem patiatur aliquis illorum ad eum qui sic est benevolus. Huiusmodi ergo homines videntur esse benevoli adinvicem, sed non possunt dici amici, cum id lateat eos qualiter se habeant adinvicem..." (*In VIII Ethic.,* lect. 2, n. 1560).

7   "...[amici] amant se [vel] propter virtutem, ... [vel] propter utile, ... [vel] propter delectationem..." (*In VIII Ethic.,* lect. 3, n. 1564). See also *In VIII Ethic.,* lect. 2, n. 1552, n. 1557, n. 1561).

sense of **grows out of,** a common context (a **communicatio**), [8] an association, in which the friends share, for whatever reason. Friendship among brothers grows out of their having their blood in common; and they share their blood because they **happen** to have been born of the same parents. Friendship among fellow travelers grows out of their having a ship in common; and they share their ship because they **happen** to have a same destination in mind. Friendship among fellow citizens grows out of their having laws and a president and a judicial system in common; and they share these because they **happen** to have been born in the same country. Friendship among fellow students grows out of their having a class in common; and they share this class because they **happen** to be at a same university, because they **happen** to have some sort of interest in taking the class, and because it **happens** [9] that they were able to work the class into their various and diversely demanding schedules.

Friends **want good** things for one another, we have said, and they know that they do; and they want these good things for the other, for the other's sake. What are these good things? Existence (life), virtue, pleasure, usefulness. I want my friend to exist (to live), and he wants that for me; and we both know that we do. I want him to grow in virtue, and he wants that for me; and we both know that we do. I want to bring him various sorts of pleasures, of body and of mind, especially of the mind; and he wants those for me; and we both know that we do. I want to be useful to him; and he wants to be useful to me. And we both know that we do.

Clearly, **wanting** good things for one another leads to **doing** good things for one another. And so, friends **do** good things for one another -- with respect to existence (life), and virtue, and pleasure, and usefulness. Doing good things for one another requires **spending time together.** And so, friends spend time together. The better the friends, the more time they spend together. Doing good things for one another, along with spending time with one another, generates a delight for one another. And this is why, as Aquinas sees it, the

---

[8]   "...talis autem mutua benevolentia [i.e., amicitia] fundatur super aliqua communicatione..." (S.T., II-II, q. 23, a. 1, c.).
[9]   It is interesting to notice that it "happens" that there is something **accidental** here.

proper activity of friends is "convivere amico cum delectatione" [10] -- living with, i.e., spending time with, one another, and delighting in it.

Why, it may be asked, do friends relate to one another in this way? The answer which Aquinas gives is this -- because a friend sees his friend as **another self,** and for that reason loves his friend **as he loves himself.**[11] When a person sees in another person the things he sees and loves in himself, he begins to look at the other as at another self, and begins to love that other as he loves himself. What are these things in the other which, when seen, generate a love for the other which is like love for oneself? These things are, primarily and especially, **the virtues,** notes Aquinas; but also **pleasure** and **usefulness.** (And going beyond **motives** to **associational contexts** -- blood, household, class, football team, city, country). And having noted that, he also notes that friendship motivated by **virtue** is **true** friendship, whereas friendship motivated by pleasure or by usefulness is **not.**[12] And this is so because virtue-friendship is **purely** benevolent, whereas other sorts of friendship are not. Other sorts are ultimately -- and if not ultimately, **at least in part** -- **for one's own sake,** whereas virtue-friendship **alone** is for the sake of the other, **and only** for the sake of the other.

---

[10] "...quidam dicuntur actu [as opposed to "secundum habitum"] amici inquantum 1) convivunt cum delectatione adinvicem, et 2) sibi invicem bene faciunt, quae duo videntur pertinere ad actum amicitiae..." (*In VIII Ethic.,* lect. 5, n. 1596). -- Whereas in n. 1596 Aquinas is concerned to note that the activity of friends consists in at least two things; in n. 1600 he notes that friends can do without the second, i.e., without doing useful things for one another **when they are not** in need, but that they cannot do without living together, spending time together, thereby delighting in one another.

[11] "...amicus secundum affectum amici est quasi alius ipse, quod scilicet homo afficitur ad amicum sicut ad seipsum..." (*In IX Ethic.,* lect. 4, n. 1811). "...cum ad aliquos superabundanter amicitiam habemus, haec assimilatur dilectioni quam habet homo ad seipsum..." (*Ibid.,* n. 1812).

[12] Following Aristotle, Aquinas notes that the word "friend" has, as a matter of linguistic fact, at least three uses: 1) virtue-friend, 2) pleasure-friend, 3) utility-friend. Only virtue friends are **true** friends. The other two sorts are **not** true friends. People call them friends because of certain similarities to virtue-friends. See *In VIII Ethic.,* lect. 4, n. 1590; nn. 1593-94; also *In VIII Ethic.,* lect. 6, nn. 1622-23.

Friendship between man and God -- *Caritas*

Since likeness is **the** cause of friendship, and man and God are infitnitely **unlike** one another, it seems that it is not possible for man God to be friends. A likeness is possible between two persons either with respect to lovable qualities (i.e., either virtue, or ability to provide pleasure, or ability to be useful); or with respect to having a common associational context, a context which relates in some way or other to the goals of human life. Now, man and God are quite unlike one another. They are alike **neither** with respect to lovable qualities: for God's virtue, God's ability to provide pleasure, and God's ability to be useful are infinitely above that of man; **nor** do they have an associational context in common: they share no way of life, no pursuit; they are not blood relatives, nor fellow travelers, nor fellow students, nor fellow citizens, etc. This is what Aristotle seems to have in mind when he notes that "when one party is removed to a great distance, as God is, the possibility of friendship ceases."[13] Something similar is also the case, even when **both** parties are **men,** and there is a great distance between them, as "in the case of kings; for with them, too, men who are much their inferiors do not expect to be friends; nor do men of no account expect to be friends with the best or wisest men."[14]

Moreover, notes Aquinas as he asks whether **caritas** (the theological virtue) is a kind of friendship, nothing is more proper to friendship than that friends should live together, i.e., spend time together, do things together. But, man and God do not do this; neither do men and the angels. And so, one might object, whatever else **caritas** might be, it cannot be friendship; since man has **caritas**, both with respect to God and with respect to the angels.[15] The underlying reason seems to be this, that men are **bodily** entities, whereas God and the angels are **spiritual** entities, and so seem to have no associational context in common.

---

13 Aristotle, *Nicomachean Ethics,* Bk. VIII, ch. 7, 1159 a 4-5.
14 *Ibid.,* 1159 a 1-2.
15 **"Nihil...est ita proprium amicitiae sicut convivere amico;** ut Philosophus dicit in *VIII Ethic..* Sed caritas est hominis ad Deum et ad angelos, **quorum non est cum hominibus conversatio,** ut dicitur *Dan.* 2: 11. Ergo caritas non est amicitia." (*S.T.,* II-II, q. 23, a. 1, obj. 1).

In response to this objection, Aquinas explains that man has a twofold life. One is a life with respect to his sensitive and bodily nature. According to this life, man has no associational context in common with God or with the angels. Man's other life is a spiritaul life according to his mental nature. And it is with repect to this life that man has to do with God and with the sngels, can spend time with them. In the present life, our spiritual contacts with God and with the angels are imperfect; but they will be perfected in the next life, when we see God face to face. And so, our friendship with God (caritas) is an incipient and imperfect friendship in the present life. But in patria, this friendship (caritas) will be perfected.[16]

What, as Aquinas sees it, makes it possible for man and God to be friends? For even with respect to man's spiritual life according to his mental nature, God is infinitely above man. What makes such friendship possible is the fact that God has decided to share with man something which is really God's. This can happen even among men, i.e., that a superior decides to share something which is his with an inferior, thereby making for a kind of equality (for friends ought to be equals in some way or other, to some extent or other), thereby making it possible for friendship to arise. The superior can decide to share with the inferior his knowledge, his possessions, his home, or any other good by which he surpasses the inferior. Now, God has decided to share with man His eternal beatitude, an endless and blessed life -- something by which God obviously surpasses man. And so, man and God do have an associational context in common. There is thus a basis or a foundation out of which friendship can arise -- friendship, which is a benevolent, and mutual, and mutually recognized love. Thus it is that Aquinas writes:

> . . .since. . .there is something in common between man and God, inasmuch as God communicates, i.e., offers, His beatitude to us, some sort of friendship ought to be founded on that offer. . .[17]

---

[16]   *Ibid.*, ad 1.
[17]   "...cum...sit aliqua communicatio hominis ad Deum secundum quod nobis beatitudinem communicat, super hac communicatione oportet aliquam amicitiam fundari..." (*S.T.*, II-II, q. 23, a. 1, c.).

Since man and God have something in common, i.e., God's eternal and blessed life offered to man as God's gift, it is **possible** for friendship to arise. For, "...if there were nothing in common, there could be no friendship..."[18] But, this is **only a possibility.** **Not** every human being enters into **actual** friendship with God. Even so, **it is fitting** -- "oportet," writes Aquinas -- that some sort of friendship be founded on, arise out of, this offer of eternal and blessed life, simply beause it has been offered **as a gift.** Whenever two persons, a superior and an inferior, have very little, or even nothing, in common, but the superior offers a **shareable gift** to the inferior; not only do the two begin thereby to have something in common -- some sort of associational context, i.e., "communicatio," as Aquinas would put it --, but it **becomes fitting** that the inferior respond to the invitation of the superior by taking steps to contribute whatever he can to help actualize the friendship to which he has been invited.

Love of neighbor as of self

Man's friendship for God -- **caritas** -- manifests itself in two activities: 1) loving one's neigbor as one loves oneself, and 2) loving God above all else. This is the "convivere amico cum delectatione," which flows over into "tribuere bona amico" (or "sibi invicem bene facere") whenever the **human** friend is in need.[19] To love one's neighbor as one loves oneself, is to spend time with the neighbor, **as much time as posssible,** delighting in his company -- and taking care of the neighbor's needs, to the extent that there **are** such needs, and to the extent that one **can** take care of them. To love God above all else is to spend time with God, **all of one's time** (to the extent that this is possible), delighting in His company -- and God has no needs. To be sure, spending **as much time as possible** with one's neighbor is somehow included in, **somehow a part of,** spending **all of one's time** with God. One cannot spend **all** of one's time with God without spending **as much time as possible** with one's neighbor.

---

[18] "...si nulla esset communicatio, non posset esse amicitia..." (*In VIII Ethic.*, lect. 9, n. 1661).
[19] See above, p. 91, footnote 10.

But, how is one to love **all** of one's neighbors as one loves oneself? For there are **so many** of them, indeed **countless** numbers of them. It might be helpful to note that the English word "neighbor" derives from the Old English words "neah," meaning **near** or **close,** and "gebur," meaning **dweller.** A neighbor is a near-dweller, or a close-dweller. And the Latin word which Aquinas uses for neighbor is "proximus," which is the superlative form of the **comparative** form **"propior,"** which means **nearer** or **closer.** And so, "proximus" means **the nearest,** or **the closest.** Now, since there are so many who count as **neighbors** -- i.e., **all** human beings -- it might be better to call them simply **others (alii)** when one is speaking of **all** of them. And then, moving on to speak of **some** of them, to grade them according to degrees of closeness or nearness, so that **some** (indeed, **most**), one might suggest,[20] could be called simply **propinqui** (close), others (fewer by far) could be called **propiori** (closer), still others (fewest by far) could be called **proximi (closest).** Thus, loving others as oneself would mean **loving most** those who are **nearest or closest** (the **proximi**), and **loving less** by grades those who are **further away** (the **propiori** and the merely **propinqui**), on a meaning of "closest" and "further (furthest) away" to be specified in terms of criteria like degrees of blood connection, or various sorts of friendship.

Having made these very general points, one can profitably turn to a number of specific ones. To the question: Whether one should love oneself more than other human beings,[21] Aquinas responds as follows. In man, there are two things to take into account: a) his spiritual nature, and b) his bodily nature. Man should love **himself** more than he loves others [22] **with respect to his spiritual nature.** And this becomes clear if one considers the **reason** for the loving. God is loved as the source of the good on which the love which is

---

20 To avoid confusion, it is to be emphasized that this suggestion with respect to the words "propinqui," "propiori," and "proximi" is **only a suggestion.** I do not find these words so used by Aquinas. Nonetheless, the suggestion does seem helpful.

21 Utrum homo ex caritate magis debeat diligere seipsum quam proximum (*S.T.*, II-II, q. 26, a. 4). It is to be noted that the love of which Aquinas speaks here is **caritas** -- for he speaks of "diligere ex caritate;" and that "proximum" here means simply **another (any other) human being.**

22 "Others," here, is to be taken to mean: others, **after** God, as Aquinas himself explicitly notes: "...secundum hoc [sc. secundum naturam spiritualem] debet homo magis se diligere, **post Deum,** quam quemcumque alium..." (*S.T.*, II-II, q. 26, a. 4, c.).

caritas is founded. Now, a man loves **himself** **(ex caritate)** because he is a participant in that good of which God is the source; a man loves **others (ex caritate)** because they belong to the society of participants in that good. For a man to love others in this way is for him to love them because of a certain sort of **union** which orders him and them to God. Since oneness **(unitas)** is something stronger than union **(unio)**, a man is said to be **one** man in a stronger sense of "one" than a society is said to be **one** society. And this is why **one's own** participating in the divine good is a **stronger reason** for being loved that is **another's** being associated with him in that participation. And so, a man should love **himself (ex caritate)** more than he loves others.

To the question: Whether one should love another more[23] than he loves his own body,[24] Aquinas makes the following response. That is to be loved more **ex caritate** which has within it **more which can be loved,** i.e., that which is intrinsically more lovable. The **soul** of **another** is intrinsically more lovable than is **one's own body,** since the spiritual is more noble than the bodily.[25] Moreover, one's body participates in God's eternal and blessed life only by a kind of **overflow (per redundantiam),** inasmuch as one's body is the soul's instrument; whereas the soul participates in this eternal and blessed life in a full and direct way. Now, the **reason** why we love **another (ex caritate)** is the fact that the other is **associated with** us in a **full and direct** participation in God's eternal and blessed life. And this is clearly a stronger reason for loving than is participation by a kind **of overflow.** And so, one should love another more than one loves his own body, but with respect to the **soul** of that other. Nonetheless, one ought to love **his own body** more that he loves the **body** of another, because one's own body is **closer to** one's own soul than is the body of the other, with respect to the makeup of his own nature as a human being. For body and soul are united in one's substance.

---

[23] "To love more" can mean either 1) to want **greater goods** for the loved one because of the level of the loved one's **intrinsic** goodness and lovableness; or 2) to want **more intensely** for the loved one whatever it is (even a lesser good) which the one who loves wants for the loved one, because of the degree of closeness which the loved one has to the one who loves.

[24] Utrum homo magis debeat diligere proximum quam corpus proprium. (*S.T.*, II-II, q. 26, a. 5).

[25] Though **not** explicitly made here (in *S.T.*, II-II, q. 26, a. 5) by Aquinas, this point is quite clearly implied in his explicit remarks.

To a number of other specific questions, Aquinas responds in terms of a **common** principle which appeals to the distinction between the **object which is loved (ex caritate)** and the **one himself who is loving (ex caritate).** The common principle is this one: to decide who (or what) should be loved **more,** and who **less,** one should consider the question both with respect to the **object loved (ex parte objecti),** and with respect to the **one who loves (ex parte ipsius diligentis).** The object which is **better,** which has in it a **greater** measure of goodness **(id quod habet maiorem rationem boni),** which therefore has within it more which is lovable, is to be loved more[26] than the object which has a lesser measure of goodness. Thus, one should love one's father more than one's son, since we love our fathers to the extent that they are the **sources of our being (sub ratione principii);** a **source** of being has a greater measure of goodness than that which **derives from** the source, and has a greater similarity, as source, to God.[27] Nonetheless, from the point of view of the **one who loves (ex parte ipsius diligentis),** those who are **closer (coniunctius)** to the **one who loves,** are to be loved more[28] than those who are **further removed.** Thus, one should love one's **son** more than one loves one's **father.** And this, for the following reasons. 1) Parents love their children as something which is their own, something which is **of** themselves, something which belongs to them **(aliquid sui).** The father, however, is **not** something **of** the son (...pater...non est aliquid filii...). And so, the love by which a father loves his son is very much like the love by which one loves himself; and so is a stronger love. 2) Parents have a better knowledge of who their children are than children have of who their parents are; and so a stronger love. 3) A son is closer to a parent, being in some sense a **part (though a separated part)** of the being of the parent, than the father is to the son, to whom he is related as **source.** A **part** of the being of a thing is, clearly, **closer** to that thing than is its **source;** and so a stronger love. 4) Parents love their children longer than children love their parents. A father begins to love his son as soon as he is born, indeed even prior to birth; the son, however, does not begin to love the father, until some time later. The longer the love,

---

[26] "More" means that **greater goods** are wanted for the object loved.
[27] S.T., II-II, q. 26, a. 9, c.
[28] "Loved more" means **loved more intensely.**

the stronger the love.[29]

This same common principle -- i.e., from the viewpoint of the **object loved,** the **better** the object, the more it should be loved; and from the viewpoint of the **one himself who loves,** the **closer** the object **to the one who loves,** the more it should be loved[30] -- is used by Aquinas to respond to other specific questions as well. As a first case, we should love **better people** more than people who are not as good, because they are closer to God, the best of all objects, Who has within Himself infinite goodness. This means that we should want for these **better people** a more perfect participation in God's blessed and eternal life. Nonetheless, we should love **more intensely** those who are **closer to us.** This means that though we should want for them a **less perfect** participation in God's blessed and eternal life, to the extent that they are (may be) **less good** than other people; we should want for them this lesser good **with a greater intensity** than that with which we want for the **better** the **greater good.**[31] -- As a second case, one should love his father more than one loves his mother, because though both are sources of one's natural origin, the father excels the mother **as source.** The father is an active source, an agent; whereas the mother is a passive source, a material source.[32] -- A third case. One should love one's parents, both father and mother, more than one's wife, because parents are the **sources** of one's being, and as such, are **lovable objects** with a higher degree of intrinsic goodness and lovableness. Nonetheless, from the viewpoint of **closeness to the one who loves,** one should love one's wife with a **greater intensity** than that with which one loves one's parents. For, a wife is as close to the husband as is his own body; since the wife is joined to her husband so that both exist as one body.[33] -- A fourth case. One should, from one point of view, love one's benefactors more than one loves those whom he benefits; yet, from another point of view, one should love those whom he benefits more than he loves his benefactors. For persons can be

---

[29] *S.T.,* II-II, q. 26, a. 9, c.

[30] It is to be noted that this common principle was also used in deciding the question: **Whether one should love another more than he loves his own body** (above, p. 82 at footnote 24).

[31] *S.T.,* II-II, q. 26, a. 7, c.

[32] *S.T.,* II-II, q. 26, a. 10, c.

[33] "...secundum autem rationem coniunctionis, magis diligenda est uxor: quia uxor coniungitur viro ut una caro existens..." (*S.T.,* II-II, q. 26, a. 11, c.).

loved for two different reasons: 1) either because they are intrinsically of a higher level of goodness and lovableness, or 2) because they are more closely conjoined to the one who loves.[34] Thus, the **benefactor** should be loved more than the benefitted, because the benefactor is intrinsically of a higher level of goodness and lovableness. But, the **benefitted** should be loved more than the **benefactor,** because the benefitted is more closely joined to the benefactor than vice versa. And this is so, for four reasons. 1) The benefitted is, in a sense, something made by the benefactor ("...est quasi quoddam opus benefactoris..."), but not vice versa. Now, it is natural for the maker to love what he has made; for example, as a poet loves his poem. And this is so, because each thing loves its own **existence** and its own **life,** which is manifested in **what it does.** 2) The benefactor sees in the benefitted a **virtuous** good, which he (the benefactor) has put therein; whereas the benefitted sees in the benefactor only a **useful** good. And the **virtuous** good is intrinsically more lovable than the **useful** good. 3) The benefactor **acts,** whereas the benefitted **receives. To act** is better than **to receive.** To love **by acting** is greater than to love **by receiving.** 4) We love more what we work hard at doing or getting. To be a benefactor is to **work hard** at benefitting another; whereas the benefitted, as such, does not work at all. And so, the benefactor loves the benefitted more than vice versa.[35]

These brief reflections, on how one is to love **all** of one's neighbors as one loves himself, can be brought to an instructive conclusion, by emphasizing that love **ex caritate** is not limited by Aquinas to love based on the **nobility,** i.e., on the level of intrinsic goodness and lovability, of the **object being loved;** in which case, one wants greater goods for those who are intrinsically more lovable. It extends also to love based on **bodily ties,** on **closeness** to others **because of blood connections;** in which case, one wants **more intensely** even lesser goods for those who are **closer** to the one who loves. And the reason for this, as Aquinas sees it,[36] is the fact that love **ex caritate,** which is an

---

34 "...aliquid magis diligitur dupliciter: uno quidem modo, quia habet rationem excellentioris boni; alio modo, ratione maioris coniunctionis..." (*S.T.,* II-II, q. 26, a. 12, c.). This, it ought to be noted, is just a very shortened form of the **general principle** which is being used by Aquinas in handling these specific cases.
35 *S.T.,* II-II, q. 26, a. 12, c.
36 See *S.T.,* II-II, q. 26, a. 6.

inclination of the gift of God's grace, is no less ordered than love **ex natura,** i.e., than a **natural** love, which is an inclination of the nature of a thing. For each of these inclinations proceeds from God's wisdom. And grace perfects nature. By our human nature, we are inclined to love **more intensely** those who are **closer** to us because of blood connections. The inclination of grace perfects this natural inclination, just as it perfects our natural inclination to want greater goods for those who are intrinsically more lovable.

Love of God above all else

It was said above[37] that to love God above all else **(ex caritate)** is to spend time with God, **all of one's time,** delighting in His company. **Why,** one might ask, should one love God above all else? And what exactly does it **mean** to love God above all else?

To love God above all else *means* 1) to love God more than one loves **other human persons,** and 2) to love God more than one loves *oneself.* Why should one love God more than one loves **other persons?** Aquinas explains this as follows. Every sort of friendship has its primary reference to that which has in itself, in a primary way, the good upon the communication of which that friendship is based. For example, political friendship bears primarily on the ruler of the state, on whom the common good of the state depends; and this is why the citizens of the state owe it to their ruler to believe in him and to obey him. And domestic friendship bears primarily on the father, on whom the common good of the family depends; and this is why all family members should love the father more than they love one another. Now, the friendship which is **caritas** is based on the common good[38] which is God's blessed and eternal life, the first principle of which is God Himself, from Whom it derives to all who are capable of such life. And this is why God should be loved **before all others** (i.e., **principaliter**) and **more than all others** (i.e., **maxime**); that is, because He is the first cause of blessed and eternal life.

---

[37] Above, p. 94.
[38] God's blessed and eternal life can be called a **common** good, i.e., common to God and to all men, only because God has freely chosen to offer it to **all** men.

All others are to be loved **after** God, and **less than** God. And this is so, because all others participate with us in the blessed and eternal life which derives to all of us from Him.[39]

Why should one love God more than one loves **oneself?** One might begin by objecting that one should love **oneself** more than one loves God. For, as Aristotle points out, the friendly acts and goods which one does and gives to others derive from the friendly acts and goods which one does and gives to oneself. So that, if one does not love oneself more than others, even more than God, one could not love those others, or God, at all.[40]

In arguing for the claim that one should love God more than one loves oneself, Aquinas proceeds as follows. We receive two sorts of goods from God: 1) natural goods, and 2) the goods of grace. Now, since a **part** naturally loves the common good of the **whole** more than it loves its own particular good as the part which it is, it is clear that all things love God, the source of the **natural** goods they have in common, more than they love themselves. And that is why one often sacrifices a part of one's body for the health and good of the whole body, and why a citizen often sacrifices his own life for the welfare and good of the whole state. Similarly, and to a greater degree, man should love **(ex caritate)** God, Who is the common good of all things, more than he loves himself. For God's eternal and blessed life is in God as in the absolutely original and **common source,** from Whom this life derives to all who are capable of participating in it.[41]

In reply to the objection mentioned above,[42] Aquinas notes that Aristotle's point about the source of the friendly acts and goods which one does and gives to another is made in the context of **another** in whom the loveable qualities, or goods, which motivate one's love are **these or those particular** qualities. The lovable qualities, or goods, which are found in God, on the other hand,

---

[39] "...et ideo principaliter et maxime Deus est ex caritate diligendus: ipse enim diligitur sicut beatitudinis causa; proximus autem sicut beatitudinem simul nobiscum ab eo participans..." (*S.T.*, II-II, q. 26, a. 2, c.).
[40] *S.T.*, II-II, q. 26, a. 3, obj. 1.
[41] *S.T.*, II-II, q. 26, a. 3, c.
[42] See just above, footnote 40.

and which motivate man's love **ex caritate,** are found in God **not** as these or those particular goods, but as goods which are the **common** goods of grace for **all** men. Thus, a man ought to love himself more than he loves another man, for the other man is but a particular good. But, he ought to love God more than he loves himself (as well as, more than other men), for God is the **common** good, the **common** eternal and blessed life, the **common** gift of grace, for **all** men.

Deus amator sui

God loves Himself. And above all else. Is God to be said, then, to be selfish? For, if God loves Himself **above** all else, and if God is infinite both as loving and as loved, can there be any of His love left for anything else? Must infinite love of self be selfish love?

In his commentary of the *Nicomachean Ethics* of Aristotle, Aquinas, following Aristotle, pursues the question: Whether a man should love himself the most, or someone else more than himself. What is said there about **man** may be capable of some sort of application to God.

There are probable arguments on both sides of the question, notes Aquinas. First of all, some say that the man who loves himself most of all does things only **for himself,** for his own advantage or utility; and never for others. But, a man who does things **only** for himself, they continue, and **never** for others, is an evil man; and the more he does this, they say, the more evil he is. Therefore, one who loves himself most of all is a most evil man, as they see it, and so is to be reproached.

The virtuous man, on the other hand, does not, they observe, do things only for himself. Rather, in pursuing what is good, he does things for his friends as well as for himself. And very often, he even puts aside and foregoes what is to his own advantage or utility. And so, it is clear, they conclude, that a man who loves himself the most is **not** a virtuous man. Hence, is reproachable.[43]

On the other side of the question, continues Aquinas, men commonly say that we ought to love **most** those who are our best friends. But, our **best** friend is he who wants good things for us, for our own sakes, and wants them for us **in the highest degree (maxime).** Now, each man wants good things for himself, for his own sake, and wants them in the highest degree. And so, each man is his own best friend. Hence, should love himself most of all.[44] And without reproach; indeed, with praise.

Secondly, all the other things by which friendship is identified and judged -- namely beneficence and benevolence and concord -- are found in a man with respect to himself, and in the highest degree **(maxime).** And so, again, a man is his own best friend; and should, therefore, love himself most of all.[45] And with praise.

Thirdly, there are proverbs which suggest that friendship consists in a kind of **oneness (unitas),** proverbs like: there is **one** soul for two friends; friends have all things in common, i.e., as **one;** friendship is a kind of equality, i.e., a kind of **oneness;** friend is to friend as the knee is to the tibia, i.e., close enough to be **one.** Now, oneness belongs most to a person with respect to himself. And so, a man is his own best friend. He should, therefore, love himslef most of all.[46] And with praise.

What is to be made of these arguments? Is the man who loves himself most of all an evil man? Or is he a virtuous man, a good man? And what about God? Is God infinitely evil? After all, He does love Himself **infinitely more** than anything else. Or, is He infinitely good?

---

[43] *In IX Ethic.,* lect. 8, n. 1857.
[44] *Ibid.,* n. 1858.
[45] *Ibid.,* n. 1859. For more details, see *In IX Ethic.,* lect. 4, nn. 1798-1810, in which Aquinas gives careful descriptions of beneficence, benevolence, and concord; and argues, following Aristotle, that a virtuous man is beneficent, benevolent, and has concord, with respect to himself.
[46] *In IX Ethic.,* lect. 8, n. 1860.

If one reflects even briefly on the arguments for each side of this question, one can see that there is a different notion of self-love (or, self-lover) underlying each side. Underlying the arguments for the first side is the notion of a self-love which is **reproachable** or **blameworthy.**   Underlying the arguments for the second side, by way of contrast, is the notion of a self-love which is **laudable** or **praiseworthy.**   God's self-love, to be sure, would have to be a **laudable** or **praiseworthy** self-love, the believer would say; indeed, an **infinitely** laudable self-love.

Further reflection will make explicit what characterizes each of these different notions of self-love. Those who find self-love reproachable or blameworthy, point out accusingly not only that such self-lovers do nothing for others but only for themselves; but also that they provide themselves with an abundant measure of **bodily** goods, goods like money and honors and the bodily pleasure of food and sex. These goods, which such self-lovers take to be the **best** of goods, are goods which all people cannot have at the same time and in abundant measure; and this is why such self-lovers argue and fight over these goods. And those who do succeed in having them in abundant measure, turn this abundance toward satisfying their concupiscence and other bodily passions generally. Thus, such self-lovers love themselves with respect to the irrational, i.e., sensory, part of the soul.[47]

Those, on the other hand, who find self-love laudable or praiseworthy, observe approvingly not only that such a self-lover, in pursuing what is good, does things for his friends as well as for himself, and that he is his own best friend; but also that he provides himself, and always, with an abundance of the goods of the mind, which are not only **thought** to be the best of goods, but **are indeed** the best of goods; that he always obeys his reason or intellect; that he does many things for the sake of his friends and of his country; that he does not abandon his friends, or his country, even if he must die for them; that he gives up money and honor and all **bodily** goods for the sake of his friend; that he even gives up performing virtuous acts himself, so that his friend might do them instead, and thereby grow in virtue and become deserving of praise;

---

[47] *Ibid.*, nn. 1863-1864.

that he would rather live **excellently** for a short time than **mediocrely** for a long time, or even perform just **one great** act of virtue, and even die in the doing of it if necessary, rather than perform **many lesser** acts of virtue. Thus, such a self-lover loves himself with respect to the rational, i.e., the intellectual and volitional, part of his soul. And this part of the soul is, clearly, what is best in man, immeasurably better than the sensory part of the soul.[48]

Deus amator sui. God loves Himself. But, how exactly are we to understand God's self-love? To begin with, His self-love must be of the laudable or praiseworthy sort. Clearly, not of the reproachable or blameworthy sort. For, God is goodness itself, goodness-of-every-conceivable-sort itself; with no admixture of even the slightest bit of evil of any sort at all. Nor does God have an irrational and sensory nature. God's nature is purely intellectual.

Does God the Father love the Son more than the Son loves the Father? And what about the Holy Spirit? Does the Father love the Spirit more than the Spirit the Father? Does the Son love the Spirit more than the Spirit the Son? Do any two of the divine persons taken together love the third more than that third loves the other two taken together? If we use the **common** principle[49] which appeals to the distinction between the **object which is loved** (in terms of its intrinsic goodness) and the **one himself who is loving** (in terms of his **closeness** to the object loved), we can say the following. With respect to the **object which is loved,** there is **nothing** in God which is **better** than, or has a **greater** measure of goodness than, anything else which is found in God. And so, since each divine person is in God, no one of them is better than the other two, whether taken singly or together. Hence, each wants for the other two, both singly and taken together, **exactly as much as** the other two, whether singly or taken together, want for the first -- i.e., eternal and blessed life in triune frinedship. Similarly, with respect to the **one himself who is loving.** There is nothing in God which is **closer to (or further removed from)** anything else which is found in God. And so, since each

---

[48] See *In IX Ethic.,* lect. 9. This **lectio,** in its entirety, sings the praises of the laudable self-lover.
[49] See above pp. 97-98.

divine person is in God, each is as **close to** the other two, taken either singly or together, as the other two, taken either singly or together, are to the first. Hence, each loves the other two, taken either singly or together, **as intensely as** the other two, either singly or together, love the first.

Nonetheless, although each wants for the other two exactly **the same thing,** i.e., blessed and eternal life in triune friendship, since each is an equally, i.e., infinitely, good and lovable object; and although each loves the other two with an equal, i.e., infinite, **intensity,** since each is equally close to the other two, i.e., by a oneness and identity of nature; the love of each for the other two is of a **different** sort. And this is so, because each of the persons is really different or distinct from the other two. No father loves his son with the same sort of love with which the son loves the father; for the father is the **source** from which the son derives, whereas the son is **that which derives** from the source. So, too, the divine Father and the divine Son. Similarly, the Father and the Son together love the Spirit as a **source** loves that which derives from it, whereas the Spirit loves the Father and the Son together as the joint source from which the Spirit derives. -- The Father says: I love the Son because **I know** (generate) the Son. The Son says: I love the Father because **I am known by** (am generated by) the Father. The Father (the knower) and the Son (the known) together say: We love the Spirit because **we** (knower and known) **love one another** (i.e., spirate the Spirit). The Spirit says: I love the Father and the Son, because **I am loved** (spirated) by them (knower and known).

Should God love Himself the most, or someone else more than Himself? The answer is clear and simple. Since God is the most lovable of **objects,** God should love Himself the most (as should any and every being which is capable of loving). Moreover, since God is infnitely lovable, to love HImself the most is to love Himself **infinitely,** i.e., to want for Himself (and He does) an infinite good. And this is intellectual and volitional life without beginning and without end, total and simultaneous. Further, since God is **one** with Himself (and this is **as close as** one can get to an object of love), God should love HImself with infinite **intensity.** And He does.

If God loves Himself infinitely, both with respect to **what He wants** for Himself and with respect to the **intensity** of the wanting; can there be any of His love left for anything else? The answer to this question, too, is clear and simple. God's love, being infinite, is inexhaustible, and overflowing. Its very inexhaustibility is what motivates God's love into an overflow, i.e., motivates Him to create. And having created, God sees in His creations what He sees in Himself. God's creations are God's reflections. And this is why He loves what He creates. He sees and loves in what He creates what He sees and loves in Himself. Each creation is, in a way, something of Himself. And so, God's love of Himself is the source of God's love for all created things. And beyond that, God's **friendship** for Himself, and that of the divine persons for one another, is the source of God's friendship for all created persons, for all intellectual and volitional creations. God (as the Father) **created** all intellectual beings to make it possible for them to have Him as a friend, and for Him to have them as friends. Then He (as the Son) **redeemed** them (i.e., those of them who are of a bodily nature, i.e., human beings) to restore for them that possibility. And having redeemed them, He (as the Spirit) works ceaselessly at **sanctifying** them, in order to actualize that possibility. God's infinitely inexhaustible triune love is an inexhaustible overflowing love -- a ceaselessly creative, redemptive, and sanctifying love. God's triune love can even be said to be a **restless** love. It will not rest until It finds its rest in loving **all that can possibly be loved,** Divine and creaturely; just as **we,** as Augustine proclaims, will not rest until we find our rest in loving **Him.** God's restless love even led Him to assume human nature, thereby enabling Him to do something which He, as God, could never have done, i.e., to die for His friends, the most noble and the most intense of the acts of human friendship. Greater love has no one than he who lays down his life for another. And God has done that for all.

CHAPTER SIX

THE INCARNATION

THE LIMITLESSLY FRIENDLY TRIUNE GOD, Who is His own best friend, and each created person's best friend as well, has decided -- we noted above[1] -- to share with man His eternal beatitude, an endless and absolutely blessed life, so that man and God might have **something in common,** a **communicatio,** by means of which man can come to have a **Divine** Friend. By means of this **communicatio,** God intended to elevate man to a higher level of life; i.e., to make it possible for man, while remaining man, to become a god. But, God did not stop there. In the person of the Son, God chose, while remaining God, to become a man. He decided to share with man man's humbler level of life, a life which is neither endless nor absolutely blessed, a life which enabled Him to have **something else in common** with man, another **communicatio** -- a **communicatio** by means of which God was enabled to do what **human** friends do for **their** (human) friends; indeed, and especially, to lay down His **human** life for them; in order to restore to them the possibility, lost by sin, of eternal friendship with Himself.

The present chapter is concerned with some of the things which Aquinas has to say about the Incarnation.

---

[1]   See above p. 93.

Only one way to preserve intact what the Scriptures say about Christ

In Christ, there is not only the divine nature (in its totality, complete or perfect) but also a human nature (in its totality, complete or perfect). That is, a human nature made up of a rational soul and a human body. So that Christ, the incarnate Son of God, is not only truly God, but also truly man. Moreover, these two natures are united in Christ in one hypostasis, one supposit, one person. This must be so, for it is only in this way that one can preserve intact, unharmed and undiminished, what the Scriptures tell us about the Incarnation. Since the Scriptures attribute **to this man** what belongs to God, and **to God** what belongs to this man, without separating the divine from the human; it must be that it is of one and the same thing that both the divine and the human are predicated.[2] For sometimes Jesus attributes to himself humble and human things, as when he says, "The Father is greater than I am,"[3] and "My soul is sorrowful even unto death,"[4] which belongs **to Him** according to His assumed human nature. But, at other times Jesus attributes to Himself sublime and divine things, as when he says, "I and the Father are one,"[5] and, "All things which the Father has are mine,"[6] which quite clearly belong **to Him** according to His divine nature.

Furthermore, the things Jesus **did,** in addition to the things he said about Himself, manifest the same Scriptural attribution of the divine and of the human to the same thing (person). For we read that Jesus feared, was sad, was thirsty, and died; all of which **He did,** but as human. But He (the very same He) also healed the sick, brought the dead back to life, expelled demons, forgave sins, arose from the dead, then ascended into Heaven; all of which **He did,** but as divine.[7]

The preceding can be made clearer by appealing to the distinction between **that about which (id de quo)** something is predicated, and **that according to**

---

2   C.G., IV, cap. 39, *in principio.*
3   St. John, 24: 28.
4   St. Matthew, 26: 38.
5   St. John, 10: 30.
6   St. John, 16: 15.
7   C.G., IV, cap. 27, *ad finem.*

which (id secundum quod) something is predicated.[8] One must remind oneself that the divine things which are predicated of Christ are **opposed to** the human things which are said of Him. For example, Christ suffered, **(passus)** and Christ cannot suffer **(impassibilis)**; Christ has died **(mortuus)**, and Christ is immortal **(immortalis)**. Clearly, opposites cannot be truly predicated of one and the same thing from the same point of view **(secundum idem)**. Hence, it must be that the divine things which are predicated of Christ are predicated from one point of view, and the human things from another point of view **(secundum aliud et aliud)**. But, both sorts of things are predicated of the **same** Christ. Since the **id de quo** is one and the same, the **id secundum quod** must be twofold; otherwise the divine and the human predications could not be truly made. There must, therefore, be in **one** Christ **two distinct** natures, one human, the other divine. Christ must, therefore, be but **one** hypostasis, or supposit, or person; but **one** person with **two** distinct natures.

Aquinas draws an interesting conclusion from the immediately preceding. Although the Son of God became a man, it is not necessary that the Father and the Holy Spirit also became that same man. For the Incarnation took place not according to a union in nature, which the Three Persons have **in common;** but according to a union in hypostasis or supposit, by which the Three Persons are distinguished. And so, just as in the Trinity there is **more than one** person subsisting in **one** nature, so in the mystery of the Incarnation there is **one** person subsisting in **more than one** nature.[9]

Some errors concerning the Incarnation

Any view of the Incarnation which **explicitly** denies to Christ either human nature or divine nature or both, or the divine personhood of the Word, is in error. Indeed, any view which even **implies** any such denial is in error. A consideration of some examples of such erroneous views will be instructive.

---

8   *C.G.*, IV, cap. 39, *in medio.*
9   *Ibid., ad finem.*

1. There was the view that Christ had a human nature, but that Christ's divinity did not consist in having, in addition, the divine nature. Rather, Christ was said to be divine by means of some kind of superior or excelling participation in the divine glory, which Christ was said to have merited by the works he performed.

This view, argues Aquinas, destroys the mystery of the Incarnation. For, on this view, God would not have taken on flesh, so as to become a man; rather, a man of flesh would have become God. And so, what the evangelist John says would not be true, namely: **Verbum caro factum est;**[10] but rather the exact opposite, namely: **Caro Verbum facta est.**[11]

Moreover, if one considers this view just a bit further, one will see that the God which this man of flesh would have become, would **not** be the **true** God. For, a god by participation in the divine glory, however superior and excellent this participation might be, is for all that **only** something created -- a **created god.** The true God, quite clearly, cannot be both Uncreated and created.

2. There was the view that the Son of God took on (assumed) not a true human body, but only an imaginary human body, i.e., something which **appeared to be** a human body, but in reality was **not** a human body.

Such a view, quite plainly, implies a denial of Christ's true humanity. For, if Christ's body was not a true human body, Christ could not have been a true man. Thus, Christ could not have been truly born, could not have truly eaten, could not have truly drunk, nor truly walked, nor truly suffered, nor truly died, nor truly risen from the dead; nor therefore could He have truly redeemed us. The Scriptures, thus, would have told many lies about Christ; God, their author, would be a liar; and there would have been no need, or use, for Christ's existence at all.[12]

---

10 St. John, 1: 14.
11 C.G., IV, cap. 28, *in medio.*
12 C.G., IV, cap. 29.

3. There was the view that Christ's body was not an earthly body, and that it was not taken from the matter of the Virgin Mary's body; that His body was, rather, a heavenly body. The proponents of this view thought that all earthly matter had been created by the devil, and they thought it unacceptable, therefore, that Christ's body should be a body of earthly matter. They concluded, therefore, that Christ passed through the Virgin Mary's earthly body as if through some sort of aquaduct or water-carrying reed or pipe, without receiving anything from her body which could enter into the composition of His body.[13]

This view, quite clearly, implies a denial of Christ's true humanity. For, if Christ's body were not an earthly body made up of earthly materials, like water and air, it would **not** be a **true** human body. And so, Christ would not be truly a man.

Moreover, if the body of Jesus received nothing from **Mary's** body to enter into the make up of **His** body, Mary could **not** be **truly** the mother of Jesus. The Scriptures, thus, would again be telling a lie, for the Scriptures explicitly state that Mary was the **mother** of Jesus.

Lastly, it is abundantly clear that it is God who created earthly matter, and not the devil. For God, and **only** God, is the creator of **all** things.[14]

4. There was the view that not only was the body of Christ not taken from the matter of the Virgin Mary's body (agreeing to this extent with the immediately preceding view), but that something of the Divine Word itself was **converted into** the flesh of Christ, in the same sense in which the water, at the marriage feast in Cana of Galilee, was **converted into** wine.[15]

This view, it is to be noted following Aquinas, deprives Christ of the personhood of the Word. For the Word of God, being God, is simple. So that, if **something of** the Word of God had been converted into flesh, the **whole** of

---

13 C.G., IV, cap. 30.
14 *Ibid.*
15 C.G., IV, cap. 31, *in princ.*

the Word would have been so converted. Now, what is converted into something else, ceases to be what it was before being converted; the water, once converted into wine, is no longer water, but wine. Thus, on the view being considered, the Word of God, once converted into the flesh of Christ, would no longer be the Word of God. And so, Christ would not have had the divine personhood of the Word.[16] Moreover, this view is impossible, to begin with. For God is absolutely immutable. Since the Word of God is truly God, it is impossible for the Word to be converted into anything at all, let alone into the body of Christ. Besides, the Word of God is eternal, i.e., without beginning or end; and the Scriptures call Christ the Word of God even **after** the Incarnation.[17]

5. The preceding views fell into error concerning the **body** or **flesh** of Christ. But there were other views which were erroneous with respect to the **soul** of Christ.

There was the view that there was **no human soul** in Christ, that Christ took only a human body, and that Christ's divinity took the place of the soul. This view seemed to take too literally the words of St. John, saying: **Verbum caro factum est,**[18] taking these words to mean that the Word of God took on **only** human flesh **(caro).**

But, argues Aquinas, this view is unacceptable because God cannot be the form of a body. This view, recall, holds that Christ's divinity took the place of the soul; and so Christ's divinity would have been the form of Christ's body. Now, the form of a body is not existence itself, but a principle of existence. But God is existence itself. Therefore, God cannot be the form of a body. Moreover, something composite results from the union of matter and form. Thus, both matter and form are related to the composite as potentiality to actuality. But there is no potentiality in God. And so, God cannot be a form united to a matter. Besides, what exists **in itself** is more noble than what exists **in another.** Now, the form of a body has existence **in another,** namely

---

16   C.G., IV, cap. 31, *in medio.*
17   *Ibid., post medium.*
18   St. John, 1: 14.

in the body of which it is the form. Since God is the most noble of beings, God must be something which exists **in itself,** and so cannot be the form of a body.[19]

Moreover, if Christ did not have a human soul, He could not have been a true man. Whereas, Scripture has it that Christ was a true man.

Besides, a human body without a human soul cannot be a human body. So that, if Christ did not have a human soul, neither did He have a human body. Thus, Christ would not have been a human at all.

Then too, If Christ did not have a human soul, He could not have been of the same species as other men. Thus, He could not have been Mary's son, nor Mary His mother; for what is born of a living thing must be of the same species as that from which it is born, in order to be called the latter's son.[20]

Furthermore, Scripture has it explicitly that Christ had a soul, as in Matthew: **Tristis est anima mea usque ad mortem;**[21] and as in John: **Nunc anima mea turbata est.**[22]

On the union of *body* **and** *soul* **and** *divinity* **in Christ**

From the preceding,[23] notes Aquinas, it is clear that in Christ there is not only the **divine nature,** but along with that a true **human body** and a true **human soul.**   How, then, is one to understand how the three -- i.e., divine nature, human body, and human soul -- are joined, or united, or put together, in Christ?[24] As Aquinas sees it, the three are joined in Christ **in one person,** as was made clear in section one.[25] And this one person is the **person**

---

19   *C.G.,* I, cap. 27. This chapter contains additional arguments for the claim that God cannot be the form of a body.
20   *C.G.,* IV, cap. 32.
21   St. Matthew, 36: 38.
22   St. John, 12: 27.
23   That is, from what was considered in *C.G.,* IV, cap. 28-33.
24   *C.G.,* IV, cap. 34, *in princ.*
25   That is, in the section entitled: **Only one way to preserve intact what the**

of the Son of God, the Divine Word, as will become clear, it is hoped, in what follows in the present section.

1. There was the view that a true human soul and a true human body, joined by a natural union, were found in Christ, so that Christ was of the same nature and species as other human beings. Moreover, according to this view, God inhabited, dwelled in, **this** human being as in a temple, i.e., by grace, and by a loving joining of wills, just as God inhabits (dwells in) other **holy** human beings. But, there was a **fuller measure** of God's grace **in this man,** so that Christ was God's temple in a prior and special way, and so that his will was joined to God's will more closely that the wills of other holy men. And this is why Christ was called a **god,** and a **son of God,** and **lord,** and **holy,** and **Christ,** in a prior and fuller sense than other holy men. But, on this view, the **person of this man** and the **person of the Divine Word** were not one and the same person. And so, things said of the one could not be said of the other. For example, it could be said that **Christ** was born of the Virgin Mary, and that he suffered, died, and was buried; but this could *not* be said of the Divine Word, **not** of the Son of God. Whence, further, though one could say that the Blessed Virgin was the mother of Christ, one could not say that she was the mother of God, or of the Word of God.[26]

Aquinas finds this view unacceptable. For, on this view, the Word of God was joined to this man **only** by an indwelling of grace, from which followed the union of their wills. And, notes Aquinas, such an indwelling of the Divine Word in a buman being is not the same as the Incarnation of the Word. For the Word of God, God Himself, was joined by an indwelling of grace **to every holy person** since the beginning of the world. Such a joining, clearly, is not an incarnation; otherwise, God's Incarnation would have taken place **countless** times since the beginning of the world. But, the Incarnation of God is a unique and singular event. -- Nor does it suffice to say that the Word of God, God Himself, dwelled in this man with a **fuller measure** of grace. Since **more and less** would not diversify the nature or species of the union, union by way of a fuller measure of grace could **not** amount to the **Incarnation**

Scriptures say about Christ, pp. 109-110.
[26]   *C.G.,* IV, cap. 34, *post principium.*

of the Word of God.[27] It must be, therefore, that the union was a union in **one person,** as was made clear above in section one;[28] and that this one person is the **person of the Word of God,** as will become clear from the following.

Demonstrative pronouns refer to the person (or hypostasis, or supposit). For no one would say, "I am running," when **someone else** is running; unless figuratively, as in the case in which someone else is running **for me, in my place.** But the man who was called Jesus said about himself, "Before Abraham came to be, I am;"[29] and "I and the Father are one;"[30] and many other things which manifestly pertain to the **divinity** of the Word. It is clear, therefore, that the person (or hypostasis, or supposit) of the man saying these things is the person itself of the Son of God.[31] -- It follows, thus, that what is said of **this man** can also be said of the **Word of God,** and vice versa. And so, both Christ and the Divine Word (since they are **one** in the **person** of the Son) were born of the Virgin Mary, and suffered, and died, and were buried; and Mary is the mother of the divine Word as well as of the man Christ.[32]

2. There was the view that in Christ there was only **one nature,** just as there was only **one person.** Before the union of the divine and the human in Christ, on this view, there were **two** natures; but in their union, they became one, namely the divine. So that, on this view, it was said that the person of Christ was **of** two natures, but not that it **subsisted in** two natures. This view was put forward to try to avoid a difficulty, namely this one. If there are **two** natures in Christ, i.e., the human and the divine, there must be two **persons** as well, i.e., a human person and a divine person. For, whatever subsists in an intellectual or rational nature is a person of that nature. Thus, if Christ subsists in a human nature, he must be a **human** person; and if he subsists in a divine nature as well, he must be a **divine** person, too. Two natures seem to

---

27   *Ibid.*
28   That is, in the section entitled: **Only one way to preserve intact what the Scriptures say about Christ,** pp. 109-110.
29   St. John, 8: 58.
30   St. John, 10: 30.
31   C.G., IV, cap. 34, *ad medium.*
32   Chapter 34 of Bk. IV of the *C.G.* is a very long chapter, offering many arguments, and in great detail, for the claim that the person of Christ is the person of the Divine Word. *Quod videte.*

require two persons.[33] It seems impossible, therefore, that there be in Christ **one** person and **two** natures.

Aquinas finds this view unacceptable for many reasons. Without going into all of them, one can note, following Aquinas, that it makes no sense to speak of **two** natures **before** their union in Christ. **Before** the union of the divine and the human in Christ -- whatever the mode of the union --, neither **Christ** nor his **human nature** (and this includes **both** his body **and** his soul) existed. And thus, it is impossible to maintain that **before** their union in Christ there were **two** natures; and after their union, only **one**.[34] It would be better to say, one wants to note, that before their union in Christ, there was but **one** nature, i.e., the divine; and only **after (or at)** their union were there two.

Furthermore, if the person of Christ was **of** two natures, **each** of the two natures would have remained in Christ, either as **not** becoming one, or as **becoming** one. If they did **not** become one, then Christ had **two** natures. But, if they **did** become **one,** namely the **divine,** as this view has it; then Christ could not be a true man, indeed not a man at all.

Besides, if Christ's one nature were something **one** constituted out of **two** component natures, these two natures would be related to one another either as bodily parts, or as matter to form. How else could they be related? But the divine nature is not something bodily; hence cannot be related to human nature as a bodily part to another bodily part. Nor is the divine nature **matter,** nor can it be the **form** of some matter.[35]

What, now, is to be said by way of responding to the objection, noted above,[36] that **two** natures seem to require **two** persons? So that it appears impossible that there be in Christ **one** person and **two** natures? -- The proper response to this objection seems to be the following. Christ has two natures,

---

33 C.G., IV, cap. 35, *in princ.*
34 C.G., IV, cap. 35, *in fine.*
35 C.G., IV, cap. 35, *ad finem.*
36 Just above, p. 116.

but so that though He subsists **in** both of them, He does **not** subsist **through** both of them. Though Christ subsists **through** (as well as **in**) the divine nature, He subsists only **in** the human nature. To clarify. **Two natures** require **two** persons only if **both** natures are that **through which** the persons subsist, i.e., through which they **exist as individual substances.** Now, the person of the Divine Word subsists **only** through the **divine nature** itself -- and **in no way** through the **human** nature of Christ. Indeed, the Son of God subsists through the divine nature **from all eternity to all eternity** -- always did, does now, and always will -- and so both **before** and **after** He became Christ the man, by assuming a human nature. Thus, whereas the Son of God both **exists** and **is divine** because of the divine nature; it is not the case that He both **exists** and **is human,** because of the human nature. Thus, it is **not necessary** that there be **two** persons in Christ.[37]

---

[37] *C.G.*, IV, cap. 49, the replies to objections 3 and 4. The objections themselves were recorded earlier, by Aquinas, in cap. 40 of *C.G.*, IV.

CHAPTER SEVEN

PAIN AND SUFFERING

THE INCARNATE GOD is a limitlessly loving God. His desire to share His eternal and infinitely happy life with countless freely created **free** human persons is so intense that He does not hesitate at anything, that He is prepared to go to the greatest lengths, in order to **persuade** these persons to **choose freely** to accept a share in that life. He is prepared to undergo pain and suffering, and of the most unbearable sort; indeed, even death. It has been said that pain and suffering and death are required to prove love. How, then, could they -- pain and suffering and death -- not have been required to prove **Divine** love? In the Person of the Son, God freely chose, while remaining God, to become man, to take on human nature. And this, in order to be able to suffer and to die. Moreover, He does not hesitate to ask that men, too, choose to suffer and to die, and **alongside Himself,** and for the same reason, i.e., to prove their love. God loves, and proves it. Since men are made in God's image, God asks, invites (indeed, at times, even requires) them to love, and to prove it; and in the same way that He does.

The present chapter is concerned with some of the things which Aquinas has to say about pain and suffering -- that of God, and that of man.

The suffering of God

In His human nature

The agony in the garden, the scourging at the pillar, the crowning with thorns, the carrying of the cross, the crucifixion -- the five sorrowful mysteries of the rosary are a poignant summary of the suffering of the incarnate God, the Son of the Father, the Lord Jesus Christ. And His crying out in deepest **mental** anguish, as he was hanging on the cross dying, "Deus meus, Deus meus, ut quid dereliquisti me?" and in matching **bodily** distress, "Sitio," are the peak points of that poignant summary.

1. But **none** of this suffering belongs to the incarnate God in His divine nature. To make this clear one must consider that the union of the human nature with the divine nature took place in the **person** of the Son of the Father, in the **hypostasis,** in the **supposit;** and in such a way that the distinction of these two natures was preserved. That is, the human nature did not become the divine, nor did the divine become the human. Rather, the person of the Son became human, while remaining also divine. The Lord Jesus is one person with two distinct natures, each nature retaining what is proper to it. Human nature is passible, i.e., capable of suffering; the divine nature is impassible, i.e., incapable of suffering. And so, whereas this suffering is to be attributed to the supposit of the divine nature, i.e., to the person of the Son of God, it is **not** to be attributed because of the divine nature, which is **not** passible, but rather by reason of the human nature, which **is** passible.[1]   If God had not become man, God would not have been able to undergo these sufferings. It is the Son of the Father who underwent these sufferings, but because He had become a man.

---

[1] *S.T.*, III, q. 46, a. 12, c.

2.   What is to be said by way of describing these sufferings? Since the Son of the Father suffered in His human nature, He suffered in both body and soul, these being the two essential parts of human nature.   What is to be said by way of describing His suffering **in body**?   By way of describing His suffering **in soul**?

In body, He endured **every** human suffering, i.e., suffering in **every** bodily member. In His head, he suffered from the crown of piercing thorns. In His hands and feet, he suffered from the nails by which He was fastened to the cross. On His face, he suffered from blows and spit. Over His entire body, from the lashes, and from the weight of the beam of the cross as He carried it, staggering and with Simon's help, to Calvary. In addition, He suffered in **every** sense: in touch, by being flogged and nailed; in taste, by the vinegar and gall He was given to drink; in smell, by the place of crucifixion which reeked with the stench of corpses; in hearing, by the outcries of blasphemers and scorners; in sight, by seeing the tears of His mother and of the disciple whom He loved.[2]

Moreover, the pain of this bodily suffering was very great, indeed the **very greatest.**[3] This can be seen, first of all, from the **sources** of this bodily pain, in particular from the facts that 1) the crucified are pierced in bodily parts which are filled with highly sensitive nerves, i.e, in the hands and in the feet; 2) that the weight of the hanging body intensifies the agony; 3) that the crucified do not die at once, like those slain by the sword, but linger for a considerable period of time; 4) that loss of blood, perspiration, and rapid and labored breathing cause dehydration, and as a consequence unbearable thirst.

This can be seen, secondly, from the fact that His **body** was endowed with a **most perfect constitution,** having been fashioned by the power of the Holy Spirit; and consequently, His sense of touch, the sensitivity of which is the reason why humans feel pain, was most acute.[4]

---

[2] *S.T.,* III, q. 46, a. 5, c.
[3] *S.T.,* III, q. 46, a. 6, c.
[4] *Ibid.*

This can be seen, also, from the fact that He accepted all this pain **voluntarily** to the all-embracing end of delivering **all** men from **all** sin; and consequently, he embraced the amount of pain which was proportionate to achieving this all-embracing end.[5]

In soul, He suffered from sadness, weariness, and fear;[6] from anxiety and distress, from feelings of helplessness and abandonment; and in such a way that His whole soul suffered, both in its essence and in all its faculties -- with but one exception, the following. The reason or intellect of the Lord Jesus did not suffer from its highest **object,** which is God; for God was the cause, not of any of the sadness or weariness or fear he was feeling, but rather of the delight and the joy He was experiencing at the same time. Nonetheless, all the faculties of Jesus' soul **did** suffer, inasmuch as they are all rooted in the essence of His soul as in their **subject;** and this subject suffered, when the body, of which the soul is the act, suffered.[7]

Furthermore, the pain of His suffering **in soul** was the **very greatest,** just as was the pain of His suffering **in body.** For He accepted this suffering, too, **voluntarily,** just as He had accepted His bodily suffering, to the all-embracing end of delivering **all** men from **all** sin; hence the proportionate magnitude of the pain.[8]

3. What is to be said, now, about what the Lord Jesus achieved by His suffering?

To begin with, His suffering won for us the forgiveness of our sins, for these reasons. First, because it moves us to acts of love, and love procures pardon for sins. Secondly, because it was the price, paid by His love and obedience, of our redemption from sin. Thirdly, because His suffering, though in His **human** nature, was the suffering of a **divine** person, and so with divine power for expelling sin.[9]

---

[5] *Ibid.*
[6] *S.T.,* III, q. 46, a. 5, c.
[7] *S.T.,* III, q. 46, a. 7, c.
[8] *S.T.,* III, q. 46, a. 6, c.
[9] *S.T.,* III, q. 49, a. 1, c.

Secondly, His suffering freed us from the devil's power over us; first of all, by winning for us the forgiveness of our sins, as noted just above. Secondly, by reconciling us with God, as noted just below, at "Fourthly His suffering reconciled us . . ."   Thirdly, by vanquishing the devil, inasmuch as His **human** suffering, at the hands of the power of the devil, was undeserved and **unjust,** requiring therefore by **divine justice** that **humans** be freed from the power of the devil.[10]

Thirdly, His suffering freed us from the punishment of satisfaction required by sin. First of all, directly -- since His suffering, as belonging to a **divine** person, was of itself not only sufficient, but superabundantly so, as satisfaction for the sins of the whole human race. Secondly, indirectly -- since His suffering is the cause of the forgiveness of sins, upon which the debt of punishment rests.[11]

Fourthly, His suffering reconciled us with God, in two ways. First, because His suffering takes away sin, by which men become God's enemies. Secondly, because His suffering is a most acceptable sacrifice to God, appeasing God perfectly and for every offense of the human race, inasmuch as His suffering was **voluntary** and **human** (in His human nature) and **divine** (in His divine person).[12]

Fifthly, His suffering opened up to us the gate of the kingdom of heaven; for that gate was closed to us by sin -- by the sin of our first parents, which is somehow **common** to the whole human race, as well as by the **personal** sins of each one of us committed by our own individual acts. And His suffering freed us from sin -- from the common sin of the whole human race, both as to guilt and as to debt of punishment; and from our personal sins, too, since we share in His suffering by faith and love and the sacraments.   And so, His sufferings opened up to us the gate of heaven.[13]

---

[10] *S.T.*, III, q. 49, a. 2, c.
[11] *S.T.*, III, q. 49, a. 3, c.
[12] *S.T.*, III, q. 49, a. 4, c.; a. 1, ad 4.
[13] *S.T.*, III, q. 49, a. 5, c.

Lastly, by His suffering He merited to be exalted -- by His Resurrection, by His Ascension, by being seated at the right hand of the Father, and by being made judge of the living and of the dead. He merited these things -- this fourfold exaltation -- in justice, for by His suffering He had humbled himself beneath His dignity in four ways: 1) by suffering and dying -- and so He merited the Resurection; 2) by being put into a tomb (in body), and into hell (in soul) -- and so, He merited the Ascension; 3) by the shame and mockeries he endured -- and so, He merited being seated at the right hand of the Father to show forth His divinity; 4) by being delivered up to the power and judgment of men -- and so, He merited being given His power and judgment over them.[14]   When one strips himself, through his just and loving will, of something he ought to have, he deserves that something further be granted to him as a reward for his just and loving will.

It is easy to see that **love** is what was at the bottom of the suffering of the Lord Jesus. Love moved Him to embrace His suffering. And His suffering freed us from our sins, from the power of the devil over us, and from the debt of punishment for our sins; it reconciled us to God, opened up the gate of heaven for our entry, and merited His being exalted. -- Love requires suffering. Suffering proves love. Love and suffering merit freedom, entry, and exaltation. His love and suffering, for Him. Our love and suffering, through His, for us.

In His divine nature

It is of the nature of a person, as person, to love others. To love others is, among other things, to sympathize with these others, i.e., to be glad and to rejoice when these others are glad and rejoice, to sorrow and to suffer when these others sorrow and suffer. Moreover, to love is to sorrow and to suffer when freely given love is not freely returned. -- One might want to conclude from this that, since God is a person, He sorrows and suffers when

---

[14] *S.T.*, III, q. 49, a. 6, c.

human persons sorrow and suffer, as well as when human persons, by sinning, do not freely return His freely given love; and this, in His **divine** nature. One might want to conclude further that, since God is eternal, He has sorrowed and suffered from forever; and that, since He is infinite, He has suffered with infinite intensity; for He had determined from forever to create man and the angels, and had known from forever that some of these would not freely return His freely given love. Suffering after all is **mental** as well as physical. Can one conclude that God, the infinite and eternal, has been undergoing eternally enduring, and infinitely intense, mental suffering?

Moreover, if there are created persons in hell -- whether human persons or angelic -- and if being in hell means, whatever else it might mean, having irrevocably, for forever, unto eternity, chosen not to return God's freely given love; can one conclude from this that God, the eternal and infinite, will sorrow and suffer forever, into the future (i.e., for the eternity for which the damned have condemned themselves to hell), and with infinite intensity? Can one conclude, further, that God's future eternal suffering will cause future eternal suffering to the blessed in heaven, who see Him face to face? How can a friend, face to face, not suffer with his suffering Friend? How can an **eternal** friend, face to face, not suffer **eternally** with his **eternally** suffering Friend? Must one conclude that the eternal happiness of the blessed, whether created or Uncreated, is accompanied, and perhaps necessarily, by eternal suffering? Must one conclude that God, **by creating persons,** has sentenced Himself, and them as well, to eternal suffering?

1. If God suffers in His **divine** nature, then He must, it seems, **be changed** in His divine nature, by what happens in the world He has created, e.g., by the pain and suffering of the child dying of cancer; by the pain and suffering of the victims of tornadoes, erupting volcanoes, earthquakes; by the pain and suffering of the victims of AIDS; but especially by the bad free choices, i.e., the sins, of the **persons** He has created. But, then, what becomes of God's immutability? Further, being changed takes **time.** What, then becomes of God's eternity? Would God's suffering be compatible with His immutability? With His eternity? And so, one is brought to ask: What exactly does it mean to say that God is immutable? That He is eternal? That

He suffers in His divine nature?

2. As St. Thomas sees it, to say that God is immutable is to say that there is in God no potentiality to change. -- What this means can be made understandable by considering briefly that everything not God is in some way mutable. In physical things, there is an intrinsic potentiality (their matter) to change as regards their substantial being, for they can go out of existence in change; and as regards many sorts of accidental being (because of their substance), e.g., color, size, relations, location. In human souls there are intrinsic potentialities (intellect and will) to change with respect to knowledge and virtue. In the intelligences, there are intrinsic potentialities (intellect and will) to change with respect to acts of knowledge and acts of choice, and as regards applying their powers to diverse objects, and thereby to be found in different places. With respect to all beings created by God, they are extrinsically mutable by the power of God, inasmuch as their existence (by creation) and their non-existence (by annihilation) are in His infinite power.[15] -- Now, God is pure act, without any admixture of potentiality. Everything which is in any way changeable is in some way in potentiality. Thus, God is not only immutable, but absolutely immutable, in every conceivable respect immutable. -- Further, whatever undergoes change remains in part the same, and becomes in part different; as, for example, what is undergoing a change from being white to being tan remains the same in substance. But, God is absolutely simple, altogether without composition of any kind. Therefore, God is immutable. -- Moreover, whatever undergoes change acquires, or loses, something by being changed. But God is infinite, comprehending in Himself the fullness of all perfections, and so cannot acquire anything which He does not have. And He is absolutely simple, and so cannot lose anything He already has. Thus, God is absolutely immutable.[16] -- In addition, God's existence and non-existence are neither in His own power (for nothing can be its own cause), nor in the power of another (for God is Pure and Subsistent Existence, and so both Uncreatable and Unannihilable).

---

[15] *S.T.*, I, q. 9, a. 2, c.
[16] *S.T.*, I, q. 9, a. 1, c.

3.   In the view of Aquinas, to say that God is eternal is to say **both** that God neither begins to be nor ceases to be, **and** that for God's being there is no succession as there is for the being of things in time, that His being is total and simultaneous.[17]

To make this clearer, one should consider that just as we come to a knowledge of simple things by way of compound things, so too we come to a knowledge of eternity by way of time, which is nothing but the before and after, i.e., succession, in movement (motion, change).   Now, if a thing cannot undergo change and is always the same, there is for it no before and after, no succession.   And so, just as our apprehension of time consists in our apprehension of the before and after, the succession, in change; so too our understanding of eternity consists in our understanding that that which cannot change, i.e., cannot be in motion, has no before and after, no succession; that its being is total and simultaneous.

Moreover, whatever is in motion (and is therefore measured by time, inasmuch as its existence has a before and an after) can have a beginning and an end to its existence. So that, what cannot be in motion, i.e., is immutable, can have no succession, no before or after; and therefore can have neither a beginning nor an end to its existence.

One can see, thus, that eternity is known by means of two negations: 1) by a negation of beginning and end, and 2) by a negation of succession. And this is what Boethius had in mind when he noted -- to paraphrase him -- that eternity is existence which is total and simultaneous (i.e., without succession) and interminable (i.e., without beginning and end).[18]

---

17   *S.T.*, I, q. 10, a. 1, c.

18   Boethius' actual words are the following: Aeternitas est tota simul et perfecta possessio interminabilis vitae. (*De Consolatione Philosophiae*,   v.)   This definition notes the two negations: 1) tota simul (negation of succession),   and 2) interminabilis (negation of beginning and end). But it does more.   The word "perfecta" is used to exclude the *now* of time, which, *as flowing*, is imperfect (*S.T.*, I, q.10, a.1, ad 5); eternity can be described as a *now* which does *not* flow. The word "possessio" is used to designate the immutability and permanence of eternity; for whatever is *possessed* is held firmly and quietly (*S.T.*, I, q. 10, a. 1, ad 6). And the word "vita" (life) is used rather that the word "esse" (existence) in order to express the *duration* which belongs to eternity, since duration is better expressed by a word which designates operation or

4. If Aquinas could be brought to admit that God can suffer in His **divine** nature, how would he understand this suffering?

Perhaps as follows. God's suffering would have to be without change (since He is immutable), without succession (since He is eternal), and trinitarian (since **all three** persons have the **same divine nature,** and not just the Son, Who is alone, among the Three, in having a human nature as well).

Shall we say that suffering without change is impossible? Or, that God's suffering is **with** change, but change of an appropriate sort? Of what sort would that be? It could not be physical change; for God has no body. Could it be mental change? God does have a mind. But, doesn't change of any sort, mental or other, entail potentiality? And isn't God pure actuality, without any potentiality at all? Is there a sense of potentiality in mental change, or at least in God's suffering, which is compatible with God's pure actuality? -- Shall we say that suffering without succession is impossible? Or, that God's suffering is **with** succession, but with succession of an appropriate sort? Of what sort would that be? It could not be temporal succession; for God has no body. Could it be mental succession? God does have a mind. But doesn't succession of any sort, mental or other, entail being in time? And isn't God eternal? Is there a sense of succession in mental change, or at least in God's suffering, which is compatible with God's eternity?

These questions are difficult questions. Perhaps unanswerable. Nonetheless, Aquinas might be brought to admit that God can suffer in His **divine** nature by the suggestion that we pattern our understanding of His **suffering** over things other than Himself on our understanding of His **knowledge** about things other than Himself. According to Aquinas, God knows all that there is to be known about things other than Himself **without** being changed or affected **by them** in any way; for He knows them all **by His own essence.** Can it be that God sorrows and suffers when created persons sorrow and suffer, and especially when they do not return His freely given love, **but without** being changed or affected **by them** in any way? That

---

activity, e.g., the word "vita," than by a word, e.g., "esse," which does not. Besides, what is truly eternal, not only exists, but lives. (*S.T.,* I, q.10, a.1, ad 2).

He **sorrows and suffers** over them **by His own essence,** just as He **knows** them **by His own essence**? That His **knowing** that **they** sorrow and suffer, and that **some of them** refuse to return His freely given love, entails **His sorrowing and suffering** over them? That His **knowing** these things about them is (in Him) identical with His **sorrowing and suffering** over them, and that both (i.e., His **knowing** and His **suffering**) are identical with His essence? That the divine **suffering,** like the divine **knowledge,** is a **perfection** in God, without any attendant imperfection or potentiality of any sort? Wouldn't this preserve God's immutability and His eternity, both of which, it seems, Aquinas would want to preserve? Wouldn't it also preserve the insight that God, **as a person, must** suffer, since, but **only** since (the following four points are to be emphasized), 1) there are **created** [19] persons who **did not, do not,** or **will not** return His freely given love; **only** since 2) there are **created** things, both bodiless (the intelligences) and bodily (including human persons), that **have** sorrowed and/or suffered (physically or mentally, or both), or **are now** sorrowing and/or suffering, or **will** sorrow and/or suffer; **only** since 3) there was the Lord Jesus who sorrowed and suffered in His **human** nature, and since 4) God knows all these things? And wouldn't the fact that God knows all these things **with His knowledge of vision,** which is a glance **(intuitus)** without succession,[20] allow one to say that God's sorrow and suffering is an **eternally present** sorrow and suffering, just as His glance **(intuitus)** is an **eternally present** glance; and that His sorrow and suffering extend over all time, and to all things (i.e.,things capable of sinning, and/or sorrow and suffering) which actually **existed,** or actually **do exist,** or actually **will exist,** and **without succession**?

To make the immediately preceding a bit clearer, one should consider that just as two things are needed for pleasure or delight, i.e., 1) the presence of some good, and 2) perceiving the presence of this good; so too two things

---

[19] The persons of the Trinity are *Uncreated.* If there were *no created* persons, it would be neither necessary nor possible for God to sorrow and suffer in His *divine* nature. *Uncreated* persons cannot fail to return freely given love.

[20] "...cum intelligere Dei, quod est ejus esse, aeternitate mensuretur, quae sine successione existens totum tempus comprehendit, praesens intuitus Dei [i.e., His knowledge of vision, which is a *glance,* i.e., *intuitus,* without succession] fertur in totum tempus, et in omnia quae [actualiter] sunt in quocumque tempore [whether past, present , or future], sicut in subjecta sibi praesentialiter." (*S.T.,* I, q. 14, a. 9, c.).

are needed for sorrow and suffering, i.e., 1) the presence of some evil (which, as evil, deprives of good), and 2) perceiving the presence of this evil.[21] And it makes no difference, we might add, whether the one to whom the good (or the evil) is present, and the one perceiving their presence, is the same one or not. Now, when those **created** things which are capable of sorrowing and suffering, **do** sorrow and suffer, or **have** sorrowed and suffered, or **will** sorrow and suffer; and when those which are capable of returning God's freely given love **do not** do that, or **have not** done that, or **will not** do it; some evil, whereby **they** have been deprived of some good, is present **to them,** and **God** perceives this. Thus, God sorrows and suffers over them, over all time and without succession. God **must** sorrow and suffer -- but **only** because He has created. And **that,** He has done **freely.**

But, someone might ask, what exactly does it **mean** to say that God sorrows and suffers over things other than Himself? A not unreasonable suggestion is this, namely that God experiences distress, anguish, pain, hurt, agony, torment (mental, of course, not physical) of an infintiely intense sort -- not as a process, but **as though** the **term** of a process -- rooted in His perception of the evils, of whatever sort they may be, which are present to His sorrowing and suffering and sinning creatures. This divine experience, it must be emphasized, occurs **by His essence,** without change and without succession; and only because He Himself has permitted and embraced it, having freely chosen to create things which He knew would sorrow and suffer and sin. Moreover, God takes pleasure or delight which is beyond measure, i.e., infinite, in the fact that He can (and does) sorrow and suffer beyond measure over the sorrow and suffering and sinning of the **creatures** He loves beyond measure. -- This can perhaps be likened to what St. Augustine has in mind when he observes in the *Confessions,* that in stage plays sorrow itself gives us pleasure (Bk. III, ch. 2), and that weeping is a bitter thing, and yet it sometimes pleases us (Bk. IV, ch. 5); and to St. Thomas' comment on Augustine's observation, namely that we derive

---

[21] "...sicut ad delectationem duo requiruntur, scilicet conjunctio [i.e. praesentia] boni, et perceptio hujusmodi conjunctionis; ita ad dolorem duo requiruntur, scilicet conjunctio alicujus mali (quod ea ratione est malum, quia privat aliquod bonum); et perceptio hujusmodi conjunctionis ." (*S.T.*, I-II, q. 35, a. 1, c.).

pleasure from the pains and sorrows and sufferings depicted on the stage, inasmuch as, in witnessing them, we perceive a certain **love** arising in us toward those whom the actors portray.[22] -- To be sure, life is not a stage play, nor a rehearsal. The pain of life is **real** pain. God's pain is **real** pain. God's love (from which arises His pain, and the pleasure deriving from that pain) is love for **real,** not portrayed stage-play, persons.

Perhaps it can also be likened, from another point of view, to what St. Thomas has to say about **man's** contemplation of truth, and of things divine, and of our future happiness in heaven; namely that our contemplation of such things has a comforting, a soothing, an assuaging effect on pains and sorrows and tribulations of various sorts; and the more so, the more perfectly we **love** such things.[23] Now, no one loves such things more perfectly than God. Thus, the absolutely perfect love with which God contemplates such things has an infinitely comforting, soothing, assuaging effect on His infinitely intense sorrow and suffering. -- God sorrows and suffers, **because He loves.** God delights in being able to sorrow and suffer, **because He loves.** God's sorrow and suffering is assuaged, **because He loves.**

5. If the preceding can be accepted, one can see that God's suffering in His **divine** nature would be compatible with His immutability, as well as with His eternity. God's sorrow and suffering over things other than Himself, like His knowledge about them, is without change, without successsion, without imperfection or potentiality of any sort, and **by His own essence.** God's sorrow and suffering is an **actus perfecti.**

Now, motion **(motus),** i.e., change or process, in the physical world, is an **actus imperfecti,** i.e., the actuality of something which is **imperfect,** inasmuch as the thing in motion, i.e., in process of being changed or of becoming, is -- while in a state of actuality, up to a point -- also, and at the same time, in a state of potentiality (and so, imperfect). It is in a state of actuality as related to

---

[22] "...dolores in spectaculis possunt esse delectabiles, inquantum in eis sentitur aliquis amor conceptus ad illos qui in spectaculis commemorantur." (*S.T.,* I-II, q. 35, a. 3, ad 2).
[23] *S.T.,* I-II, q. 38, a. 4, c.

the term **a quo,** and simultaneously in a state of potentiality as related to the term **ad quem.** And it retains this status of actuality-potentaility just so long as the process continues. This is why motion (physical) has been defined as an "actus existentis **in potentia,** inquantum hujusmodi," the word "actus" relating it to the term **a quo,** and the words "in potentia, inquantum hujusmodi," relating it to the term **ad quem.** This implies, further, the need for something other, which can -- because it is in a state of actuality surpassing the state of the actuality which is the motion itself -- actively account for that emerging actuality. Imagine the process in which a block of marble **is becoming** a statue. I mean, imagine the sculptor actually at work with hammer and chisel. Imagine seeing **the shape of the statue slowly emerging** in the marble as the sculptor is wielding his tools. **The shape of the statue slowly emerging** is the **actus imperfecti;** it is successive, and in time.

But motion **(motus)** can be taken in a second sense, namely as an **actus perfecti,** i.e., **existentis in actu.** This is the sense in which understanding **(intelligere)** is a **motus,** along with sensing **(sentire)** and willing **(velle)** and delighting **(delectari).** And this is the sense, I have been suggesting, in which God's sorrow and suffering is a **motus,** an **actus perfecti.** Such a *motus* -- **motus** as an **actus perfecti** -- is neither successive, nor of itself in time.[24] Such a **motus** may be the term of a process, as is the case with **human** knowing and willing and delighting and sorrowing. As terms of a process, these are **acquired** actualities. But in God's case, the **motus** which is sorrowing and suffering **is not** the term of any process. It is an **un**acquired actuality. This is why it was said above (p. 95) that God's experience of distress, anguish, pain, hurt, agony, torment (mental, of course, not physical) is **as though** the term of a process. And why it was said (p. 120) that the divine **suffering,** like the divine **knowledge,** is a **perfection** in God, without any attendant imperfection or potentiality. And this is why God's sorrow and suffering does not need something other than God as its active cause. God's sorrow and suffering is **by His own essence.**

---

24 "... motus dupliciter dicitur. Uno modo, qui est *actus imperfecti,* scilicet *existentis in potentia, inquantum hujusmodi;* et talis motus est successivus, et in tempore. Alius autem motus est *actus perfecti,* idest *existentis in actu;* sicut intelligere, sentire, et velle et hujusmodi, et etiam delectari. Et hujusmodi motus non est successivus, nec per se in tempore." (*S.T.,* I-II, q. 31, a. 2, ad 1).

The suffering of man

Just as the dying Jesus cried out in the grip of crushing bodily and mental suffering, "Deus meus, Deus meus, ut quid dereliquisti me?" -- "Why, for what purpose, in order that what (ut quid?) have you abandoned me?" -- so too we humans often cry out, "My God, my God, why, for what purpose, in order that what (ut quid?) am I suffering? Why are You **causing** me to suffer? And if it is **not** You Who are causing it, then what (or who) **is causing** it? But, then, **why** are **You allowing** it? And You most certainly are **at least** allowing it. Why don't You put an end to it? You most certainly **can;** for You are said to be infinitely powerful. And You most certainly **should want to;** for You are said to be infinitely good. Is it that You have some **good reason** for allowing it? Or, is it that You don't care? Or, is it that You don't exist at all?"

There are some, as we all know, who have come to just that conclusion, i.e., that God does not exist; or, at least, that an infinitely good and provident God does not exist; and precisely because they see the suffering and the evil in this world. "If God exists," they ask, "whence this suffering and this evil?" Has there ever been a man who has not, at some time or other, asked himself that question? St. Thomas suggests, as a kind of pleasantly surprising twist, that one turn this argument around; that one argue rather as follows, "If there is suffering and evil, then God exists." For there would be no evil in the world, he explains, if there were no good in it, inasmuch as evil is the privation of good in something which exists, and as existing is good. And there would be no good in the world, if God did not exist.[25] God is the ultimate source of what is good. And so -- God exists, one might admit. But **why** (the persisting question), then, does He **cause** and/or at least **allow** suffering and evil?

---

[25] "...[sunt aliqui] qui propter hoc quod mala in mundo evenire videbant, dicebant Deum non esse; sicut Boetius,... [introducens] quendam philosophum quaerentem, *Si Deus est, unde malum?* Esset autem e contrario arguendum, *Si malum est, Deus est.* Non enim esset malum sublato ordine boni, cuius privatio est malum. Hic autem ordo [boni] non esset, si Deus non esset. " (*C.G.,* III, cap. 71, ad finem).

The providence of the good God, by which He governs the world, argues Aquinas, does not require the conclusion that God totally exclude the corruptions and failings and evils which are found in our world.[26] Nor therefore, Aquinas would want to add, does it require the conclusion that God totally exclude the **suffering of man** (since that too is a kind of evil).

Things created by God, notes Aquinas, are like God not only in **being,** but also in **being causes.** [27] But unlike God, continues Aquinas, created things can fail (and at times do fail) in the exercise of their causality, thereby introducing failings or defects in their effects. These failings or defects, of course, are failings or defects in being or goodness, and a defect in goodness is an evil. Since created causality is part of God's providential plan for the governance of the world, so too is evil.[28]

It must be emphasized that, as Aquinas sees it, evil and suffering are **not** effects of God's causality -- at least not when His causality is **taken by itself alone. By itself alone,** God's causality cannot fail. **By itself alone,** God's causality produces only what is good. Evil and suffering are rather the effects of the causality of created things. But their causality, it is to be noted, is a kind of instrumental extension of the causality of God. Created things are such, explains Aquinas, that they can and do fail in the exercise of their causality. And they fail even though (perhaps, even because) they act according to their God-given natures, and with dependence on, and as extensions of, the governing causality of God. This means that evil and suffering are the effects of a **joint** causality, that of God as **unfailing First Cause,** and that of created things as **failing secondary** causes. It is like what happens, for example, when a defect appears in the effect of an artist who has perfect mastery of his art, but is using a defective instrument; as when Mozart's piano performance is here and there unpleasantly dissonant, because some of the strings in his piano are out of tune. Or, when a man, who has a strong walk, walks with a limp,

---

26   C.G., III, cap. 71.
27   "...[Deus ex immensitate bonitatis suae] suam similitudinem rebus communicare voluit, non solum quantum ad hoc quod *essent,* sed etiam quantum ad hoc quod aliorum *causae* essent..." (C.G., III, cap. 70, ad finem).
28   This is the thought underlying the arguments of C.G., III, cap. 71.

not because of a failing in the strength of his walk, but because of a defect in the tibia of his leg.[29]

But, what accounts for the fact that created things fail, at times, in the exercise of their causality, thereby bringing about the suffering of man (as well as the suffering of animals, and myriad other sorts of evil)? What accounts for the fact that the piano which Mozart is playing is out of tune? Quite clearly, the twofold fact that 1) the piano **can come to be** out of tune, i.e., has a **passive potentiality** for coming to be out of tune, and 2) that there is something with the **active potentiality or power** to bring this about. That is, 1) the strings of the piano can be loosened, and 2) the mischievious child from next door comes into Mozart's music room, and actually loosens some of them. -- What, now, accounts for the fact that the limping man's tibia is defective? Quite clearly, the fact that 1) the tibia **can be affected** by a cause(s) which can shorten and bend it, and 2) the fact that such a cause(s) actually did the shortening and the bending. For example, this person's right leg was run over by a car, which broke the leg, which, when healed, turned out bent and shortened. These are facts which **precede** these failings, these defects -- the dissonant music, the limping walk -- and are related to them as material and agent causes.

It is because created things **can** fail, that they **do in fact** fail (at times), in the exercise of their causlaity. Created things have inherent potentialities for such failure; both to **undergo** the failure, e.g., matter, a finite will; and to **bring it about,** e.g., the power to wield hammer and chisel, a strong will. Only God's causality is inherently unfailing, indeed unfailable. For there are no passive potentialities for change in God, nor are there anywhere (nor can there be) any agent causes which might be able to bring about any changes in

---

[29] "Divina gubernatio, qua Deus operatur in rebus, non excludit operationem causarum secundarum,.... ... Contingit autem provenire defectum in effectu propter defectum causae secundae agentis, absque eo quod sit defectus in primo agente; sicut cum in effectu artificis habentis perfecte artem, contingit aliquis defectus propter instrumenti defectum; et sicut hominem cujus vis motiva est fortis, contingit claudicare, non propter defectum virtutis motivae, sed propter tibiae curvitatem. Contingit igitur in his quae aguntur et gubernantur a Deo, aliquem defectum et aliquod malum invenire, propter defectum agentium secundorum, licet in ipso Deo nullus sit defectus..." (C.G., III, cap. 71, in princ.).

Him.

To make this clear, it must be considered that the agent causality of created things, unlike God's, is not **ex nihilo.** Created things exercise their agent causality **on other created things** (which have the role of a pre-existing matter), changing them in various ways, at times affecting their active causal powers and rendering these powers defective; at times even causing these things to go out of existence, thereby bringing other things into existence. For example, the human male eats food, part of which is changed into sperm; the human female, too, eats food, part of which is changed into ova. A sperm fertilizes an ovum, and the effect is a new human being. Thus, **generatio unius** (that of the human being) **est corruptio alterius** (that of the food, e.g., a piece of beef steak). Something good for the newly generated human being (existence); something bad (suffering, and the evil which is death) for the slaughtered steer. Moreover, this particular human female had used the sedative thalidomide during pregnancy, and the drug so affected the reproductive powers of her body, and the developmental powers of the foetus, that her infant was born deformed. -- Another example. A deadly virus attacks the human body, changing parts of certain cells of that human body into more viruses of its own kind, and thereby in the end changing certain organs of that human body so radically that the human being dies. Something good for the viruses (existence); something bad (suffering, and the evil which is death) for the deceased human being. Moreover, the brain of this particular individual was so affected by the multiplying virus that, for three months before death, this individual, a sculptor, was scarcely able to wield hammer and chisel; and when he **was able** to do so from time to time, it was without his heretofore skilled control, so that his sculptures turned out uncharacteristically gross and ugly.

What, now, is God's **good reason** (without which He could not be an infinitely good and provident God) for permitting the suffering of man? That is, what is it that **follows** man's suffering, and is related to it as some sort of **goal** or **final cause**?

The underlying assumption, here, is that it belongs to the infinite goodness and power of God to allow evils (including the suffering of man) to exist, and to extract in various ways something good out of them.[30] For, to extract something good out of evil is very much like making something out of nothing **(creatio ex nihilo),** inasmuch as evil is a kind of non-being.

There are many good things in our world, explains Aquinas, which would not be there at all, if there were no evils in it. In the **natural** world, there would be no generation, if there were no corruption, for the generation of one thing is always the corruption of another. And in the **moral** world, i.e., the world of man, there wouldn't be the **patience** of the upright, if there weren't the **maliciousness** of their persecutors. Nor would there be the **justice of punishment,** if there were no **crimes.** [31] Nor would there be any **unselfishness, courage, generosity, kindness,** or other like virtues; if there were no earthquakes, no hurricanes, no erupting volcanoes, or any other like **environmental or natural** mishaps; and if there were no murders, no thefts, no oppression, no racial discrimination, no unjust wars, or any other like **sins.** -- This now, it appears, is God's **good reason,** as Aquinas sees it, for permitting the suffering of man -- through failing secondary causes in the **natural** world, as well as through failing secondary causes in the **moral** world, i.e., through failing human wills which have freely chosen to sin. That is, this suffering (our own and that of others) provides us with **occasions** for the possibility of growth (our own and that of others) in the virtues, i.e., with opportunities to prove that we **love.** It provides us as well, of course, with occasions for the possibility of growth (our own and that of others) in the

---

[30] "Hoc...ad infinitam Dei bonitatem pertinet, ut esse permittat mala, et ex eis eliciat bona." (*S.T.,* I, q.2, a.3, ad 1).

[31] "Multa bona sunt in rebus quae, nisi mala essent, locum non haberent; sicut non esset patientia justorum si non esset malignitas persequentium. Nec esset locus justitiae vindicanti si delicta non essent. In rebus etiam naturalibus non esset unius generatio nisi esset alterius corruptio. Si ergo malum totaliter ab universitate rerum per divinam providentiam excluderetur, oporteret etiam bonorum multitudinem diminui." -- "Impossibile est quod agens operetur aliquod malum nisi propter hoc quod intendit aliquod bonum,.... ...Prohibere autem cujuscumque boni intentionem universaliter a rebus creatis, non pertinet ad providentiam eius qui est omnis boni causa; sic enim multa bona subtraherentur ab universitate rerum; sicut, si subtraheretur igni intentio generandi sibi simile, ad quam sequitur hoc malum quod est corruptio rerum combustibilium, tolleretur hoc bonum quod est generatio ignis, et conservatio ipsius secundum suam speciem." (*C.G.,* III, cap. 71, ad medium).

vices, i.e., with opportunities to prove that we **hate,** or at least that we do **not** love. For we men have from God the gift of free choice. And this gift is among the greatest of the good things in our world.

There are questions which persist. Why do created things fail at times in the exercise of their causality? Why do they fail at all? Is it **necessary** that they fail at times? Does it **simply happen,** i.e., without being necessary, that they fail at times? Is it the case that created things ca**nnot** produce good without at the same time producing some evil? Is some further good to be derived from this evil? Would this further good be impossible without the prior evil? Are there some goods such that even God cannot get them except out of some prior evil? If there are, would this be a limitation on God's infinite power? Wouldn't our world be a better governed world, and wouldn't created causes be better likenesses of the Divine Cause, if created causes never failed in their causality? -- These are pressing and difficult questions. Some of them have already been pursued in this chapter; others have not. For the time being, these others shall not be pursued herein, but left rather to be considered at a later and better time.

CHAPTER EIGHT

THE RESURRECTION

THE SUFFERING GOD is a limitlessly powerful God. Having proved His love for us human persons by becoming a man, and by suffering and by dying for us, He rose from the dead. His resurrection was not only a manifestation, but a crowning and a pledge. A manifestation of His limitless power. A crowning of His overflowing love. And His pledge that we, too, shall rise from the dead.

This chapter is concerned with some of the things which Aquinas says about resurrection from the dead -- the resurrection of God, and that of man.

The resurrection of God

The resurrection, the ascension, the descent of the Holy Spirit, the assumption of blessed Mary, her coronation -- the five glorious mysteries of the rosary -- are a stirring summary of the many-splendored magnificence of what was achieved by the pain and suffering of the incarnate God, the Son of the Father, the Lord Jesus Christ. But among these five glories, the resurrection holds first place: it is the gently and continuously erupting source of the other four.

How, then, is the resurrection of the Lord Jesus to be understood? That is, exactly what kind of resurrection was it? And secondly, was His resurrection a resurrection caused by His own power, or by that of another?

As regards the first question, i.e., the question: exactly what kind of resurrection was the resurrection of the Lord Jesus?, Aquinas begins by noting that resurrection is a restoration from death to life. But this, he continues, can occur in two ways.[1] In one way, when a person begins to live again after having been actually dead, but remains subject to the necessity of dying again. Such a resurrection is an **imperfect** resurrection; such was the resurrection, about which we read in the Old Testament, of certain persons raised to life by Elias and Eliseus. Such, too, was the resurrection of the three persons whom the Lord Jesus raised to life, about which we read in the New Testament.[2] In a second way, when a person is not only raised from death, but is freed from the necessity, indeed from the possibility, of dying again. Such a resurrection is a **perfect** resurrection; for, so long as a person lives as subject to the necessity, even to the possibility, of dying, death has some measure of dominion over him. The resurrection of the Lord Jesus was a perfect resurrection. Not only was He raised from death to life, but to utterly immortal life, with no necessity, indeed with no possibility, of dying again, as is written in the letter to the *Romans*, 6: 9, **"Christ being raised from the dead will never die again."**[3]

As regards the second question, i.e., the question whether the resurrection of the Lord Jesus was caused by His own power, or by that of another, i.e., by that of the Father, Aquinas reflects as follows. It is true that the Lord Jesus was raised to life by the power of another, i.e., that of the Father, as is said in the *Acts of the Apostles*, 2: 24, and in the letter to the *Romans*, 8: 11. And whoever is raised to life by the power of another, one might object, cannot be the cause of his own rising.[4] Nonetheless, replies Aquinas, the power of God, which is what raised the Lord Jesus, is not only the power of the Father, but also that of the Son; it is one and the same power. Thus, to say that the Lord Jesus was raised by the power of another, i.e., by the power of the Father, is to say as well that He was raised by His own power. For, though the Father is other than the Son, the power of the Father is not other than the power of the Son.[5] And the Lord Jesus is not a phoenix, which is said by some to rise by its own power from the ashes of the fire of its death; and by others to be incapable of this, since what is dead, no longer exists; and, as not existing, can do nothing

---

1   *S.T.*, III, q. 53, a. 3, c.
2   *Ibid.*, obj. 1.
3   *Ibid.*, c.
4   *S.T.*, III, q. 53, a. 4, obj. 1.
5   *S.T.*, III, q. 53, a. 4, ad 1.

at all. Though Jesus, as man, was dead; Jesus, as God, was quite alive.   And with infinite power.

One might want to ask at this point whether the Lord Jesus **really** died. For resurrection, whether perfect or imperfect, requires that the person who begins to live again was **actually** dead.   Now, for one who accepts the Bible as the word of God, or as a believable historical document, or as both, there is no problem here.   As Aquinas points out, the body of the Lord Jesus lay in the tomb for a day and two nights, so as to demonstrate the **truth** of His death.[6] And again, putting it somewhat differently, the rising of the Lord Jesus was **deferred** until the third day to establish the **truth** of His death. An **interval** between His death and His rising (three days are sufficient, notes Aquinas) shows conclusively that He had **really** died; for some signs of life would certainly have appeared within three days if He had not actually died.[7] And if He had risen **directly** after death, it might seem that His death was not genuine. -- In addition to the time spent in the tomb, there is the account, in the gospel of *St. John*, 19, 31-34, of the breaking of the legs, and of the piercing of the side. The soldiers broke the legs of the two who had been crucified with the Lord Jesus, one on each side of Him. Neither of the two had yet died. But when they came to Jesus, they found Him already dead. And so, they did not break His legs. Instead, one of the soldiers pierced His side with a spear -- as though for good measure -- and immediately blood and water flowed out of the opening. If the Lord Jesus had not already died **before** the piercing, He most certainly did die **after** the piercing. For it seems quite clear that the spear was intended to pierce His heart, or at least to sever a major artery, say the aorta, so that He might bleed to death, just in case He had not already died. After all, the soldiers had been sent of set purpose to determine whether the three had died; and if they hadn't, to see to it that they did die. And this, in order that the three might not remain hanging on their crosses, and slowly dying, on the sabbath, which was fast approaching. The Jews wanted them down, and taken away.

---

[6]   *S.T.*, III, q. 52, a. 4, c.
[7]   *S.T.*, III, q. 53, a. 2, c.

What is to be said, now, to those who do not accept the Bible either as the word of God or as a believable historical document? What can be said to make it clear to them that the Lord Jesus **really** died? Are there any documents generally accepted as historically believable which record the death of the Lord Jesus? There are accounts like that of the Jewish historian Flavius Josephus (37?-95?), and that of the Roman historian Publius Cornelius Tacitus (55?-117?), which record the fact that there was a Jesus of Nazareth, and that He died by crucifixion. But neither one nor the other, it might be objected, given the tentative date of the birth of each (37 A.D. for the one, and 55 A.D. for the other), could have been an eye witness to the crucifixion and death, which took place about the year 33. Thus the questions: whose word do these historians take? who was their eye witness to the crucifixion and death? to whose historically believable documents do they appeal?

Returning now to those who accept the Bible as the word of God, or as a believable historical document, or both, there are other questions which would be of interest to them. What about the body of the risen Christ? Was it a **true** body, or an imaginary body, i.e., **not** really a body, but only the **appearance** of a body? Was it a **glorified** body? What exactly is a glorified body? Was it a complete, or **integral,** or entire human body, i.e., did it contain flesh and bones and blood, and all other natural parts? Did it contain all the bodily humors (fluids)? And what about the **scars** which remained, the scars made by the wounding from nails and spear? Why would (should) a glorified body retain such scars; aren't scars blemishes of sorts? Should a glorified body have any blemishes?

By what sort(s) of proof(s), and why, did Christ manifest His resurrection to His disciples? Does proof give rise to faith? Does proof make faith impossible, or at least unnecessary? If not, were Christ's proofs sufficient to show somehow the **glory** of His resurrection, in addition to showing that it was a **true** resurrection? Would its glory need to be shown? Why?

The body of the risen Christ was a **true** human body, i.e., **really** a human body, argues Aquinas, and not simply the appearance of a body; otherwise Christ's resurrection would not have been a true or real resurrection, he argues, but only the **appearance** of a resurrection. Clearly, for Christ's resurrection to have been a **true** resurrection, the **same real** body must have been united again to the **same real** soul, so as to have the **same real** Christ.[8] And so, one can easily agree with Aquinas' argument, since the appearance of a body is not a **real** body at all, let alone the **same** real body as before death.

Besides, in the gospel of *Luke* toward the end of chapter 24, the risen Christ says to the troubled and frightened and questioning disciples -- the Eleven, and others, including the two who had walked with Jesus to Emmaus -- "It is I myself. Touch me and see; no ghost [i.e., appearance, or something with an imaginary body] has flesh and bones as you can see that I have." (*Luke*, 24: 39-40). "Come, **touch** what you **see**," Christ was saying in effect. And to make the reality of His body more convincing still, "He took and ate before their eyes" a piece of fish which they had cooked, and had offered to him at His request (*Luke*, 24: 42-43). Can an **imaginary** person with an **imaginary** body eat a piece of **real** fish? The resurrected Christ ate and drank with His disciples, not as needing food and drink, but in order to show that His risen body was **truly** a human body, **really** a human body.[9]

The body of the risen Christ was a **glorified** body, i.e., a body with a special sort of **impassibility,** a special sort of **subtlety,** a special sort of **agility,** and a special sort of **clarity.**[10] Christ's risen body was a **glorified** body, argues Aquinas, because the resurrection of Christ is the cause, both agent and exemplar, of the coming resurrection of saintly human persons; and **they** in their resurrection will have **glorified** bodies, as is written in *I Cor.*, 15: 43-49. Since a cause, whether agent or exemplar, is mightier than its effect, the risen Christ was clearly a glorified Christ, and so His body was a glorified body, and even more glorious, as cause, than the glorified bodies-to-be of the saints. Moreover, Christ's soul was a glorified soul from the instant of His conception. Nonetheless, His soul's glory was held back from passing into His body, especially with respect to its special sort of impassibility, in order that

---

8   *S.T.*, III, q. 54, a. 1, c.
9   *S.T.*, III, q. 54, a. 2, ad 3.
10   See below, pp. 156-161, for a discussion of the question: What exactly is a glorified body?

by His passion and death, He might redeem us. And so, after His passion and death had achieved our redemption, His glorious soul immediately communicated its glory, in its fullness, to His risen body.[11]

Moreover -- besides being 1) a **true** human body, i.e., not just an appearance, and so the **same** body as before death, and 2) a **glorified** body -- the body of the risen Christ was also a **complete or integral** human body, i.e., a body with all the parts and organs which are required by human nature, **and each in its entirety.** Flesh and bones, therefore, and everything else which belongs to the nature of the human body, such as the four elements, the four bodily fluids or humors (one of which is blood), the heart, the liver, entrails, hands, feet, hair, nails, etc. -- **all** of these were found in Christ's resurrected body. This must be so, argues Aquinas -- and quite rightly -- because otherwise Christ's resurrection would not have been a **complete** resurrection, if whatever had been lost by his death had not been restored. And so, not only were **all** the parts and organs restored, but each was there **integrally or completely,** i.e., without any diminution.[12]

What, now, is to be said about the **scars** on the body of the risen Christ, the scars from being wounded by the piercing nails and spear? Don't wounds and scars imply corruption? Aren't scars considered to be defects, deformities, blemishes? Aren't scars opposed to bodily integrity, since they break the continuity of bodily tissues? These scars, argues Aquinas, are fitting accompaniments of Christ's resurrection into glory. They helped make it clear that the risen body was the **same** body which had suffered, and so helped to confirm the hearts of His disciples in their faith in His resurrection. But there are other reasons, reasons which show also that these scars will remain in His body **forever.** A first such reason. Christ will keep these scars, not because He cannot heal them, but rather as a trophy or badge of His power and victory and love, and so as **an increase** of His glory -- and **forever.** These scars are not defects or deformities or blemishes. Nor do they imply any sort of corruption. They are, rather, perfecting accompaniments of His glory, adding dignity to it, and beyond that a certain beauty -- most fittingly,

---

11 *S.T., III,* q. 54, a. 2, c.
12 *S.T., III,* q. 54, a. 3, c.

therefore, to be retained **forever.** Secondly, Christ will keep them forever so that as He pleads for us with God the Father, He may always keep before the Father the kind of suffering and death He endured out of love for us. These arguments, based on fittingness, are eminently reasonable and persuasive. There are others too, though perhaps somewhat less persuasive, such as 1) to serve as **eternal** reminders of His loving mercy, reminders to those He has redeemed, and 2) to serve as **eternal** reminders of His loving justice, reminders to the condemned, i.e., to those who have refused His loving mercy.[13]

The risen Christ gave His disciples many **proofs** of His resurrection, and over a period of some forty days. But these were proofs of a special sort, proofs which do not interfere with faith, proofs which do not make faith impossible or unnecessary; proofs which rather are helps to faith. There are two sorts of proofs, points out Aquinas. First, there are proofs in the sense of **arguments drawn from human reason,** i.e., based on principles **known** by human reason. Such proofs are useless or inefficacious with respect to things of faith, things like the resurrection of Jesus. For things of faith are **beyond** human reason. Secondly, there are proofs in the sense of **evident sensible signs** which can be used to manifest the truth. The many proofs of Christ's resurrection, over the forty days, were all of them proofs in the sense of evident sensible signs, i.e., Christ showed His disciples a **visible, touchable, palpable, integral, scarred** human body, **capable of eating and drinking,** and **visibly and palpably the same** body as before death. And what the disciples saw was **one thing,** i.e, the evident sensible signs; but this led to a belief in **something else,** i.e., in the **resurrection,** and in the **divinity,** of Christ. This becomes very clear if one considers the case of doubting Thomas; for wounds were what Thomas saw and touched, but God, i.e., the divinity of the risen Christ, was the object of Thomas' belief. What Thomas saw and touched were helps to his belief. One can see from this, notes Aquinas, that the faith of someone who does not need such helps is a more perfect faith, and that such a one is more blessed than the one who does need such helps.[14]

---

[13] *S.T., III,* q. 54, a. 4, c.
[14] *S.T., III,* q. 55, a. 5, ad 3

Christ's proofs, argues Aquinas -- and eminently plausibly -- were sufficient to show **not only** that his resurrection was a **true** resurrection, but also that it was a resurrection into **glory.** And it was necessary to show its glory as well as its truth, notes Aquinas, so that together they, glory and truth, might serve as stronger sign-proofs to nudge the hearts of His disciples toward, and to confirm them in, belief or faith in His resurrection and in His divinity.

Some sign-proofs were used by Christ to show the truth of His human nature, and thereby that His resurrection was a true resurrection; others were used to show forth the **glory** of His rising.[15] That it was a **true** resurrection He showed first **on the part of the body,** and this in three ways. First, by offering His body **to be touched,** He showed that it was a true and solid body, and not simply a phantasm (i.e., something imagined), or rarefied (like the air). Secondly, by presenting Himself **to be visually perceived,** His disciples recognized Him in His unique and unrepeatable features, thereby showing that His body was the **same** body which He had before He died, and so a **true** human body. Thirdly, by showing His disciples the scars of His wounds, He showed again that His risen body was **identically the same** body which He had before His death.

Secondly, Christ showed His disciples the truth of His resurrection **on the part of His soul** as reunited with His body. And this He showed by exercising the operations of nutritive life, of sensitive life, and of intellectual life -- of nutritive life, by eating and drinking with them; of sensitive life, by replying to the questions of His disciples, showing thereby that he **heard** them speak; and by greeting them when they were in His presence, showing thereby that he **saw** them; of intellectual life, by talking with them about what the prophets had written about Him in the Scriptures.

Lastly, to make the manifestation of His resurrection complete, Christ showed also that He was **divine,** by working the miracle of the catch of fishes, and by ascending into heaven before their very eyes as they stood watching.[16]

---

15 *S.T., III,* q. 55, a. 6, ad 2.
16 *S.T., III,* q. 55, a. 6, c. , ad finem.

As regards sign-proofs to manifest the **glory** of His rising, He entered in among His disciples through closed doors, showing thereby the glorified property of bodily subtlety. He also vanished suddenly from before their eyes, as it is written in the last chapter of Luke, showing thereby that it lay within His power to be seen or not to be seen, which belongs to a glorified body inasmuch as it is a spiritual body, i.e., a body entirely subject to the will (power) of the spirit (soul).[17]

The resurrection of man

As Aquinas sees it, the body perishes because of death, but the soul does not. The soul survives death. So that the resurrection of man is the resurrection of the **body** -- by the power of God, of course.

There are some, by way of contrast, who believe that the **whole person** perishes at death, i.e., that both soul and body cease to exist when the person dies. So that the resurrection of man is the **re-creation** of the **whole person** -- again, by the power of God. But this view is impossible, one can readily see, since even God's power cannot re-create **the very same thing** which has totally and utterly perished (here, an annihilated human soul), though such power can surely create a **replica** or **duplicate** or **copy** of it. To be sure, God's infinite power can gather together the elements into which the **body** after death has disintegrated, and reunite them into the same body as before death; for the elements remain in existence as retrievable and re-composable ingredients. But, there appears to be no way that God's power can bring back into existence the **same soul;** for the soul, being a spiritual thing, cannot go out of existence by disintegrating into elements, or into other sorts of retrievable and re-composable parts. It has no such parts. The soul's going out of existence must be by annihilation. Moreover, this view is theologically untenable, since Revelation makes it quite clear that, though the body perishes because of death, the soul survives.

---

[17] *S.T., III,* q. 55, a. 6, c., in fine; *S.T., III,* q. 54, a. 1, ad 2.

Of interest at this point are the questions: 1) whether there is **to be** a resurrection of the body? 2) whether **all** will rise, the wicked as well as the good? 3) in what way(s) will all resurrected bodies **be alike,** i.e., what will they have **in common?** 4) what will be distinctive of the resurrected bodies **of the good?** 5) what will be distinctive of the resurrected bodies **of the wicked?**

There *will be* a resurrection of the body

With respect to the question **whether there will be** a resurrection of the body, [18] Aquinas argues that since a man cannot be happy in this life, and since the soul is related to the body not only as a worker (or doer) to an instrument, but also as form to matter, it is necessary that there be a resurrection of the body.

To explain, Aquinas points out that differing opinions with respect to **man's nature** and the **attainability** of his last end, i.e., happiness, generate differing opinions with respect to the **resurrection of the body.** Some have been of the view that man can attain his last end, perfect happiness, in this life. This led them to conclude that there is no need to admit another life after this one, in which man would be able to attain to this last end. And so, they denied the resurrection of the body. But the view that man can attain perfect happiness **in this life,** argues Aquinas, can be put aside with sufficient probability by considering that luck or fortune is so very changeable, that the human body is very weak, that our knowledge is very imperfect and unstable, so too our virtue. And all of these things are, quite clearly, hindrances to being perfectly happy.

Because of these hindrances, others held that after this life there is another life, in which human beings lived **only as souls,** and that such a bodiless life was sufficient, indeed necessary, for perfect happiness. The soul, it is often claimed, must avoid and give up everything bodily, in order to be perfectly happy. And this is attainable only in a bodiless state.

---

[18] *S.T., III, Suppl.,* q. 75, a. 1.

But, argues Aquinas, this view is based on an unacceptable foundation, i.e., on the conviction that everything bodily derives from the principle of evil, the devil (since what is bodily is **intrinsically** evil); and that everything spiritual derives from the principle of good, God (since what is spiritual is **intrinsically** good). From which it follows, they argue, that the soul cannot reach the height of its perfection, unless it be separated from the body, since the body draws the soul away from its principle, God, in union with Whom the soul's perfect happiness consists. But this is unacceptable, points out Aquinas, because nothing can be intrinsically, or essentially, evil. For every being, as such, is good; and evil can exist only in **what is good** as in its subject.[19]

Others, in turn, held that man is **simply a soul,** rather than something made up of soul and body, and that the soul is related to the body **only** as a worker (or doer) to an instrument, or as a sailor to his ship;[20] or only as a mover to the thing moved, or as a man to his clothes.[21] From which it follows, they argue, that perfect happiness can be attained by the soul alone, which is the **whole** man. And so man's natural desire for perfect happiness will not be thwarted in a bodiless existence after death.

But this is unacceptable, argues Aquinas, for Aristotle has shown, and rightly, that the soul is related to the body as a form to its matter, and not only as a doer to an instrument (or as a sailor to his ship, or a mover to the moved, or a man to his clothes). From which it follows that the soul alone is not the whole man. The whole man is the composite of body and soul. And only the whole man can be perfectly happy. Thus, since man cannot be perfectly happy in this life, it follows that there must be a resurrection of the body for a life to come.[22]

---

19   *S.T., I,* q. 49, a. 3, c., in princ.
20   *S.T., III, Suppl.,* q. 75, a.1, c., in fine.
21   *S.T., III, Suppl.,* q. 79, a.1, c., in medio.
22   *S.T., III, Suppl.,* q. 75, a.1, c.

All will rise, the wicked as well as the good

Will all rise, **the wicked (the damned)** as well as **the good (the just, the blessed)?** Is belief in the resurrection of the body a belief applicable to all, to the wicked as well as to the good? Aquinas argues, simply and persuasively, that **all** will rise. Since the soul is related to the body as a form to its appropriate matter,[23] he argues, it follows that the soul **alone** cannot be the **whole** man; that it is rather the composite of soul and body which is the whole man. And so, since it is the **whole** man who is to live forever, and not simply the soul which has survived death, the bodies of **all** will rise. Or, to put this somewhat differently, since the **souls of all** were made to live forever, the **bodies of all** must rise to make this possible.[24]

Moreover, just as the good are to receive a **reward** which is **eternal,** so too the wicked are to receive a **punishment** which is **eternal.** And, just as the good performed their good acts as **whole** human beings, as composites of soul and body, and thus deserve to be rewarded as whole human beings; so too the wicked performed their wicked acts as **whole** human beings, and thus deserve to be punished as whole human beings. Therefore, the bodies of **all** will rise.[25]

What *all* risen bodies will have in common

Now, all resurrected bodies -- **of the good** and **of the wicked** as well, as Aquinas sees it -- will have a number of things **in common.** First, any resurrected body will be the **same** body as before death. And this must be so, argues Aquinas, for resurrection would not be resurrection unlesss the soul receives the **same** body which was lost, or which fell, at death -- since resurrection is a rising, and what rises must be the same thing which fell.

---

23 *S.T., III, Suppl.,* q. 75, a. 1, c., in fine.
24 *S.T., III, Suppl.,* q. 75, a. 2, c.   The argument which Aquinas gives in the body of article 2 is not as clear as this. But this seems to be what he intends.
25 *S.T., III, Suppl.,* q. 75, a. 2, the third **sed contra.** Aquinas does not in this **sed contra** make explicit my reference to the **whole** human being, both **body** and soul, but this is quite clearly implied.

Moreover, if the body to which the soul returns is not the same body, it will not be a **resurrection,** but rather the **assuming of a new body.**[26]

Secondly, any resurrected body will have **all** its parts and organs, e.g., heart, lungs, liver, entrails; hands, feet, genitals; hair, nails. This must be so, argues Aquinas, for the soul would not receive the **same** body, if that body is not restored **complete** or **whole** or **integral** with respect to all its parts, like head and hands and feet, heart and lungs and liver and entrails, and genitals. Resurrection of the body implies a **complete restoration.**[27] With respect to hair and nails, Aquinas introduces an interesting and helpful distinction, prompted by his pointing out that the soul is related to the parts of the animated body as art is related to its instruments (and this is why, notes Aquinas, an animated body is called an **organed body**). Art uses certain instruments **to accomplish the operations intended,** and these instruments are its **principal** instruments, i.e., they belong to the **primary** intention of art. It uses other instruments **for the safe keeping** of the principal instruments, and these are **secondary** instruments, i.e., they belong to the **secondary** intention of art. For example, the art of warfare employs a sword for fighting, and a sheath for the safe keeping of the sword. Among the parts of an animated body, some are directed to the accomplishment of the soul's operations, e.g., heart, lungs, liver, hand, foot; some, however, are directed to the safe keeping of others, as leafs to cover fruit. And so, hair and nails are found in man for the protection of other parts. Thus, though they do not belong to the primary perfection (wholeness, completeness, integrity) of the human body, they do belong to its secondary perfection. Since man will rise with all the perfections of his nature, i.e., **complete** or **whole** or **integral** in his nature, the soul will receive a risen body with hair and nails.[28]

Thirdly, any resurrected body will have **certain** bodily humors, i.e., fluids or liquids, e.g., blood. But **not all** of them; urine, sweat, seed, and milk will not be found in the resurrected body.[29] This must be so, argues Aquinas,

---

[26] S.T., III, Suppl., q. 79, a. 1, c.; a. 2, c.
[27] S.T., III Suppl., q. 80, a. 1, c.
[28] S.T., III, Suppl., q. 80, a. 2, c.
[29] S.T., III, Suppl., q. 80, a. 3.

since whatever belongs to the completeness (wholeness, integrity) of the restored human body, and only that, will rise with that body. Thus, whatever bodily fluids belong to that integrity will rise as components of the risen body; some belong to that integrity, and some do not. Which belong, and which do not, continues Aquinas, can be seen if one considers that there are three kinds of fluids in a human being. -- One kind of fluid is such that it is **on its way out of the body,** because it is a waste of one sort or another, e.g., urine, sweat, the moisture in feces; or because it is in the seed, which is on its way to becoming incorporated into the **body of another,** i.e., the human about to be generated; or because it is in milk, which is on its way to entering the **body of another** as its food. Such fluids will not rise, argues Aquinas, because they do not belong to the completeness (perfection) of the risen person himself; such fluids are fluids **on the way out of the person himself.**

A second kind of fluid is such that it is **on the way to becoming incorporated into the body;** and this in turn is of two kinds. One kind has achieved a definite form, like blood, but has the role of producing and/or nourishing other bodily parts. Fluids which have achieved a definite form will rise, since they count as formed parts, alongside other formed parts. A second kind of fluid is in transition, and so without a definite form. These transitional fluids, whether in the beginning stages of transition, or in some later stages, will not rise, simply because they do **not** count as **fully formed** parts, and so do not belong to man's wholeness

A third kind of fluid is such that it is neither on the way out of the body, nor on the way to becoming incorporated into the body, but rather **has already been incorporated** -- in various ways, into **all** parts of the body. This fluid is called gluten, notes Aquinas. Gluten belongs to the wholeness of the body's various parts, inasmuch as it keeps each of the constituents of these parts together as within a whole, i.e., keeps each bodily part from disintegrating into its constituents, being a kind of glue or cohesive. This is why the gluten of bodily parts will rise with these bodily parts.[30]

---

[30] *S.T., III, Suppl.,* q. 80, a. 3, c.

Fourthly, any risen body will be a youthful body, i.e., a body in the prime of life, at about the age of 30 (at about which age the movement of growth terminates, and from which the movement of decrease and decline begins), without any of the imperfections of the growth toward 30, or of the decline of moving past 30.[31]   This will be the case, argues Aquinas -- and most reasonably -- because just as God **first made** human nature without any failings or weaknesses or deficiencies, so too will He **restore** human nature without any failings or weaknesses or deficiencies. If one considers human nature, notes Aquinas, one can see that it has two sorts of deficiencies: 1) the first, **on its way toward** full perfection, and so as not yet having achieved that full perfection;   2) the second, **on its way away from** full perfection, and so, **after** having already achieved it.   The first deficiency is found in children; the second, in old people.   And so, just as in the case of children the resurrection will **move them forward** to the full perfection which they had not had in this life, part of which is a body in the prime of life; so too in the case of old people, the resurrection will **move them back** to the full perfection they had had in this life, including a body in the prime of life.

This youthful body will be **of a different size** for each individual, but uniquely and unrepeatably appropriate for each individual at about age 30.[32] This will be so, argues Aquinas (and most acceptably), because God will restore, in the resurrection, not only what pertains to the nature of the human **species,** but also what pertains to the nature of the human **individual,** as unique and unrepeatable.   Now, the nature of the **species,** notes Aquinas, demands a quantity or size within cetain bounds, which it neither exceeds nor fails to achieve. The nature of each individual, however, aims at a quantity or size (within the bounds required by the species) which is unique to that individual, and achieves that unique size at the end of its growth, if there has been no error in the workings of nature by which (error) something might have been added to, or subtracted from, that unique quantity, which, because unique, is not the same for each individual.   And so, concludes Aquinas, **all** individuals will **not** rise with the same quantity.   Rather, each individual will rise with the unique bodily quantity or size which would have been his at the end of his

---

31   *S.T., III, Suppl.,* q. 81, a. 1.
32   *S.T., III, Suppl.,* q. 81, a. 2.

growth, if nature had not erred or failed. God, of course, by His power, will add or subtract whatever is needed.

This youthful body will be of the **same sex** as before death.[33] This will be so, urges Aquinas, because of the requirements of the **nature** of the human **individual,** the very same reason which was given (as noted just above) with respect to the question of the **quantity or size** of each risen body. And so, contrary to the thinking of some who held for various reasons that all, both men and women, will rise as males;[34] females, as Aquinas sees it, will rise as females, just as males will rise as males.[35] Each **individual** human has it as part of his uniqueness to be either male or female. And since each will rise in his uniqueness and unrepeatability as an individual, the risen youthful body of each will be **of the same sex as before death.** Besides, both sexes are required for the perfection (or wholeness or integrity) of the **species.** [36]

This youthful body will have **all** its nutritive and generative **powers,** but there will be no need to exercise the **activities** of these powers.[37] This must be the case, argues Aquinas, by reminding the reader of the reason why the resurrection of the body is necessary. It is not necessary with respect to the things which man **can** achieve **in this life by the action of natural causes,** such as nourishing his body or giving birth to children. Resurrection is necessary, rather, with respect to the attainment of man's ultimate perfection, which is the ultimate end of perfect happiness. And perfect happiness cannot be achieved **in this life,** because luck or fortune is so changeable, the human body is so very weak, our knowldge is very imperfect and unstable, so too our virtue. All of these things are hindrances, quite clearly, to being perfectly happy, as Aquinas had pointed out in another place.[38] And so, those operations (activities) which are directed to the things which can be achieved in this life by the action of natural causes -- those activities will not take place after the resurrection. Such are the **activities** of animal life in man, i.e.,

---

33 S.T., III, Suppl., q. 81, a. 3.
34 S.T., III, Suppl., q. 81, a. 3, obj. 1-3.
35 S.T., III, Suppl., q. 81, a. 3, c.; ad 1-3.
36 S.T., III, Suppl., q. 81, c.
37 S.T., III, Suppl., q. 81, a. 4.
38 S.T., III, Suppl., q. 75, a. 1, c., in medio.

activities like eating, drinking, sleeping, begetting;   such too are the **actions** of the elements on one another, and the **motions** of the heavens and the heavenly bodies.

Moreover, the **activities** of the **generative** powers will not be necessary after the resurrection, because by the time of the resurrection the human race will already have reached the number of individuals set by God, inasmuch as generation will have continued up to that point.   Further, each individual will have risen with the bodily quantity or size required by his nature as a unique individual, and there will be no bodily wastes to be eliminated nor bodily weight losses to be replaced.   And so, no need for the activities of the **nutritive** powers.[39]

Nor can it be argued that the nutritive and generative **powers** would have **no purpose,** if their activites are not to be exercised.   Their purpose is the **restoration** of the **perfection** (wholeness, integrity) of human nature, both as regards the **species** and the **individual.**[40]

In addition, the activities of the nutritive and generative powers do not belong to man as man.   Man has these in common with the lower animals. Man's ultimate happiness consists in the exercise of the activities which belong to man as man, i.e., knowing and loving.[41] Besides, it is only spiritual pleasures (as opposed to bodily pleasures), i.e., the pleasures of knowing (of the intellect) and of loving (of the will), which are sought for their own sake. And it is only pleasures sought for their own sake which belong to man's ultimate happiness.[42]

---

[39]   *S.T., III, Suppl.,* q. 81, a. 4, sed contra.
[40]   *S.T., III, Suppl.,* q. 81, a. 4, ad 2.
[41]   *S.T,, III, Suppl.,* q. 81, a. 4, ad 3.
[42]   *S.T., III, Suppl.,* q. 82, a. 4, ad 4.

What will be distinctive of the resurrected bodies of the *blessed*

The resurrected bodies **of the good** (the just, the blessed), as Aquinas sees it, will be **glorified** bodies. And as glorified, they will have the properties of impassibility, subtlety, agility, and clarity.

The **impassibility** of the glorified body will consist in its not being subject to changes which are against nature, i.e., which can corrupt it, as opposed to changes which can perfect it. This does not exclude the kind of change or alteration (and passibility) required for sensory experience. None of these sensory changes or alterations will be of a bodily (physical, material) sort; all of them, only of a **spiritual**, or **intentional**, sort.[43] This must be so, argues Aquinas, because a glorified body, and all that is in it, will be perfectly subject to the rational soul, just as the soul itself will be perfectly subject to God. And so, it is impossible for the glorified body to be subject to any sort change which might in any way **corrupt** it (i.e., any bodily, physical, material change), such is the controlling power **(dominium)** which the glorified soul has over its glorified body.[44]

Nonetheless, changes (alterations) which can **perfect** the body will most certainly occur. For example, the changes required for sensory experience.[45] The senses are **passive** powers, observes Aquinas, and that is why they need to be affected, changed, by **external** objects. But these sensory alterations will not include any bodily (physical, material) aspects, since these are capable of causing corruption; only the spiritual, or intentional, aspects which alone, properly speaking, cause the sensory experience. For example, clarifies Aquinas (for his thirteenth century readers), the pupil of the eye receives the form or species of a color without itself becoming colored;[46] and the air, too, as the medium of sight, receives the form or species of color without itself becoming colored.[47] Or, the eye receives the form or species (visual) of a tree into eye-matter, without itself becoming a tree; and air receives the form or

---

43 *S.T., III, Suppl.,* q. 82, a. 3, c., in fine.
44 *S.T., III, Suppl.,* q. 82, a. 1, c., in fine
45 *S.T., III, Suppl.,* q. 82, a. 3, c.
46 *S.T., III, Suppl.,* q. 82 a. 3, c., in fine.
47 *S.T., III, Suppl.,* q. 82, a. 3, ad 2.

species (visual) of a tree into air-matter, without itself becoming a tree. In physical change, by way of contrast with sensory change, when matter receives the form of a tree, it is received into tree-matter, and actually becomes a tree.

The **subtlety** of the glorified body will be of a special sort, notes Aquinas. To explain. "To be subtle" means basically **to be able to penetrate** -- ". . . nomen "subtilitatis" a virtute penetrandi est assumptum . . . "[48] Now, there are two reasons why a body might have the ability to penetrate. 1) First, because its **dimensions** are so **small** -- **at least two** of its three dimensions, e.g., a needle. To be sure, something which is small in **all three** dimensions, like a grain of sand, is also subtle, capable of penetrating, in this sense. 2) Secondly, because it has such a **small amount** of **matter,** which is why we say that bodies which are rare (not dense) are subtle, e.g., fire is rare; indeed more rare than, and so more subtle than, air; air, more than water; and water, more than earth. Now, from this second meaning of "subtle" derives a third meaning. Since it appears that the form of a body with rarer matter has more controlling power over its rarer matter than the form of a body with denser matter has over its denser matter (the form of fire has more controlling power over its **very rare** matter than the form of earth has over its very dense matter); 3) the word "subtle" has been extended to describe those bodies which are **to a high degree subject to their forms, and so to a high degree perfected by them;** e.g., the sun and the moon, and other heavenly bodies; similarly, gold or silver which have been **highly refined** and made as **pure** as possible. 4) Further, there is a fourth meaning for the word "subtle," deriving from the first and the second. Since incorporeal things have **no quantity** at all (a reference to the first meaning), and **no matter** at all (a reference to the second meaning), and so are capable of penetrating in a special sort of way, they too are said to be subtle. For example, just as the thinner needle (which can penetrate one's finger more quickly and deeply than a thicker one) is said to be the more subtle; so too the intellect which can penetrate to the truth more quickly and deeply is said to be the more subtle. He has such a subtle, such a penetrating, mind, we say. Similarly, the eye which can see the smallest of things at a very great distance is said to have

---

[48]   *S.T., III, Suppl.,* q. 83, a. 1, c., in princ.

subtle, or penetrating, vision. He has such subtle, such penetrating, eyes, we say. And such a sharp (penetrating, subtle) sense of hearing; such a sharp sense of taste, of smell, of touch.

The subtlety of the glorified body, we said above, will be of a special sort. It will consist in **perfection of the most complete sort.** This is "subtle" in the third meaning distinguished just above. But, this most complete sort of perfection, points out Aquinas, will **not** be due to the **fifth** essence (the matter of heavenly bodies), as some have maintained; for that sort of matter does not belong to the integrity of the human body, and so will not be of the essence of the risen and glorified body. The matter of the human body is the matter of the **four** elements. This most complete perfection will be due, rather, to the complete controlling power **(dominium)** which the glorified human soul has over the glorified human body, the controlling power by reason of which the glorified body is said to be a **spiritual** body, which means: a body **wholly, in every respect,** subject to the controlling power of the spirit (soul). Thus, to say that the risen body is a subtle body is to designate the primary effect of its being a spiritual body, the other effects being agility, and lightsomeness, and impassibility. And all of these qualities of glory are rooted in the controlling power **(dominium)** which the glorified human soul has over the risen body: ". . . dicta completio [i.e., completissima corporis perfectio] ex qua corpora humana dicuntur subtilia [sc. omnino spiritui subjecta) erit ex dominio animae glorificatae . . ."[49]

Now, the subtlety of the glorified body (this is subtlety, recall, in the **third** sense noted just above) will **not** make it possible for that body to be in the same place as another body (whether this other is glorified or not), argues Aquinas, because subtlety does not rid the body of its dimensions. And dimensions are what makes it necessary for a body to occupy a place of its own, distinct from that of any other body.[50] To be sure, a glorified body can be in the same place with another body **by the power of God,** as was the case with Christ's risen body when He passed through the closed doors, and when He

---

49 *S.T., III, Suppl.,* q. 83, a. 1, c., in fine.
50 *S.T., III, Suppl.,* q. 83, a. 2, c., in fine; a. 4, c.

passed through the closed womb at His birth.[51]

Nor will the subtlety of the risen and glorified human body render it impalpable. To make this point clear, Aquinas distinguishes between tangibility and palpability. A body is **tangible** if it has qualities by which the sense of touch, given the nature of touch, can be affected, e.g., hot, cold, wet, dry. And so, fire (hot) and air (dry) and water (wet) and earth (cold) are tangible. But, a **palpable** body, besides being tangible, is also such that it offers resistance to other bodies which are in contact with it, or try to enter its space, i.e., try to pass through it. Thus air, which never resists what passes through it because it is most easily parted or pierced, exemplifies Aquinas, is tangible (dry) indeed, but not palpable. Water (wet) and earth (cold), however, are not only tangible, but palpable (resist) as well.

Now, a glorified body is by nature such that it has the qualities which are capable of affecting the sense of touch. Nonetheless, because such a body is wholly subject to the spirit (soul), it is within the power of the risen person to use those qualities either so as to affect touch, or so as not to affect touch. Similarly, it belongs to the nature of such a body to resist other bodies which try to pass through it, and thus to keep these other bodies from being together in the same place with it. Nonetheless, such a body can be in the same place with another body by not resisting it (if a person so chooses -- by appealing to God).   But this would take place, emphasizes Aquinas, only miraculously, only by the power of God.[52]   Thus, the subtlety of the glorified body does not remove its palpability. Indeed, palpability belongs to the integrity of the human body. Moreover, subtlety is one thing; impalpability is another. And subtlety does not entail, does not cause impalpability.   Indeed, it can be said that a body is subtle, in another sense of subtle (i.e., in the sense of being capable of penetrating another), precisely because it is palpabable. There is no way one body could pierce another, if it itself, the piercing body, were not palpable, i.e., such that it offers resistance.   A needle could not pierce one's skin and flesh, if the needle could not offer resistance; indeed, a needle, qua piercing flesh, is considerably more palpable, considerably more resisting, than

---

51   *S.T., III, Suppl.,* q. 83, a. 2, ad 1.
52   *S.T., III, Suppl.,* q. 83, a. 6, c.

the flesh which it pierces.

The **agility** of the glorified body will consist in a special sort of movability -- movability without any difficulty, without any hard labor or work, of any sort. One must keep in mind, observes Aquinas, that the soul is united to the body not only as its **form,** but also as its **mover.** [53] And just as the body's **subtlety** is rooted in its being perfectly subject to the soul as to its **form,** which (subjection) makes the human body as complete and perfect as a human body can be as to **what it is** (like highly refined gold, which is as complete and perfect, i.e., **as pure,** as gold can be); so too its **agility** is rooted in its being perfectly subject to the soul as to its **mover,** which (subjection) makes the human body as complete and perfect as a human body can be as to **what it does** -- not only with respect to activities like walking, running, jumping, and other such physical endeavors, but also as regards sensation, imagination, memory, and other soul-directed activities which depend on **bodily** organs.[54]

One must also keep in mind that, as Aquinas sees it, the glorified body, in being wholly subject to the soul as to its form and as to its mover, will **not only** be such that there will be nothing within it whereby it could reisist the will of the spirit (soul), **but** it will **also** be such that there will be in it a certain perfection to render it in a special way accepting of, receptive of, that complete subjection, that complete absence of resistance to the controlling power of the spirit. This is a kind of double subjection, that is, subject to the soul, and subject to being subject to the soul. It is almost to say that the body receives a sort of will, so that not only does it **do** what the soul wants it to do, but it also **wants to do** what the soul wants it to do. And it gets this wanting power from the glorified soul itself, rather than from the fifth essence (as some maintain), since the only matter which will be in the human body after the resurection will be the same as in this life, i.e., the matter of the four earthly elements.[55]

The **clarity** of the glorified body will consist in its being lightsome, i.e., glowing, bright, dazzling, resplendent (recall the Transfiguration of Jesus).

---

[53] *S.T., III, Suppl.,* q. 84, a. 1, c.
[54] *S.T., III, Suppl.,* q. 84, a. 1, ad 2; ad 3.
[55] *S.T., III, Suppl.,* q. 84 a. 1, c., in fine.

This must be so, argues Aquinas, simply because the Scriptures make this promise.[56]   But its being resplendent cannot be caused by matter from the heavenly bodies, i.e., the fifth essence, as some think, simply because the matter of the risen body, preciesly because it is a **risen** body, must be the same sort of matter which was in that body **before** death. And that pre-death matter is the matter of the **four earthly** elements, and only that, the fifth essence being in no way included therein. Its being resplendent will be caused, rather, by the glory of the soul, as that glory overflows into the body. The glorified soul, one must keep in mind, is the **substantial form** of the **now glorified body,** just as it was the substantial form of that body before death.

The **resplendence** of the glorified body will not deprive that body of the color which it has because of the nature of its component parts, points out Aquinas. Nor will the **density** of the glorified body, he continues, deprive it of being transparent. Its resplendence and transparency result from the soul's glory, as that glory overflows into the body of which it is the substantial form, whereas its color and density are caused by the nature of the composing four elements. Glory, emphasizes Aquinas, does not destroy nature, but perfects it. Glory adds to nature. Glory adds resplendence and transparency to the color and density which belong to the body because of the nature of its composing matter, the four elements.[57]   Indeed, glory **adds** impassibility, subtlety, agility -- in a word, all the special qualities of the **risen** bodies of the saints   -- without destroying any of the **non-corrupting** qualities which the body has because of the nature of its composing four elements.

Moreover, the **visibility** of the glorified body will be within the controlling power of the glorified soul. This does **not** mean that the glorified soul will be able to rid the body of its color, any more than the glorified soul can rid the body of its dimensions, or change the size of these dimensions, without requiring the body to undergo some alteration which is at odds with its impassibility.   It means, rather, that the glorified soul can, by willing it, prevent the color (natural) of its body, as well as the resplendence (glorified) of that body from acting on the eyes of the beholder. The soul, by its bidding,

---

[56]   *S.T., III, Suppl.,* q. 85, a. 1, c., in princ.
[57]   *S.T., III, Suppl.,* q. 85, a. 1, ad 2; ad 3.

does not remove the color itself of the body, or its resplendence. What it does, rather, is to suspend the activity of these qualities.[58]

What will be distinctive of the resurrected bodies of the *damned*

The resurrected bodies **of the wicked** (the damned) will have certain sorts of defects (or deformities), a certain sort of incorruptibility, and a certain sort of passibility.

Defects or deformities

With respect to the sorts of defects or deformities which the resurrected bodies **of the wicked** will have, Aquinas raises the question: Whether the bodies of the wicked will rise with the defects or deformities which they had **before** death? He responds by reminding the reader that the risen bodies of **all** -- of the damned as well as of the blessed -- will be as perfect as human bodies can be, given the requirements of human nature, i.e., they will be the **same** bodies as before death, they will be **complete or whole** with respect to all their parts, they will have **certain** bodily fluids though **not** all of them, they will be **youthful** bodies in the prime of life (about age 30), they will be of a **unique size** for each individual, they will be of the **same sex** as before death, they will have **all** their nutritive and generative **powers** but without need to exercise the **activities** of these powers.[59]

Now, the defects or deformities which a human body can have before death are of two kinds. One kind is brought about by corruption, or by weakness in natural principles. With respect to the kind brought about by corruption, people who have been mutilated or maimed are said to be ugly or deformed, because certain bodily parts, like fingers, have been crushed or mangled, or the eyes have been gouged out, or the ears have been cut off, or the skin of the face has been burned. With respect to the kind brought about by weakness in natural principles, people who are born with stubs for arms or

---

58 *S.T., III, Suppl.,* q. 85, a. 3, ad 2.
59 See above, pp. 150-155: **What *all* risen bodies will have in common.**

legs, or with two or three fingers, or with no toes, are said to be ugly or deformed. There is no doubt that deformities of this sort will not be found in the bodies of the wicked, since God will resurrect the bodies of **all** -- of the wicked as well as of the good -- with every bodily member present, and every one complete or whole or integral.

But there is another kind of defect or deformity which a human body can have before death, the kind which is a natural consequence of the natural principles which make up a human body. Thus, people who are excessively overweight (excessively fat, obese), because of prolonged overeating, are said to be ugly or deformed. Similarly, those who are excessively underweight (excessively thin, skinny, emaciated), because of prolonged undereating, are said to be ugly or deformed. Defects or deformities of this kind, it is quite reasonable to hold, notes Aquinas, will remain in the bodies of the wicked, **not only** because such defects or deformities are not incompatible with the presence of every bodily member, and each member present in its wholeness, **but also** because such defects are compatible with, and contribute to, the punishent which the damned deserve.[60]

Incorruptibility

As regards the sort of incorruptibility which the risen bodies of the damned will have, Aquinas points out that the contraries, the four elements, out of which these bodies must be composed (since they are **risen** bodies) do not suffice of themselves to cause corruption. For the agent causality of the elements is but a **secondary** (or instrumental) agent causality; and instruments can act only under the causality of the primary agent(s). The primary agent cause of the corruption of physical substances, of substances composed of the four elements, is, as Aquinas sees it, the local motion of the heavens. And so, given the motion of the heavens, it is necessary that bodies composed of the

---

[60] S.T., III, Suppl., q. 86, a. 1, c., in medio et in fine. This article is, in many places, very difficult to follow and to understand. However, given the context -- i.e., what is distinctive of the risen bodies **of the wicked** by way of difference from the risen bodies **of the blessed** -- my interpretaion of its message makes good sense.

four elements undergo corruption, unless there be some cause with more power, like grace or glory, to prevent this corruption. But, after the resurrection, when the local motion of the heavens will have ceased, there will be no agent cause which can by appropriate alterations cause a body which is composed of the four elements to go out of existence by corruption. And so, the risen bodies of the damned will be incorruptible in this way, that is, **not** as though there were some prinicple(s) **intrinsic** to them (like grace or glory) which can prevent corruption, but rather because something **extrinsic** to them, namely the local motion of the heavens, which is the **primary** agent of corruption, has ceased to excercise its causality. -- This is by way of difference from the risen bodies of the blessed, which will be incorruptible not only because the local motion of the heavens has ceased, but also because of an intrinsic principle which can prevent corruption, i.e., the glory of the glorified soul, by which the risen bodies of the blessed are wholly subject to the will of that soul.[61]

Moreover, since death is the greatest of punishments, it would seem inappropriate, one might object, to withdraw death from those who, as damned, are to be in the greatest misery and unhappiness. And so, the bodies of the damned will be corruptible.[62] Aquinas responds to this objection by granting that death is indeed the greatest of punishments. But, since death brings **life** to an end, it also beings **punishment** to an end. From this it follows that the withdrawal of death contributes to an **increase** of punishment by making punishment **everlasting**. Punishment without end is greater by far than punishment by death.[63] Besides, the Scriptures make it clear that the damned will be punished with an unending, an everlasting, an eternal punishment, in body as well as in soul. Thus, it must be the case that the risen bodies of the damned will be eternal, and so incorruptible.

---

[61] *S.T., III, Suppl.*, q. 86, a. 2, c.
[62] *S.T., III, Suppl.*, q. 86, a. 2, obj. 3
[63] *S.T., III, Suppl.*, q. 86, a. 2, ad 3.

Passibility

With respect to the sort of passibility (i.e.,. capacity for undergoing change) which the resurrected bodies of the damned will have, Aquinas points out, in the **sed contra,**[64] that just as the body works together with the soul in gaining merit, so too does it work with the soul in committing sin.   And just as the risen bodies of the **blessed** will be rewarded along with their souls, because these bodies worked with these souls in the gaining of merit; so too will the risen bodies of the **damned** be punished along with their souls, because these bodies worked with these souls in the committing of sin.   It is clear therefore that the risen bodies of the damned must be **in some way** passible (i.e., in some way capable of being affected, of being altered, of undergoing change).

But **in what way** will their bodies be passible? By way of answering this question, Aquinas begins by noting that it is God's justice which requires that the bodies of the damned be given **unending** punishment, and thus God's justice will be the principal cause which keeps their bodies from being consumed by the fires of Hell.   But, adds Aquinas, it is also the case that God's justice is served by certain natural dispositions in bodies as being altered **(ex parte corporis patientis)** as well as in bodies as doing the altering **(ex parte agentium).**   Now there are two ways of being altered, of undergoing change **(duplex est modus passionis),** according to which there are correspondingly two ways of being received **(secundum quod aliquid in aliquo recipi potest dupliciter).** A form can be received into something either **materially,** i.e., in its (the form's) natural being, **or spiritually,** i.e., in an intentional way. It can be received in its natural being, as when **heat** is received into air from fire, making the air actually and physically hot. Corresponding to this sort of reception is a sort of undergoing of change which is called an undergoing of change of nature, or natural undergoing change **(passio naturae).** Or a form can be received into something in an intentional way, as when the **likeness of whiteness** is received into the air and into the pupil of the eye (in order to bring about actual seeing) without making either the air or the pupil of the eye

---

[64]   *S.T., III, Suppl.,*   q. 86, a. 3, the second **sed contra.**

actually and physically white. Corresponding to this sort of reception is another sort of undergoing of change called an undergoing of change of the soul **(passio animae)**, since it is like the reception by which **the soul** receives the likenesses of things. Now, after the resurrection, the motion of the heavens will cease, and this is why, as noted above (see, pp. 130-131), no body composed of the four elements can be altered so as to be corrupted. And so, the bodies of the damned will not undergo or experience material changes -- **nullum corpus pati poterit passione naturae.** But, even when the motion of the heavens has ceased, there will remain the undergoing of change which is like that of the soul, since the air will **both** receive light from the sun **and** deliver to sight all the many different colors. It is with respect to this sort of undergoing of change that the bodies of the damned will be passible. And so, the bodies of the damned will experience pain and suffering and punishment in a way which is like this spiritual (intentional) way, without undergoing any accompanying material (natural) changes. The risen bodies of the damned will, thus, be naturally or materially impassible, but spiritually or intentionally passible.[65] The damned will experience bodily pain and suffering and punishment **without** any **physical** change to their bodies. The intense heat of the fires of Hell will be experienced by the damned. They will feel the pain, in all its intensity, of being burned by fire, but the fire will not consume their bodies.[66]

---

[65] *S.T., III, Suppl.,* q. 86, a.3, c.
[66] *S.T., III, Suppl.,* q. 86, a.3, c., in fine. See also *ibid.,* ad 2: . . . species quae materialiter est in igne, recipitur spiritualiter in corporibus damnatorum. Et sic ignis sibi assimilat damnatorum corpora, nec tamen ea consumet.

CHAPTER NINE

THE EUCHARIST

THE RESURRECTED GOD is an ever present God, a God ever with us. But He is an ever hidden God. He is present in bread and wine, yet completely hidden therein. On the cross we saw **only** the man. In the bread we see **not even** the man. **In cruce latebat sola deitas. At hic [in pane] latet simul et humanitas.**

The present chapter is concerned with some of the things which Aquinas has to say about the Bread and the Wine.

As with respect to the Trinity, so too with respect to the Eucharist, the main task of the philosophy of religion is to show **that,** and **how,** it is possible, or at least not impossible.[1] The belief is that Christ himself begins to exist in the sacrament of the Eucharist, i.e., that the **substance** of the bread is converted into the **substance** of the body of Christ, when the priest speaks the words: "This is my body," and that the **substance** of the wine is converted into the **substance** of His blood, at the words: "This is the cup of my blood." And, of course, that this happens by the power of the Holy Spirit. To show that it is possible, or at least not impossible, presupposes that it has been shown to be intelligible, understandable, to us humans. That it is possible, or at least not impossibile, can be shown by removing the objections which some use to point to what they take to be inner contradictions in claims about the Eucharist. And that it is intelligible can be shown by reflecting carefully on something we humans can very easily experience, and for that reason can

---

[1] See above p. 72.

come to understand, i.e., the fact of change in the physical world. It is said that the bread **is changed** into, **converted** into, the Christ's body, and that the wine **is changed** into, **converted** into, His blood. How is this change, this conversion, to be understood? How is it **like** physical change; how is it **unlike** physical change?

Intelligible

When bread is changed into, and **begins to be,** the body of Christ, and wine is changed into, and **begins to be,** the blood of Christ, something **begins to be** which **is already** in existence. Christ is already in existence, having been conceived in the womb of, and having been born of, the Virgin Mary.[2] How is this being changed, this beginning to be -- this beginning to be **again or anew** -- to be made intelligible to us, understandable to us?

In any ordinary physical or natural change (or conversion), there **remains** a **subject,** in which diverse forms succeed one another, either accidental forms, as when something white is converted into something black, the subject which remains being a substance; or substantial forms, as when the element air is converted into the element fire (for a thirteenth century reader), the subject which remains being prime matter. Such conversions can be called **formal** conversions, since a given form is succeeded by another and diverse form, and in such a way that **something new begins to be**. -- Now, when bread is converted into, and begins to be, the body of Christ, it is a given **substance** which is succeeded by another and diverse **substance,** what remains being the set of accidents which belonged to the **succeeded** substance. This conversion can be called a **substantial** conversion, since in this case it is **not** a **form** which succeeds a prior form, but a **substance** which succeeds a prior **substance;** and **not** in such a way that something new begins to be, but rather in such a way that something **which already exists** (the body and the blood of Christ) **begins to be here or there** (on the altars where the words of consecration have been pronounced).

---

2   *C.G., IV,* cap. 62, paulum post princ.

Now, this does **not** happen by the power of any **natural** agent. It takes place, rather, by the power of God. Just as a natural agent converts **this** whole into **that** whole by causing this **form** to succeed that **form,** in this given **presupposed, underlying and remaining, subject**; so too God converts **this** whole into **that** whole, by causing this **substance** to succed that **substance,** no underlying and remaining subject being presupposed.

Although no common subject remains after the conversion of the bread into His body, something must remain in order to keep true the words, **Hoc est corpus meum,** for it is these words which both signify and cause the conversion, and it is clear that something of what is referred to by the word **"hoc"** must remain. Since the **substance** of the bread does not remain; since something which belonged to the bread must remain (for it is the **bread** which became the Body); and since there is nothing besides the substance of the bread but the **accidents** of the bread; it is these accidents which remain.[3] Thus, what happens in this conversion is in a way the opposite of what happens in **certain** natural changes, in which the **substance** remains, whereas the **accidents** are varied. In this conversion, the **accidents** remain, whereas the **substance** is varied.

But there are different sorts of accidents, and they are differently related to the substance in which they inhere. Dimensive quantity is the first among the physical accidents to inhere in substance; it inheres immediately. Then come the qualities. These too inhere in the substance, but mediately, i.e., by way of inhering first and immediately in dimensive quantity; for example, color by way of inhering in the surface of the substance. Further, certain qualities are the principles of the actions of a substance, like warming or burning another; and of the passions of a substance, like being warmed or burned by another; as well as of certain of its relations, like being a father or a son, a master or a servant. And there are still other relations which follow **immediately** on quantity, like bigger and smaller, double and half.[4]

---

[3]   *C.G., IV,* cap. 63, in medio.
[4]   *C.G., IV,* cap. 63, paulum post medium.

Reflecting on these things, one can see that the accidents of bread remain in this conversion in such a way that dimensive quantity alone remains as something without the subject it had prior to the conversion. The qualities, on the other hand, remain as inhering in their prior subject, i.e., in their dimensive quantity; and similarly the actions, passions, and relations, as inhering in their appropriate qualities. -- One can also see that such a conversion cannot be properly said to be a motion **(motus)**, the motion which is considered by the Natural Philosopher, since that motion requires an underlying and remaining **subject.** It is rather a certain sort of **succession,** a **substantial** succession, which can be likened **in a way** (but only in a way) to creation, which is also a sort of succession, in which existence follows on, or succeeds, non-existence, without any presupposed, underlying and remaining subject. Nonetheless, whereas in creation **something new begins to be,** in a substantial conversion something which **already exists** begins to be **elsewhere, and without ceasing to be where it now is.**

And so, it is not difficult to see how this conversion is both like, and unlike, physical change, and thereby to see that it is something intelligible, or understandable, to us humans.

Possible

There are several difficulties which Aquinas addresses in this regard. Some of these difficulties arise   1) from the claim that the bread and the wine are changed into, i.e., become, something which **already exists,** i.e., the body and the blood of Christ (see below pp. 171-173).   2) Others arise from the claim that the body and the blood of Christ **occupy the place** occupied by the bread and the wine by reason of their dimensive quantity (see below pp. 174-176).   3) Others arise from the obvious fact that the accidents of the bread and of the wine **remain the same** after the conversion (see below pp. 176-178). 4) Others arise from the obvious fact that the actions and the passions of the bread and of the wine **remain the same** after the conversion (see below pp. 178-180).   5) Still others arise from the claim that though the bread and the wine can be, and are, divided into many parts or portions, by reason of their dimensive quantity, this does not result in dividing the body and the blood of Christ into their many parts. The body of Christ remains whole and entire in each of the pieces of bread, and His blood remains whole and entire in each of the portions of wine (see below pp. 180-182).[5]

The bread and wine *become* something which *already exists*[6]

It is difficult to see, some object, how Christ's body can begin to exist on the altar where the Eucharist is being celebrated. For, they point out, there are two ways in which a thing can begin to exist where it did not exist before: 1) either by being moved locally, i.e., from one place to another, or 2) by coming into existence at the ceasing to exist of something else, i.e., when one thing becomes, or is changed into, another **in a substantial change.** Fire, a good example for a thirteenth century reader, begins to be somewhere either 1) because it is moved locally, brought there, moved there, from some other place, or 2) because the fire is started there anew. -- Now, it seems impossible to say that something becomes, or is changed into, the body of Christ in a substantial change, because the body of Christ **already exists,** having been born of the Virgin Mary; and it is clear that that into which something else is changed, or converted, in a substantial change, **begins to exist** precisely because of that change. Similarly, it seems impossible to say that the body of Christ **begins to exist** on the altar of celebration by being moved to that place from another place, i.e., from Heaven, where He is believed to have ascended. It is clear that what is moved from one place to another begins to exist in that other place in such a way that it ceases to exist in its former place. Does Christ cease to exist in Heaven when He begins to exist on this altar? Furthermore, nothing which is moved from place to place can be moved in such a way that it ends up simultaneously in **more than one** new place. And isn't it clear that the Eucharist is celebrated on many different altars at one and the same time?

Aquinas responds by agreeing that the body of Christ can**not** begin to be on the altar of celebration **by being moved locally,** i.e., from one place to another,

---

5   C.G., *IV*, cap. 62.
6   C.G. , *IV*, cap. 63.

because 1) it would follow that His body would cease to exist in Heaven whenever a consecration took place, 2) because consecration could not take place at the same time on different altars, since one local motion can terminate in but one location, and 3) because local motion takes time, rather than being instantaneous, and the bread becomes His body instantaneously, i.e., in the instant in which the last syllable of the consecrating words has been pronounced.

Aquinas also agrees that the body of Christ cannot begin to be on the altar of consecration in a substantial change, i.e., at the ceasing to be of the bread. For, even though a substantial change is instantaneous, the terminus ad quem of such a change begins to be, whereas the body of Christ already exists.

How then, i.e., by what sort of change -- as Aquinas sees it -- does the body of Christ, which already exists, begin to be on the altar where Mass is being celebrated? By a substantial conversion, answers Aquinas. That is, in a change in which: 1) a whole substance of one kind is succeeded by a whole substance of a different kind, but not in such a way that that succeeding substance begins to be (for it already exists), 2) there is no matter which underlies and remains, and 3) what remains is the collection of accidents which belonged to the succeeded substance. Now, though this cannot happen by the power of a natural agent, it can happen by the power of God. For all things -- substances, accidents, matter, forms -- are subject to the power of God, Who not only brings them into existence, but keeps them in existence.

And so, in this special sort of change, a substance which already exists begins to exist elsewhere. And it is clear that there is nothing intrinsically impossible about such a change. It is in no way like a square circle.

To make this a bit clearer, one should reflect a bit on matter and dimensions, and on their role in individuating and locating. An ordinary substantial change in the physical world presupposes an underlying and surviving prime matter, which as dimensively quantified individuates the newly generated substance, and thereby locates it. To be sure, it is the substantial form which confers dimensive quantity on prime matter. But prime matter is never, even for an instant, without some substantial form, either that of the about to be corrupted substance, or that of the about to be generated substance; for substantial change is instantaneous. Prime matter exists as always with a substantial form, and so as always dimensively quantified, and therefore as individuated and located, by reason of the individuation and location of the substance of whose essence it is an ingredient.

Now, when the bread becomes the body of Christ, and the wine becomes His blood, the accidents of the bread and of the wine remain, though **without** the substance of the bread and of the wine. **All** of the accidents of the bread and of the wine remain, including their dimensive quantity. And all of them are kept in existence by the power of God. What God can do **through** the receptive causality of prime matter, He can do **directly and immediately** without that receptive causality; just as He can do anything **either** through **or** without any sort of secondary cause(s). Now the **remaining** dimensive quantity individuates the **other** remaining accidents, e.g., the color, the taste, the bouquet, thereby giving them **this** location or **that** one. The dimensive quantity which remains **after** the conversion is the dimensive quantity by which the bread was individuated, and by which it had the location which it had, **before** the conversion. And so, the substance of the bread, which was changed into the body of Christ, becomes, is **succeeded** by, the body of Christ, **but with** the dimensive quantity (and all the other accidents) which **formerly** belonged to the substance of the bread: ". . . substantia panis in corpus Christi mutata fit corpus Christi sub quantitate dimensiva panis . . . ," as Aquinas puts it, clearly, briefly and elegantly. And the body of Christ takes on the individuation, and thereby the location, which the bread had, by reason of its dimensive quantity, before the conversion. The body of Christ which **already exists** (in Heaven) begins to exist **elsewhere** (in **this** bread, **located on this** altar) without ceasing to be in Heaven; and this it does by reason of the dimensive quantity of something else, i.e., of the bread which was there before the conversion.[7]

---

[7]   . . . cum quantitas dimensiva panis remanet post conversionem, per quam [sc. quantitatem] panis hunc locum sortiebatur, **substantia panis in corpus Christi mutata fit**

The body and the blood of Christ *occupy the place* **which had been occupied by the bread and the wine**[8]

It is difficult to see, as a first objection, how it can be claimed **both** that the parts of a thing are at a distance from one another, i.e., in different places, **and** that the thing itself remains whole or integral. In the sacrament of the Eucharist, it is clear that the bread is **here** on the paten, and that the wine is **elsewhere, there** in the chalice. Now, if the body of Christ is under the species, i.e., the outer appearances, of bread, and His blood under the species of wine, it follows that Christ does not remain whole or integral; but rather that each time this sacrament is celebrated, that part of Him which is His body is separated from that other part of Him which is His blood.[9]

Aquinas responds to this objection with an illuminating distinction. In the sacrament of the Eucharist, there is that which is there **as deriving directly from the conversion,** and that which is there **as a natural accompaniment** of that which derives directly from the conversion:

> ... in hoc sacramento [est] aliquid ... ex vi conversionis [sc. illud ad quod directe conversio terminatur], aliquid autem ex naturali concomitantia [sc. omnia alia quae sunt realiter conjuncta ei in quod conversio terminatur] ... (C.G., IV, cap. 64, in princ,).

The **body** of Christ **derives directly** from the conversion, as is clear from the words of consecration, Hoc est **corpus** meum; similarly the **blood** of Christ, as is clear from the consecrating words, Hic est calix **sanguinis** mei, etc. Everything else which is present in the now consecrated bread, and in the now consecrated wine, is there **as a natural accompaniment** of the body and of the blood. For example, the conversion of the bread does not terminate in the **divinity** of Christ, nor in the **soul** of Christ. Nonetheless both His divinity

---

corpus Christi sub quantitate dimensiva panis; et per consequens locum panis quodammodo sortitur, mediantibus tamen dimensionibus panis. (*C.G., IV,* cap. 63, in fine).
[8]   *C.G., IV,* cap. 64.
[9]   *C.G., IV,* cap. 62, in medio.

and His soul are there in the now consecrated bread, because both are really conjoined to His body. Similarly, both are there in the now consecrated wine, because both are really conjoined to His blood. Similarly, again, though the conversion of the bread does not terminate directly in His blood, His blood is there in the now consecrated bread, because His blood is really conjoined to His body. And His body is there in the now consecrated wine, because His body is really conjoined to His blood.[10]

It is also difficult to understand, someone might point out as a second objection, how a body can be included in a place which is smaller than that body itself. Now, it is obvious that the true body of Christ is considerably larger than the piece of bread which is being offered on the altar; from which it follows that the body of Christ, whole and entire, can**not** be where **this piece** of bread is seen to be. And so, if the whole body cannot be there, then only a part of it, at most, must be there. And thus a form of the first difficulty returns, i.e., that whenever this sacrament is celebrated, **this** part Him is separated from **that other part** of Him.[11]

Aquinas responds to this objection, too, by appealing to the distinction between what is in this sacrament **ex vi conversionis** and what is there **ex naturali concomitantia.** The **substance** of the bread, points out Aquinas, is directly converted into the **substance** of the body of Christ, i.e., is in the sacrament **ex vi conversionis.** The **dimensions** of the body of Christ, on the other hand, are in this sacrament **ex naturali concomitantia,** not **ex vi conversionis.** And this is so, since the dimensions **of the bread** remain. And so, the body of Christ is related to **this** place, i.e., the place where the outward appearances of the bread are located, not by reason of Christ's body's own dimensions, as though these dimensions ought to fit that place exactly. i.e., be of the same size as that place; but by reason of the **remaning** dimensions of the bread, which fit exactly, i.e., are of the same size as, the place which **they** occupy.[12]

---

[10] C.G., IV, cap. 64, in princ.
[11] C.G., IV, cap. 62, in medio.
[12] C.G., IV, cap. 64, ad finem.

As a third objection, someone might argue that it is impossible for **one** body to exist in **several** places at one and the same time. Now, it is clear that this sacrament is celebrated in many different places at one and the same time. It seems impossible to claim, therefore, that the body of Christ is truly present in this sacrament; unless of course one were to say that **a very small part** (particula) of Christ's body is **here,** and another very small part (particula) is **there.** But then, it would follow again that Christ's body is divided into parts by the celebration of this sacrament. Moreover, the body of Christ is not big enough to be divided into as many parts as would be required by the great number of places in which this sacrament is celebrated.[13]

This objection, too, points out Aquinas, can be met in the same way as the second objection just above. Christ's body exists in but **one** place **by reason of His own dimensions,** i.e., in Heaven (and His own dimensions are in this sacrament only **ex naturali concomitantia**). But, **by reason of the dimensions** (which remain after the conversion) **of the bread** into which His body is changed, Christ's body exists in as many places as this conversion is being celebrated; and not as divided into parts, one part in each place of celebration, but whole and entire in each of these places. Each piece of bread which is consecrated is converted into the **whole** body of Christ.[14] Thus, **here** in Heaven by reason of His own dimensions, **there** in countless other places by reason of the dimensions of countless pieces of bread.

The *accidents* of the bread and of the wine *remain the same* after the conversion[15]

The difficulties here arise from what our senses perceive in this sacrament. And what we perceive by our senses, even after the conversion, is **all** the accidents of the bread and of the wine: color, taste, smell, shape, amount, weight.

---

13   *C.G., IV,* cap. 62, in fine.
14   *C.G., IV,* cap. 64, in fine.
15   *C.G., IV,* cap. 65.

As a beginning difficulty, one might point out that accidents of this sort cannot exist in the body of Christ **as in their subject.** Nor can they exist, **as in their subject,** in the surrounding air. And this is so because these accidents need a subject of a **determinate** nature, and the human body does not have that determinate nature; neither does air.[16]

Aquinas points out in reply that neither the body of Christ nor His blood can be affected by, i.e., **take on themselves as their own,** the accidents of the bread and of the wine which remain after the consecration. And this is so, because 1) this cannot happen without altering His body and His blood, and 2) His body and His blood are not of a nature which is capable of **taking on as their own** such accidents. Similarly with respect to the substance of the surrounding air. Whence it follows that these accidents remain **without** their subject, but in the way explained by him in an earlier chapter (ch. 63), i.e., the remaining dimensions **alone** subsist without a subject, while serving as the subject for the other accidents.[17]

It is not impossible, continues Aquinas, that an accident subsist without its subject **by the power of God.** God can do **without** the causality of secondary causes what He does **through** that secondary causality. For it is He Who confers on them that secondary causal power. And it is He Who, in this sacrament, keeps the accidents of the bread and of the wine in existence, even though the **substance** of the bread and of the wine are no longer there to keep these accidents in existence, as they did before the conversion.[18]

One might object, secondly, that since accidents are **forms,** they cannot be individuated except by their subject. It follows, therefore, that the remaining accidents, which are quite clearly individuated, are there in **their** determinate subject, i.e., in the substance **of the bread and of the wine.** And so, since the substance **of the bread and of the wine** must be there, the substance **of the body** (and of the blood) of Christ cannot be there. For it seems impossible for

---

[16]   *C.G., IV,* cap. 62, paulum post medium.
[17]   *C.G., IV,* cap. 65, in princ.
[18]   *C.G., IV,* cap. 65, in medio.

two substances to be there simultaneously.[19]

In reply, Aquinas points out that dimensive quantity is such by its nature that it individuates not only **itself,** but also 1) those substances which are dimensively quantified, i.e., corporeal substances, as well as 2) the accidents which inhere in dimensive quantity as in their appropriate, and immediate or proximate, subject. Since the quantitative dimensions which remain subsist **per se,** and the other remaining accidents exist in these dimensions as in their subject, one need not conclude that these accidents are not individuated because the **substance** which is ordinarily their appropriate subject has not survived. The remaining **quantitative dimensions** are the source of the individuation of the **other accidents.**[20]

The *actions* and the *passions* of the bread and of the wine *remain the same* after the conversion[21]

It is easy to observe, one can object, that the **consecrated** bread and wine **can do,** and **can have done to them,** exactly what they could do, and could have done to them, **before** they were consecrated. For example, the wine, even after consecration, if taken in great enough quantity, makes the drinker quite warm, and even intoxicates. And the consecrated bread strengthens and nourishes the one who eats enough of it. Also, if they are kept around for a long time and carelessly, they can go bad, become spoiled; the bread can be eaten up, and the wine sipped away, by mice and other animals; they can be affected by fire, the bread reduced to ashes, and the wine boiled away as steam. Now, the body of Christ is such that things of this sort canot be done to it, since the faith holds His body to be impassible, i.e., incapable of undergoing changes of a **destructive** sort. It seems to be impossible, therefore, that the **substance** of the body of Christ be present in this sacrament.[22]

---

[19]   C.G., *IV,* cap. 62, ad finem.
[20]   C.G., *IV,* cap. 65, in fine.
[21]   C.G., *IV,* cap. 66.
[22]   C.G., *IV,* cap. 62, ad finem.

Aquinas embarks on his reply to this objection by noting that there is something here which can be easily handled; but also something which presents a good measure of difficulty.[23]

There is no great difficulty, begins Aquinas, arising from the fact that the bread and wine, **after** consecration, **do** the same things they did **before** consecration, like affecting our senses, altering the air which surrounds them, or other nearby things, with respect to their smell or their color. For, the **accidents** of bread and wine **remain** in this sacrament, and among these remaining accidents are the sensible qualities which are the active principles of such changes. -- Nor is there any great difficulty concerning certain passions, i.e., certain things which the bread and wine, **after** consecration, **can have done to them**, like being warmed, or being cooled, or undergoing a change in taste. For, their remaining accidents (other than the remaining dimensive quantity) exist in the remaining **dimensive quantity** as in their subject, and can for that reason undergo the same changes as they did when they existed in the **substance** of the bread and wine **before** consecration. Besides, such changes are **not** changes of a **destructive** sort.[24]

But, there is considerable difficulty -- **maxima difficultas,** notes Aquinas -- concerning the generation and corruption which are observed to occur in this sacrament, e.g., concerning facts like nourishing the human body, spoiling, being burned to ashes, evaporating. And having said this, Aquinas undertakes a long reflection on certain difficulties which different people have seen in this matter.[25] It is not necessary to go into the details of this reflection, but one should emphasize what Aquinas takes to be the important underlying point for resolving difficulties of this sort, namely that in this sacrament the **substance** of the bread is converted into the **substance** of the body of Christ; and that this is a **miraculous** conversion. And, just as the **substance** of the bread is **miraculously** converted into the body of Christ, so too are the accidents **miraculously** given the capacity to subsist, via their inherence in dimensive quanitity, which functions **miraculously** as their **ultimate** subject.

---

23   C.G., *IV*, cap. 66, in princ.
24   C.G., *IV*, cap. 66, paulum post princ.
25   C.G., *IV*, cap. 66, a medio ad finem.

As a consequence of this, it follows that the accidents which remain can do, and can have done to them, all the things that the substance could do, and have done to it, if that substance were present. And so, **without a new miracle,** they can bring on drunkenness, they can nourish, they can be burned into ashes, they can spoil and rot away, in the same way and order as if the **substance of the bread and of the wine** were present.[26]

The bread can be broken, and the wine divided, into countless portions, but the body and the blood of Christ remain whole and entire in each[27]

This fifth difficulty arises in a special way fom the breaking of the bread -- ex fractione panis. This breaking is obvious to the senses. And it is clear that breaking cannot take place without a **subject** to be broken. It seems unacceptable to say that the subject being broken here is the body of Christ, for such a breaking would be **destructive,** and the impassibility of Christ's body does **not** permit **destructive** changes. And so, it does not appear to be the case that the body **of Christ** is here, but only the substance **of the bread and of the wine.**[28]

By way of response, Aquinas invites the reader to recall that the quantitative dimensions found in the consecrated bread and wine are dimensions which subsist **per se.** And so, one can hold that it is **these subsisting dimensions** which are the **subject** being broken (divided), and **not** the body (or blood) of Christ. And this is why the body of Christ can remain whole and entire in each piece of bread, and the blood of Christ whole and entire in each portion of wine.[29]

To make this clearer, Aquinas appeals again to the important distinction he made earlier, i.e., the distinction between 1) what is here in this sacrament **ex vi conversionis** (or, as he puts it at this point, **ex vi sacramenti**[30]), and

---

26 C.G., IV, cap. 66, in fine.
27 C.G., IV, cap. 67.
28 C.G., IV, cap. 62, in fine.
29 C.G., IV, cap. 67, in princ.
30 Ibid.

2) what is here in this sacrament **ex naturali concomitantia**.[31] The **substance** of the body of Christ is here in this sacrament (i.e., in all the **places** where we find the **consecrated** bread) **ex vi conversionis (sacramenti)**; but the **dimensions** of His body are here in this sacrament **ex naturali concomitantia**, which they have with respect to the **substance** of His body. And this is quite different from (indeed, the opposite of) the way in which an ordinary body is in some given place naturally; for the ordinary body is located here or there by means of **its own** dimensions, which fit exactly the place where it is.   And this is why the consecrated bread can be broken without breaking the body of Christ contained therein.

Moreover, a **substantial** whole is related in one way to that in which it is found, and a **quantified** whole in another way. A **quantified** whole is **not**, as the whole which it is, found in each of its parts; rather only a part in each part. A **substantial** whole, on the other hand, **is found**, wherever it is found, **as the whole** which it is. It is whole and entire in the whole, and whole and entire in each of its parts. For example, **all** of the water, the **whole** of it, which is in this jar, is wholly water; and each quantitative part of that water is **wholly** water: tota natura et species aquae in qualibet parte aquae est. Similarly, just as the **whole** soul is in the **whole** living body, so too the **whole** soul is **in each part** of the living body: et tota anima est in qualibet corporis parte.[32] Now, an ordinary body is located in a place in such a way that the **whole** of it is in the **whole** place, and **parts** of it are in **parts** of that place; and this is so, because the ordinary body is in place by reason **of its own** dimensions.

Now, since the body of Christ is here in this sacrament by reason of its **substance,** into which the substance of the bread was converted, but in such a way that the dimensions **of the bread** remain; just as the substance of the bread, whole and entire, was (**before** the conversion) in each part of the dimensions of the bread; so too the body of Christ, whole and entire, is in each part of the dimensions **of the bread** which have **remained.** Thus, the breaking,

----

[31]   ... considerandum est igitur in hoc sacramento aliquid esse **ex vi conversionis,** aliquid autem **ex naturali concomitantia** ... (*C.G., IV,* cap. 64, in princ.)
[32]   *C.G., IV,* cap. 67, in medio.   See also, *C.G., II,* cap. 72: Quod anima sit tota in toto [corpore] et tota in qualibiet [corporis] parte.

the dividing, does not touch the body of Christ, as though His body was the **subject** being broken.[33]   The subject being broken or divided is, rather, the remaining and subsisting dimensions of the bread and wine.   These remaining dimensions are the subject of the breaking, just as they are the subject of the other remaining accidents.[34]

Thus, the body of Christ is located **here** and **there, in this** piece of **consecrated** bread and in **that** one, **not** by **its own** dimensions, but **by the remaining dimensions** of what was the substance of the bread before the conversion.   And so, the breaking of the bread does not break the body of Christ.

The substance of the bread (and of the wine) does not remain, neither is it annihilated, nor is it resolved into prime matter or into the four elements

What happens, it seems natural to ask, to the **substance** of the bread and of the wine, which have been converted into the body and the blood of Christ?

---

[33]   Not only is the **whole** Christ **under each species,** i.e., the whole Christ under the accidents of bread, and the whole Christ under the accidents of wine. The **whole** Christ is also **in each quantitative portion** of each species. In the *Lauda Sion*, it is put in a way which is as beautiful as it is clear and precise:

> A sumente [Christus] non concisus ,
> non confractus, non divisus,
> integer accipitur.
>> Sumit unus, sumunt mille,
>> quantum isti, tantum ille;
>> nec sumptus consumitur.
>>> . . .
> Fracto demum sacramento,
> ne vacilles, sed memento,
> tantum esse sub fragmento,
> quantum totum tegitur.
>> Nulla rei fit scissura,
>> signi tantum fit fractura,
>> qua nec status, nec statura
>> signati minuitur.

(From the Sequentia of the Latin Mass, in festo Sanctissimi Corporis Christi, feria V post festum Sanctissimae Trinitatis).

[34]   *C.G., IV,* cap. 67, in fine

Do they remain in this sacrament, along with the body and the blood of Christ, as some thought? Are they annihilated, as others thought? Are they resloved somehow into their originating matter, either the four elements, or prime matter?

First of all, the substance of the bread and of the wine cannot **remain** in this sacrament after the consecration, argues Aquinas, because to claim that they do would be to destroy the truth of this sacrament, i.e., to deny that Christ's body and blood are truly there. To make this clear, one must consider that a thing cannot begin to exist where it did not exist before, except 1) by being moved into that place from some other place, or 2) by a change in which something else ceases to be and it begins to be. For example, a fire begins to be **in my fireplace** either because I brought it there from elsewhere, or because I started it there to begin with from some combustible materials. Now, it is clear that Christ's body can**not** begin to be in this sacrament by local motion, for the reasons given above (pp. 173-174, *quod vide*). It must be the case, therefore, that Christ's body can begin to be in this sacrament **only** by a conversion, or change, in which something else ceases to be (i.e., the **substance** of the bread). But what is changed into another thing does not remain after such a change. And so, since the substance of the body of Christ is truly here -- **and only** because the substance of the bread has has been changed into His body (this is to be emphasized) -- the substance of the bread can**not** remain in this sacrament.[35] Besides, to hold that the substance of the bread does remain is to hold something which makes false the consecrating words, i.e., the words: This is my body. For it is clear that the substance of the bread is not the body of Christ, neither the whole of His body, nor any part thereof. Instead of beginning with "Hoc," meaning: **This,** the consecrating words would have to have begun with "Hic," meaning: **Here (i.e., where the bread is),** or with "Hoc loco," meaning: **Here (i.e., in this place -- hoc loco -- along with the bread).**[36]

Secondly, the substance of the bread (and of the wine) **is not annihilated.** For, to be annihilated is for a thing to be changed in such a way that it ceases to

---

[35]   S.T., *III,* q. 75, a. 2, c.,
[36]   C.G., *IV,* cap. 63, paulum post princ.; S.T., *III,* q. 75, a. 2, c., in fine.

be, and so that nothing else (absolutely nothing else) begins to be at its ceasing to be. But, in this sacrament, the ceasing to be of the bread is identically the beginning to be of the body of Christ. Thus, the substance of the bread is not annihilated, is not reduced to absolute nothingness. Rather, it becomes, is changed into, the body of Christ.[37] Furthermore, even though the substance of the bread (and of the wine), **after** consecration, remain neither in the sacramental species, nor elsewhere, this is not to say that they were annihilated; for, as just noted, they were changed into something else, i.e., the body and the blood of Christ; and when something is annihilated, it is **not** changed into something else.   This is in a way like what happens in a **substantial change,** too. In a substantial change, the term **a quo,** which is a substance of one kind, becomes a term **ad quem,** which is a substance of another kind; and, the term **a quo** exists neither here (i.e., where the term **ad quem** has begun to be), nor elsewhere. The term **a quo** has ceased to be. Yet it has not been annihilated, because its ceasing to be is the beginning to be **of something else.**[38]   Further, it is certainly to be granted that, **after** the consecration, this proposition is **false: The substance of the bread is something real,** as some rightly point out. But it should also be pointed out, and just as rightly, that this does not mean that the bread has been annihilated; for it has been changed into **something else** which **is** real, namely the **body** of **Christ.**[39] And lastly -- on the suppostion of annihilation -- more and more of the corporeal matter which was created in the beginning would have been reduced to absolute nothingness by repeated consecrations, so that the physical world would be considerably (and measurably) smaller now than it was some 2000 years ago.[40]   Clearly, therefore, the substance of the bread (and of the wine) has not been annihilated.

Thirdly, the substance of the bread (and of the wine) **cannot be resolved into prime matter,** since prime matter cannot exist except with some sustantial

---

[37]   S.T., III, q. 75, a. 3, c., ad finem.
[38]   S.T., III, q. 75, ad 1. -- Aquinas uses the example of air, which would make a good example for a thirteenth century reader. When air is changed into fire, Aquinas points out, it exists neither here, i.e., where the fire has begun to be, nor elsewhere. Though the air has ceased to be, it has not been annihilated, because its ceasing to be is the beginning to be **of something else,** namely the fire.
[39]   S.T., III, q. 75, a. 3, ad 3.
[40]   C.G., IV, cap. 63, paulum post princ.

form or other. And so, to be resolved into prime matter would have to mean, if anything, to become a **substance** of some kind, a substance composed of prime matter and substantial form. Such a substance is not, quite clearly, the same as prime matter. The substance of the bread, therefore, cannot be resolved into prime matter.[41]

Fourthly, the substance of the bread (and of the wine) **is not resolved into the four elements.** For, after the consecration, nothing remains under the sacramental species except the body and the blood of Christ. And so, it would be necessary to say that the elements into which the substance of the bread and of the wine are resolved **have departed,** and this can take place only by local motion, which would be perceived by the senses.[42] Moreover, such a resolution would entail many local motions, and bodily alterations among contraries, and these cannot be instantaneous, whereas transubstantiation is preciesly that, i.e., instantaneous.[43]

Hoc est corpus meum

Having seen something of what Aquinas has to say about the **intelligibiliy** and the **possibility** of transubstantiation, i.e., of the special sort of change which occurs when the substance of the bread and of the wine are converted into the substance of the already existing body and blood of Christ, we might move on to two other concerns (closely related to one another) of the philosophy of religion, i.e., to the question of **meaning** and to the question of **truth.** 1) What exactly do the words of consecration **mean?** How are we to understand the words which the priest pronounces, i.e., the words: **Hoc est corpus meum,** and the words: **Hic est calix sanguinis mei, novi et aeterni testamenti, mysterium fidei, qui pro vobis et pro multis effundetur in remissionem peccatorum** (as different from: **Can we understand** what these words mean? which is the question of intelligibility; see above pp.160-162)? And 2) are these statements **true,** i.e., the statements: **Hoc est corpus meum,**

---

41   *S.T., III,* q. 75, a. 3, c., in princ.
42   *S.T., III,* q. 75, a. 3, c., in medio.
43   *C.G., IV,* cap. 63, paulum post princ.

and: **Hic est calix sanguinis mei?**

Meaning

The word "Hoc" in the formula "Hoc est corpus meum" needs to be clarified. It does **not** refer to the **substance of the bread,** because the substance of the bread does **not** remain after the consecration, and the word "Hoc" refers in some way to **what remains** as well as to what precedes.[44] Neither does it refer to the **substantial form** of the bread. For, if the substance does not remain, neither does the substantial form of that substance remain. Neither does it refer to the **accidents** (and these **do** remain), for accidents are not the same as substance; and it is a **s u b s t a n c e** which is there after the transubstantiation, i.e., the substance of the body of Christ. Nonetheless, the word "Hoc" does refer, in a way, to the accidents of the bread and of the wine -- in a special **instrumental** way, i.e., seen both 1) as that which used to inhere in the substance of the bread (**before** the change), and 2) as that which now (**after** the change) locates and identifies, **without** inhering in, the **substance** of the body of Christ. And so, the word "Hoc" means: that which (i.e., a substance, though indeterminately signified) **before** the change appeared to be bread, and **in fact was** bread, and which (i.e., a substance, indeterminately) **now, after** the change, appears to be be bread, **without** being bread. Or, the word "Hoc" means: **This bread,** provided that by the words "This bread" one does not understand the **substance** of the bread, but rather **that which is contained under the species (outward appearance) of bread,** under which species there was first the substance of **bread,** and afterwards the substance of the **body of Christ.**[45]

Truth

Someone might argue that the statement: "Hoc est corpus meum" is **not** true. For, to say "hoc" is to designate a **substance.** But when the word "hoc" is

---

[44] *S.T., III,* q. 75, a. 2, c., ad finem.
[45] *S.T., III,* q. 75, a. 8. c., in fine.

pronounced, the substance **of the bread** is still there, since transubstantiation does not take place until the instant in which the last syllable of "Hoc est corpus meum" has been uttered by the priest. The last instant of pronouncing the words is the first instant in which the body of Christ is in the sacrament.[46] Now, since it is false to say that **this bread** (**before** consecration) **is the body of Christ,** it is simply false to say: Hoc est corpus meum.[47]

By way of responding to this objection, Aquinas notes that "Hoc est corpus meum" is like a pronouncement of the **practical** intellect, i.e., its truth does not presuppose the thing understood, but **produces or makes** it. Moreover, one must keep in mind that this change, this making, does not take place successively, but in an instant -- in the last instant of the pronouncing of the words. Yet, the subject of the statement, i.e., "hoc," does not stand for the term **ad quem** of the conversion, as if to say: My body is my body. Nor does it stand for that which was the term **a quo** of the conversion, as if to say, This bread is my body. Rather, "hoc" stands for something which is related to both terms, i.e., that which (unspecified as to its nature) is contained under the species, the outward appearance, of bread, namely some substance or other, but without determining or specifying for it any determinate nature; and so neither the nature of bread nor the nature of Christ's body.[48] The pronoun "hoc" does not stand for, or point to, the accidents, but **by way of the accidents** (in a **special instrumental** way, as noted just above, at the top of p. 180) points to the **substance underlying** the accidents, which at first was bread, and is afterwards the body of Christ, which body, though not informed by those accidents, is yet contained under them.[49]

Someone might object, secondly, that since the words of consecration, by their meaning, are said to be **the efficient (agent) cause** of the conversion of the bread into the body of Christ, one must note that an efficient cause **precedes** its effect. Thus, these words, and their meaning, **precede** the change of bread into the body of Christ. But, prior to the change, the statement "Hoc est corpus

---

46   *S.T., III,* q. 75, a. 7, c., in fine.
47   *S.T., III,* q. 75, a. 5, obj. 1.
48   *S.T., III,* q. 78, a. 5, c.; and ad 1.
49   *S.T., III,* q. 78, a. 5, ad 2.

meum" is false, since the body of Christ is **not** there before the change. Similarly, with respect to the statement "Hic est calix sanguinis mei."

Aquinas' response begins by pointing out that any cause is indeed prior to its effect, but **only** by nature, which is to say, **not** with respect to time. A cause and its effect are always **together with respect to time.** Or, no cause, as cause, is temporally prior to its effect, but always simultaneous with it. And this simultaneity, notes Aquinas, suffices for the truth of the statement "Hoc est corpus meum." For these words **produce** the effect at their being pronounced. And this is what is to be kept in mind here, i.e., **the producing agency** of these words. They are like a pronouncement of the **practical** intellect, which does not presuppose the thing understood, but rather brings it into existence.[50]

Hic est calix sanguinis mei, novi et aeterni testamenti, mysterium fidei, qui pro vobis et pro multis effundetur in remissionem peccatorum

What was said just above about the **meaning** and the **truth** of the words, **Hoc est corpus meum,** is to be said also about the meaning and truth of the words, **Hic est calix sanguinis mei.** And one can do this very simply, i.e., by inserting "Hic" wherever "Hoc" appears, and "sanguis" wherever "corpus" appears.

But, in the case of the words which consecrate the wine, there are two further things to consider: 1) the word "calix" which appears here has no counterpart in the words which consecrate the bread, i.e., there is **no** reference to a **container** for the body of Christ; and 2) the consecrating formula does not end with the words "sanguinis mei," but continues with: "novi et aeterni testamenti, mysterium fidei, qui pro vobis et pro multis effundetur in remissionem peccatorum."

---

[50]   *S.T., III,* q. 78, a. 5, ad 3.

Calix

Why, one can ask, do the words which consecrate the bread mention the **body** of Christ simply and directly, as **that into which** the bread is converted; whereas the words consecrating the wine mention the **cup** (calix) as **that into which** the wine is converted, adding that this cup is the cup of my blood (calix sanguinis mei).[51]

Aquinas' clarifying response points out that the words, Hic est calix sanguinis mei, are **a figure of speech,** which can be understood in two ways. In the first way, these words can be taken as a case of **metonymy,** i.e., a figure of speech in which the name of one thing is used to name another thing, of which it is an attribute, or with which it is associated, as when one speaks of the "lands which belong to the crown," the word "crown" being used to name the king. So that here, the meaning would be: This is my blood contained in the cup, the word "cup" being mentioned in addition to the word "blood" **to indicate** that Christ's blood is the **drink** of the faithful, which is **not** indicated, even by implication, by the word "blood" itself.

In the second way, it can be taken as a **metaphor,** i.e., as a figure of speech in which a word or phrase **literally** denoting one kind of object or idea is used in place of another to suggest a **likeness** or **analogy** between them, as in "the ship plows the sea," in which what the ship does to the sea **is like** what the plow does to the land. So that here, the meaning would be: This is the cup of my passion, the words "cup of my blood" being used to denote Christ's passion, in which Christ's blood **was separated from** Christ's body; and this is why, i.e., because of the **likeness,** the wine is consecrated **in separation from** the consecrated bread.[52]

---

51   S.T., III, q. 78, a. 3, obj. 1.
52   S.T., III, q. 78, a. 3. ad 1.

Novi et aeterni testamenti, mysterium fidei, qui pro vobis et pro multis effundetur in remissionem peccatorum

One can also ask, secondly, why the consecrating words do not stop at "sanguinis mei," but continue with "novi et aeterni testamenti . . . , in remissionem peccatorum"?

Aquinas answers this question by pointing out that the beginning words, i.e., "Hic est calix sanguinis mei," **denote the change** of the wine into the blood of Christ, and that the words which follow **point out the power** of Christ's blood which was shed in His passion, the power which works in this sacrament, and has three purposes. The first purpose of its power is to secure our **eternal** inheritance, which is denoted by the words, "novi et aeterni testamenti." Its second purpose is to justify by grace, which comes through faith, and this is why the words, "mysterium fidei," are added. Its third purpose is to remove sins, which are impediments to the first two, i.e., to our eternal inheritance, and to grace through faith. And this is why the words, "qui pro vobis et pro multis effundetur in remissionem peccatorum," are added. Even though the **whole** of this sacrament, i.e., **both** the body **and** the blood of Christ, is a memorial of the Passion of our Lord, and even though it is His body which underwent the Passion; it is nonetheless the shedding of the blood which indicates most intensely and graphically the Passion which His body underwent. And this is why the words, "novi et aeterni testamenti, mysterium fidei, qui pro vobis et pro multis effundetur in remissionem peccatorum," are included among the words which Christ used to consecrate the **wine,** though they could just as well have been included, *mutatis mutandis,* among the bread-consecrating words, and are certainly understood therein, without being explicitly said. Besides, Christ did say of His body, as He consecrated the bread, "quod pro vobis tradetur," (*Luke,* 22: 19; see also *I Cor.,* 1: 24)), which indicated that it was Christ's **body** which was to undergo the Passion, i.e., the shedding of the blood. Moreover, it is to be noted that nowadays these very words, i.e., "quod pro vobis tradetur," i.e., "which will be given up for you," follow the words, "This is my body," as part of the bread-consecrating formula.

Adoro te devote

One can see in various phrases of Aquinas' simple, but elegant meditation, the **Adoro te devote,** certain aspects of his theology of the Eucharist, i.e., of the ever present, but ever hidden God.   There is reflection on **what is hidden:** both the humanity and the divinity; on **what is sensed:** the accidents of the bread and the wine; on **what is done** by the power of what is hidden: it **removes** sin, **bestows and nourishes** faith and hope and love; and in the end, after this life, **reveals** the hidden God.

1.

> Adoro te devote, latens Deitas,
> Quae sub his figuris vere latitas.
> Tibi se cor meum totum subjicit,
> Quia, te contemplans, totum deficit.

In **1.,** Aquinas meditates on the **hiddennness** of God (latens Deitas; vere latitas), on God truly there, though concealed beneath these forms (sub his figuris), i.e., the forms of bread and wine; but **only** the forms, since the bread and the wine **themselves** are no longer there.   This is God's body; this is God's blood. The Most High, so lowly; the Most Extraordinary, so ordinary; the Most Believable, so unbelievable.   One's heart can do no better than to accept and to acquiesce (totum subjicit); for it cannot understand.   Though it tries, it utterly fails (totum deficit).

2.

> Visus, tactus, gustus in te fallitur,
> Sed auditu solo tuto creditur.
> Credo quiquid dixit Dei Filius,
> Nil hoc verbo Veritatis verius.

In **2.**, Aquinas meditates on **what the senses perceive.** Sight, touch, taste, and smell (not explicitly mentioned) perceive only bread and wine -- brown-white to sight, smooth to touch, wheaty to taste, and earthen to smell, the bread; amber-red to sight, cool to touch, tart-sweet to taste, and fragrant to smell, the wine. Without hearing, the other senses would be led astray. One can do no better than to believe what the ear has heard. There are no words truer than the words spoken by Truth Itself: Hoc est corpus meum. Hic est calix sanguinis mei.

3.

> **In cruce latebat sola Deitas,**
> **At hic latet simul et humanitas.**
> **Ambo tamen credens atque confitens,**
> **Peto quod petivit latro poenitens.**

In **3.**, Aquinas meditates on the **cross (In cruce).** The body on the cross shows the Man; but hides the God. Then he meditates on the **bread and wine (At hic).** These hide the Man as well. One can do no better than to believe, and to proclaim, **both** (ambo) what the **cross** hides (the God), **and** what the **bread and wine** hide, and they hide **both** (ambo) the God **and** the Man; and thereupon ask with the penitent thief to be remembered when He comes into His kingdom: Domine, memento mei, cum veneris in regnum tuum (*Luke,* 23: 42).

4.

> **Plagas, sicut Thomas, non intueor,**
> **Deum tamen meum te confiteor.**
> **Fac me tibi semper magis credere,**
> **In te spem habere, te diligere.**

In **4.**, Aquinas continues the theme of **3.**, the theme of the **cross** -- by focusing in particular on the **wounds** (plagas) from piercing nails and thrusting spear -- as that **sorrowful** theme gives rise to the **glorious** theme of the Resurrection. The apostle Thomas saw the Man -- the risen Man -- whose body, bearing the **scars** of nail and spear, hid the God from his bodily eyes; yet stirred, and awakened, then strengthened, the eyes of his faith. One can do no better than to acknowledge that the Bread (in which neither the body, nor the scars, nor the Man, nor the God can be seen) is both Man and God; and to ask for an increase in faith and hope and love: fac me tibi semper magis credere, in te spem habere, te diligere, especially love; for the greatest of these is love (*I Cor.*, 13: 13).

5.

> O memoriale mortis Domini,
> Panis vivus, vitam praestans homini
> Praesta meae menti de te vivere,
> Et te illi semper dulce sapere.

In **5.**, Aquinas returns to the **Bread,** to meditate on its **power.** The Bread points at once to **His** dying, which has conquered **our** dying; and to **His** rising, which has won **our** rising. It stirs up at once the memory of a **saving** death, and the anticipation of a **saved** life. This Bread is a living Bread (panis vivus). This Bread is the living God. One can do no better than to ask **to live with His life** (de te vivere), and **to savor it, delight in it, forever** (semper dulce sapere).

6.

> Pie pellicane, Jesu Domine,
> Me immundum munda tuo sanguine,
> Cujus una stilla salvum facere
> Totum mundum quit ab omni scelere.

In **6.,** Aquinas calls the hidden Jesus by name, and addresses Him as **the Pellican** (Pie pellicane, Jesu Domine),[53] as the One who feeds us, nourishes us, cleanses us, with **His own** Body and **His own** Blood. Aquinas meditates on the power of the Blood **in the cup,** which is the same as the Blood which began to flow **in the Garden,** continued **at the pillar** and from **amid the thorns, on the way** to the hill, and was totally drained **on the cross.** One drop, just one, would have been enough to save **all** the world from **all** its wickedness and **all** its guilt -- yesterday's, today's, tomorrow's.

7.

> **Jesu, quem velatum nunc aspicio,**
> **Oro, fiat illud quod tam sitio,**
> **Ut te revelata cernens facie,**
> **Visu sim beatus tuae gloriae.**

In **7.,** Aquinas again calls the hidden Jesus by name (Jesu, quem velatum nunc aspicio). The **hiddenness** -- **now** (nunc velatum) -- noted by the word "velatum" suggests, by a transfer of meaning from a **hiding** to a **covering** to a **crowning,** the glorious crowning of Jesus -- **then** -- after the Ascension, at the right hand of the Father. We can do no better than to pray for the fulfillment of the deepest desire of our hearts (quod tam sitio), i.e., that, after this life, we will see Jesus face to face, both the Man and the God (ut te cernens) -- no longer hidden beneath bread and wine, but fully revealed (revelata facie), and in glory; and that this seeing, this **blessed** seeing, will be **our** crowning and **our** glory as well (visu sim beatus tuae gloriae); and that it will have no end.

---

[53] "In the Middle Ages, naturalists thought the pelican used its beak to pierce its side, from which flowed blood to nourish its young -- an apt image of Christ shedding his blood on Calvary to redeem humanity and of Christ literally feeding humanity with his Flesh and Blood in the Eucharist. One version of the pelican story asserts that the mother pelican is oversolicitous of its young and inadvertently kills them with loving pecking. After three days, the father pelican comes and, greatly grieved, stands over its dead offspring and smites its own side, from which blood trickles on the young and brings them back to life." *Catholic Digest,* March 1998, p. 116.

CHAPTER TEN

THE LAST THINGS: DEATH AND PURGATORY

THE HIDDEN BUT EVER PRESENT GOD is an ever faithful God. He protects us as we pass through the door of death, helps us to keep from succumbing to the last temptations which could plunge us irretreivably into hell, and guides us through the loving cleansing of purgatory to prepare us for **our** glory, which is the vision of **His** glory.

The present chapter is concerned with some of the things which Aquinas has to say about death and about purgatory.

Death

What, as Aquinas sees it, is death? --   one might ask. Death, Aquinas would answer, is the separation of the soul (mind, spirit, capacity to know and to love) from the body. And **we** might add, by way of responding to the question one naturally wants to ask at this point, that this separation takes place at the cessation of all physiological activity -- chemical and electrical - in the brain. It would be difficut, indeed, to identify the exact moment of cessation, but that is an empirical matter, and is not relevant to an attempt at definition.

Since man is made up out of body and soul, it follows that **man** can die. **Death or dying** is a way of going out of existence. But man's **soul** cannot go out of existence by dying. And this is so, simply because man's soul is not itself made up out of body and soul. Only living things can go out of existence by dying, for only living things are made up out of body and soul. And the soul of a living thing is its substantial form. Souls and substantial forms are not made up out of body and soul.

What about man's **body?** -- one might ask. Can **it** go out of existence by dying? We often say that "the body dies." But, on this definition of death, i.e., death as separation of the soul from the body, one must conclude that man's body, too (like man's soul) cannot die. And for the same reason, i.e., because man's body is not itself made up out of body and soul. What is true of man's body is true of the body of any living thing. It cannot go out of existence by dying.

Can man's **body** go **out of existence?** Indeed, it can. And it does. This is clear. But it goes out of existence **by falling apart.** It falls apart into its physical components, however one identifies them -- whether as molecules, or atoms, or protons, or neutrons, etc. **Falling apart** is another way of going out of existence. What is true of man's body is true of the body of any physical thing. It can go out of existence by falling apart.

And, what about man's **soul?** Can **it** go out of existence **by falling apart?** As Aquinas sees it, the soul cannot go out of existence by falling apart, since the soul is simple, not made up of parts, at least not of the sort of parts into which a thing can be disintegrated. What is true of man's soul is true of any soul, indeed of any substantial form. Souls and substantial forms cannot go out of existence by falling apart.

Will man's **soul** go out of existence when **man** dies? It will, **if** man's soul is **totally dependent** on man's body. For man's body goes out of existence at man's death. Given two things, A and B (however radically different from one another they might be), such that A depends on B; if B goes out of existence, A too must go out of existence. Going out of existence **because of dependency** is still another way of going out of existence.

One might ask, further, whether God will **annihilate** man's soul when man dies? Reduce man's soul to absolute nothingness? This is certainly within God's power. For God can create, i.e., bring into existence out of absolute nothingness; and what can create can also annihilate. Both take infinite power. As Aquinas sees it, though God **can,** He **will not,** annihilate the human soul. For, He created it with an intrinsically indestructible nature, an intrinsically eternal nature. It would be contrary to God's Wisdom, argues Aquinas, to create such a thing, and then to annihilate it. **Annihilation** is another way of going out of existence.

There are, thus, at least four ways of going out of existence: 1) by dying, 2) by falling apart, 3) by dependency, 4) by annihilation. And death, it is to be emphasized, is just one of these ways. Only that can die which is made up out of body and soul; death is the separation of a thing's soul from its body.

The above will become clearer if one notices, as Aquinas does, that death (mors) can be considered in two ways. 1) In one way, it can be taken to mean the privation of life, in the sense of a **state**. Thus, in the first instant after life departs, i.e., in the first instant after the soul has been separated from the body, death **as a state of privation** is present. Death in this sense, Aquinas adds in context, is **not** physically painful, for privation of life includes privation **of sense life** as well. 2) In a second way, death can be taken to mean the alteration which precedes, and terminates in, death taken in the first way. This is a **corrupting** alteration, as different from the **generating** alteration which precedes and terminates in the state of life. Death, in this way, is a **temporal process** (as opposed to a state), a **motion toward** death as a privation of life. Death, in this way, might better be called dying. Thus, **dying** precedes and terminates in **death;** or, death **as process** precedes and terminates in death **as privation.**[1] Death in this second sense, Aquinas adds in context, is physically painful, or at least can be physically painful, for life, including the **life of the senses,** is still present.

Death is *both* natural to man *and* a punishment for our first parents' sin

Someone might feel, observes Aquinas, that death cannot be a **punishment** for **any** sin, let alone our first parents' sin, since death is natural to man. How can what is natural be a punishment? It is clear that death is

---

[1]   *S.T., II-II,* q. 164, a. 1, ad 7.

natural to man, since man's body is composed out of the elements, and the elements are contraries. Corruptibility is a necessary consequence of composition out of contraries; and for a living thing, to be corruptible is to be capable of death. This is what it means to say that death is natural to man. This is also why **mortal** is included in the definition of man: animal rationale **mortale**.[2]

Aquinas responds to this argument by pointing out that what is natural to a thing derives from the components of its nature, i.e., form its matter and its form. Man's form is his soul, the rational soul; and since the rational soul is intrinsically immortal, death is not natural to man with respect to his soul. But death **is** natural to man with respect to his body. For man's body is composed out of the elements, and these have contrary qualities. The necessary consequence of such composition is corruptibility. With respect to man's body, thus, Aquinas agrees with this argument. Further, Aquinas adds by way of explanation, it is **necessary** for man's body to be composed throughout out of the elements with their contrary qualities, since it is natural to man to have a body with **a sense of touch** which is spread throughout the **whole** of it. This would be impossible if the body were not composed throughout out of contraries, since these are necessary as means for the perception of the qualities which affect touch, qualities like wet and dry, hot and cold.[3] Touch requires a physical or natural change in its organs, as well as a spiritual or perceptual change, to be caused by the power of the qualities which are its proper objects.[4] The organ of touch must **become** hot in order **to perceive** hot, and cold in order to perceive cold, etc. Now God, the all-powerful creator, conferred on man, when He first created man, the favor of being exempt from the corruptibility which is a necessary consequence of composition out of the elements. It is clear, therefore, that death can be **both** matural to man, **and** a punishment to man. **Natural,** because it is a consequence of man's having to have a body composed throughout out of the elements with their inherent contrarieties. **A punishment,** because death is a consequence of man's having lost (by sinning) God's initially conferred favor

---

[2] *S.T., II-II,* q. 164, a. 1, obj. 1.
[3] *S.T., II-II,* q. 164, a. 1, ad 1; see also *S.T., I,* q. 78, a. 3, esp. obj. 3 and ad 3.
[4] *S.T., I,* q. 78, a. 3, ad 4.

of exempting him from death.[5]   Man's death is necessary **both** because it is possible (for man's body must be composed throughout out of the elements), **and** because it cannot be avoided (for God has withdrawn, as a just punishment, His initial exemption).

It will be helpful at this point to clarify a bit what Aquinas means when he speaks of "death as a punishment **for our first parents' sin.**" Though it is a punishment **for** our first parents' sin, it is **not** a punishment **limited to** our first parents.   It extends to every human being descended from them as well.

Someone might object, notes Aquinas, that the sin of our first parents was the sin **of two particular individuals,** whereas death affects **absolutely every** human being.   Punishment for sin ought to affect **only** those who have actually committed that sin.[6]

By way of response, Aquinas points out that God created our first parents **not only** as two particular individuals, **but also** as the originating sources or principles, i.e., the causes which were to transmit human nature, **together with the Divine favor exempting and preserving them from death,** to the whole of their posterity.   Since their sin deprived our first parents of that exemption, the human nature they passed on to their children, and to their children's children, and thereby to every human being, is a human nature deprived of that exemption.   If they had not sinned, the human nature they passed on would have retained that exemption.[7]

Someone might object further, points out Aquinas, that since all human beings are equally descended from our first parents, all should be affected by death equally.   But this is clearly not the case, since some die sooner than others, and some more painfully than others.[8]

---

5   *S.T., II-II,* q. 164, a. 1, ad 1.
6   *S.T., II-II,* q. 164, a. 1, obj. 3.
7   *S.T., II-II,* q. 164, a. 1, ad 3.
8   *S.T., II-II,* q. 164, a. 1, obj. 4.

Aquinas' response to this objection clarifies the nature of the Divine favor which was conferred on man when God first created man. It was a favor ordered toward keeping human nature whole and entire, by keeping all its components together -- body and soul together; and in the body, the four elements together. All human beings are subject **equally** to God's **withdrawal** of this initial together-keeping favor; and therefore to pain and suffering and death, which are the **necessary results** of the withdrawal. But the **time** of one's death, and the **kind and intensity** of one's pain and suffering, are certain **accidental features** of the necessary results of God's withdrawing that initial favor; just as continuing life, i.e., no death, and no pain and no suffering, would have been the **necessary results** of the continued presence of the favor. It is here, with respect to these accidental features, that all do **not** suffer equally. God, in His providence and love, has chosen to mete out these accidental features in different ways to different persons; to some as to parents being punished by seeing the suffering of their children; to others as a remedy intended for their spiritual welfare, e.g., to help them turn away from their sins, or to help them not to become proud of their virtues, or that they may be crowned for their patience.[9]

Purgatory

What exactly is purgatory, as Aquinas sees it? Purgatory, Aquinas would answer, is a place of **temporary** punishment in which **saved** human souls (vs. damned ones), in the period between death and the resurrection of the body, are **cleansed** from the **guilt** of **venial** sins, and are **enabled to pay in full** the **debt of punishment due to sin,** both venial and mortal though already forgiven, by a twofold pain: 1) the pain of loss, i.e., a delay with respect to the vision of God, and 2) the pain of sense, i.e., punishment by corporeal fire.

---

[9] *S.T., II-II,* q. 164, a. 1, ad 4.

Is there a purgatory?

There **is** a purgatory, notes Aquinas, and this can be argued from what is written in *Machabees,* 12: 46: *It is a holy and wholesome thought to pray for the dead, that they might be loosed from sins.* It is clear, points out Aquinas, that there is no need to pray for the dead **who are in heaven;** for they already see God faced to face, and so have no need of our prayers. Nor is there any need to pray for the dead **who are in hell,** for they cannot be loosed from their sins (these are **mortal** sins, and there is not even a hint of the love of **caritas** in the damned). There must be some, therefore, who, after this life, are **not yet** loosed from sins, but **can be** loosed from them (these are **venial** sins). They must, therefore, have some measure of the love of **caritas** in them, for without such love they could not be loosed from their sins. And so, they will not be consigned to the everlasting pains of hell (because of the love of **caritas** which is in them); nor can they see God face to face (because of the uncleanness of the sins which are in them). There must, therefore, be some kind of cleansing which takes place after this life, and this is what is meant by purgatory.[10]

Moreover, there must be a place called purgatory, for these reasons. 1) To make possible **payment in full** of the **debt of punishment due to sin,** even after all sins, both mortal and venial, have been forgiven by contrition and the sacrament of penance. 2) Because venial sins are not always removed when mortal sins are forgiven. 3) The justice of God requires that the disorder of sin be set aright by due punishment. To be **forgiven** one's mortal sins, and to die so forgiven, is to be saved, indeed. But in someone so saved, there may well be **unforgiven venial** sins, however few, which need to be forgiven; and the **debt of punishment** due to his forgiven sins, both venial and mortal, may well not yet have been fully paid at the time of death. Thus, because there is a God, and God is just, there must be a purgatory, **for God's sake.** Besides, the love of God requires that there be a purgatory **for our sake.** Purgatory is God's **loving cleansing** of the souls of those who have died **in his friendship,** but **imperfectly** in that friendship.[11]

---

[10] *S.T., Suppl., Append. 2,* q. 1, a. 1, sed contra.
[11] *S.T., Suppl., Append. 2,* q. 1, a. 1, c.

Can fire, which is something corporeal, affect something incorporeal, like a disembodied human soul in purgatory, so that the soul suffers from the fire?

It can, Aquinas holds, but **only** because it functions as an **instrument** of God's justice, and **only in a very special way**.

To begin with, the disembodied human soul, in the view of Aquinas, does not retain its sensory **powers,** since these powers employ certain bodily organs for the performance of their proper **activities.** By way of contrast, the powers which do **not** employ bodily organs for the performance of their proper activities, e.g., activities like understanding, considering, and willing, **do** remain in the separated human soul.[12] Since the sensory **powers** do not remain, neither do the **activities** of these powers remain.[13] And so, there is no possibility of a visual experience of fire, or of an auditory experience, e.g., the crackling of the fire, or of an olfactory experience, e.g., the smell of burning flesh. Nor can the disembodied soul **feel** the burning of the fire by means of the **sense of touch.** How, then, does the separated human soul experience the punishing fires of purgatory (or of hell) if sensory experience is impossible? Aquinas addresses this question in the third article of question seventy: **Whether the separated soul can suffer from a bodily fire?**[14]

Someone might object, observes Aquinas, that every corporeal agent acts **by contact.** But a corporeal fire can**not** be in contact with a disembodied human soul, since the human soul is an incorporeal thing, and contact can occur only between corporeal things when the outer bounds of their bodies come together. The human soul has no such outer bounds.[15]

---

12 *S.T., Suppl.,* q. 70, a. 1, c.
13 *S.T., Suppl.,* q. 70, a. 2, c.
14 *S.T., Suppl.,* q. 70, a. 3.
15 *S.T., Suppl.,* q. 70, a. 3, obj. 7.

Aquinas responds to this objection by agreeing that, although there cannot be a body-to-body contact between the separated human soul and a bodily thing, like fire, since the human soul is not a body; there can be nonetheless, and is, another kind of contact between them.[16] To make this understandable, one must point out that since fire is the **instrument** of Divine justice in the punishment of sin, the fire must affect the soul by an action whicn is **natural** to the fire itself. For **any instrument** of a principal agent contributes something which is **proper to itself,** and through that contribution functions as an instrument; for example, the pen with which I write contributes the ink. To do this, the fire must be in some way united to, joined to, the soul, and by this joining touch the soul in some way, be in contact with the soul in some way. Now, something incorporeal can be united to something corporeal in more than one way. In one way, as form to matter. Clearly, this is not how the separated human soul is united to fire, for the human soul is not the substantial form of fire. In another way, as a mover is united to the thing being moved. Neither is this how the separated human soul is united to fire; for in purgatory it would not be the human soul which moves the fire, but rather the fire which moves the human soul. In still another way, as a thing in a given place is united to that place. Now, although something corporeal can, **by its nature** or what is proper to itself, **confine** something incorporeal to a place, as the human body does with respect to the human soul during this life; it cannot, **by its nature, detain** something incorporeal in the place to which it is confined. **Confining** is one thing, **detaining** is another. The human body, for example, in confining the human soul to a place, limits the human soul to being in one place at a given time, so as not to be in another place at that time. But, the human body cannot by its nature detain it there, keep it there; for the soul by a simple act of **volition** can move its body from this place to that one, as when I **decide** to walk from here to there. Nonetheless, something corporeal **can, as an instrument** of God's justice, **detain** something incorporeal in a given place, thus producing a punishing effect -- by hindering it from doing its own will, from acting where it might will, and as it might will.

---

16   *S.T., Suppl.,* q. 70, a. 3, ad 7.

Thus, something bodily (or corporeal) is **of its nature** able to have something incorporeal united to it as a thing in place is united to that place, and so is able to **confine** it to a place. As the **instrument** of God's justice (though **not** of its nature) it can go beyond **confining,** and **detain** something incorporeal in a given place, **chain it** to that place. Thus, fire confines (by its own nature) and detains (as an instrument of God) the human soul in purgatory **for a time** (and, in hell, **forever**). As God's instrument, fire is something hurtful to the human soul, keeping it from doing its own will, from acting where it might will, and as it might will. And, perceiving that fire (something **inferior** to itself, for the fire is something **corporeal,** and the soul something **incorporeal**) is something hurtful, in this confining and detaining way (temporarily in purgatory, eternally in hell); perceiving also that what confines and detains it is something **inferior** to itself, the human soul is distressed and tormented, and so punished by that fire.[17] To be **confined and detained** is hurtful, indeed; but, by something which is **inferior** to itself, is doubly so. This is the **special way** in which fire causes the separated human soul to suffer.

---

[17] S.T., *Suppl.*, q. 70. a. 3, c.

CHAPTER ELEVEN

THE LAST THINGS: HEAVEN AND HELL

THE EVER FAITHFUL AND PROTECTING GOD is a **limitlessly loving** God. For He wants to share His blessed and endless life with us -- **all** of us. He wants us in heaven, in the love and the light and the joy of His presence. He wants us to sit at His table, to eat His bread and drink His wine, to enjoy His company and His conversation, and that of His friends and ours, forever. But, he is also a **limitlessly powerless** God. For He has made us **free.** It is **we,** it is said, who freely choose hell, just as it is **we** who freely choose heaven; and God is **powerless** to make us do otherwise. Most happy and joyous, the second choice (but, why **only** by a **certain some,** why not **by everyone?**); most tragic and sad, the first (but, why **by anyone at all?**).

The present chapter is concerned with some of the things which Aquinas has to say about heaven and about hell.

Hell

What exactly is hell, as Aquinas understands it? Hell, as he understands it, is a place of punishment in which the damned, like the saved in purgatory, suffer from a twofold pain: 1) the pain of loss, with respect to the vision of God, and 2) the pain of sense, which is a punishment by the confining (natural) and detaining (instrumental) causality of corporeal fire.   But there is this significant difference. The punishment of the damned is an **everlasting** punishment. The pain of loss, for them, is **not simply a delay,** as it is for the saved in purgatory.   And the pain of sense, for them, does not cease, as it does for the saved in purgatory when God's loving **cleansing** is finished. In hell, the pain of sense is **not** for cleansing at all; it is **not a cleansing** pain prompted by God's **love,** as it is in purgatory; its purpose is simply and only punishment -- punishment required by God's **justice.**   There is no possibility of cleansing for the damned in hell, since they have died **completely outside** friendship with God.

Is there a hell?

Someone might argue that there cannot be a hell; or, if there is a hell, that there cannot be anyone in it.   For, God is **our father.**   Jesus himself told us that God is our father.   St. Luke writes that once Jesus was praying in a certain place, and when He had finished, one of this disciples said to Him, "Lord, teach us to pray, as John taught his disciples."   Jesus responded with what we've come to call the Lord's prayer, or the Our Father, the opening words of which make it undeniably clear that God is exactly that, i.e., Our Father.[1]   St. Matthew too records this same prayer, though in a longer version.[2]

What Jesus was telling us is that God is **our father** in a special sense of "father," indicated by the words, "who art in heaven." We are to understand our father **in heaven** by way of reference to the way in which we understand our father **here on earth.** Our father **in heaven** is **like** our father **on earth,** but infinitely better.   All the perfections of our earthly fathers (of our earthly **mothers**, too; and so, of our earthly **parents**) are found in our heavenly father, but without limit, i.e., infinitely; and **without** any of our earthly parents' **imperfections.**   Consider how a father, how a parent, looks after his child. The parent wants only the best of things, and all of them, for the child; and does all in his power to bring these things about -- food, shelter, clothing, education, virtuous friends, and the like.   But most of all, the parent wants the child to become a morally good person, a person who loves God above all else, and others as he loves himself; and, because of that love, to be rewarded with eternal happiness in heaven, rather than to be condemned to eternal punishment in hell.   When the child is very young, being spanked or being made to sit in a corner or being deprived of a favorite dessert -- i.e., mild and

---

[1]   *St. Luke,* 11: 1-4.
[2]   *St. Matthew,* 6: 9-13.

loving punishments -- are the appropriate and effective means for encouraging morally acceptable behavior. But, as the child grows, these punishments cease to work. The child turns into **a conscious center of free choice,** at which time **persuasion,** rather than punishment, becomes the appropriate, and effective (it is hoped), means for encouraging morally acceptable behavior, which, at this point, is to be seen by the child, as behaviour motivated by love. The parent begins to read all sorts of things, articles and books, on the psychology of **persuasion**, begins to seek help from professionals in the art of raising children, in the hope of becoming as effective as possible **in persuading** the child to make the right **free choices,** and for the right reason, i.e., out of love. **Persuasion,** the parent is convinced, and rightly, does **not** take away **free choice.** But the parent, being only human, often fails. The parent's arguments are often simply not persuasive enough. God, however, by way of difference from an earthly parent, is the Divine Psychologist, **infinitely** persuasive -- besides being **infinitely** knowing, **infinitely** loving, **infinitely** powerful, **infinitely** patient. As such, God would want, and would be able, to persuade (**persuade,** and so **without** depriving them in any way of **free choice**) **all** people, without exception, to become morally good, i.e., loving persons, who, as morally good, would be rewarded after this life with eternal happiness in heaven. This, after all, is what God wants, and most of all, for **all** of us. From which it follows that there is no hell. Or, if there is a hell, that there is no one in it, not even one single person. Otherwise, God has failed. Either He does **not** love us, one would have to conclude, or He is **unable** to persuade us. These things, however, are impossible.

But one can also argue that there **is** a hell, and on scriptural, i.e., theological, grounds. Jesus not only gives us the Our Father, but He also tells us, and explicitly, that there **is** a hell. We read in St. Matthew's gospel how Jesus, at the end of time, will separate those who have done evil from those who have done good, that He will send out his angels to gather up "all whose deeds are evil, and these will be thrown into the blazing furnace,"[3] as he says to them, "depart from my sight, you cursed, into the eternal fire which

---

[3]   *St. Matthew,* 13: 41-42.

has been prepared for the devil and his angels."[4]   And they will go away to eternal punishment, but the righteous will enter eternal life.[5]

God puts no one into hell, it is said.   It is **we,** it is said, who freely choose hell, by willfully turning away from God (by mortal sin), and by persisting in that choice **until and through death;**[6] just as it is **we** who freely choose heaven.   Because we are free, it is said by some, God is **absolutely powerless** with respect to the choices we make.   But then, does this mean that we get to heaven **without** God's grace?   And that we fall into hell **in spite of** God's infinite persuasiveness, in spite of the fact that God's love for us is an **infinite love?**   Does this mean that God **permits** people to go to hell, though He loves each person with an infinite love, and **could have prevented** this with His infinite persuasiveness as heavenly father, as the Divine Psychologist?

Since God loves us the way He does, and since His powers of persuasion are limitless, there cannot be a hell; or, if there is, there cannot be anyone in it, **not even one person.**   Is there something wrong with this argument?   Is God **unable** to persuade us **without** depriving us of our freedom?   Is there something about God's powers of persuasion, and about human freedom, which this argument fails to understand?   And, do we go to hell **on our own,** but to heaven **only by God's grace?**   Why doesn't **everyone** choose heaven? Why does **anyone at all** choose hell?   Are some of us **born** good, and some **born** bad?   Does it in some way, at some point, come down to **heredity?**

The fire of hell

It is easy to see that the punishing fire which will torment the **bodies** of the damned **after** the resurrection **must be a corporeal** fire.   For punishment cannot be applied to a body, as Aquinas argues, and rightly, unless the means of punishment is itself something bodily.[7]

---

[4]   *St. Matthew,*   25:   41-42.
[5]   *St. Matthew,*   25:   46.
[6]   *Catechism of the Catholic Church*   (English translation), Washington, D.C.:   United States Catholic Conference, Inc., 1994;   paragraph 1037.
[7]   *S.T., Suppl.,*   q. 97, a. 5,   c.,   in fine.

And there is no difficulty with respect to maintaining that this same **corporeal** fire will torment the **souls** of the damned, both **before** and **after** the resurrection of the body, and so forever after death. The fact that human souls are **incorporeal** does **not** make this impossible; just as the fact that the **demons** are incorporeal does not make it impossible for them to be tormented by that same corporeal fire. The souls of the damned along with their bodies, it must be remembered, will be condemned to the same blazing furnace to which the demons have been condemned: "depart from my sight, you cursed," Jesus will say at the end of time, "into the eternal fire which was prepared for the **devil** and his angels."[8] What was said above about the **confining and detaining** causality of **corporeal** fire with respect to the **souls of the saved in purgatory** is to be said with respect to the **souls of the damned in hell.** Corporeal fire can contain, by its own nature, and detain, as an instrument of God's justice, and thereby torment an incorporeal thing, whether a demon or a human soul, and whether only for a time (as in purgatory) or forever (as in hell).[9]

Moreover, this fire will cause the **bodies** of the damned to feel the pain of being burned or scorched by heat of the utmost intensity. But this heat will not alter their bodies in any way. Nor will it consume them.[10] This fire is unquenchable, neither needing kindling to start it, nor fuel to keep it going .[11] The fire in hell will be of the **same species** as our fire on earth, just as the bodies of the damned will be of the same species as they were before death; but, like the bodies of the damned, it will be **incorruptible,** both because it is an instrument of God's justice, and because the motion of the heavenly bodies will have ceased.[12]

---

[8]   *St. Matthew*, 25: 41-42.
[9]   See above pp. 202-204.
[10] *S.T., Suppl.,* q. 97, a. 5, ad. 1
[11] *S.T., Suppl.,* q. 97, a. 6, c., in fine.
[12] *S.T., Suppl.,* q. 97, a. 6, ad 3.

Punishment by fire is *not the only* punishment of the damned in hell

It is in accord with divine justice, argues Aquinas, that the damned in hell be tormented in **many** ways, and by **many** things. For, in departing from the **one** God by their mortal sins, the damned have chosen as their end **an array** of things, **many** things. They have chosen not only themselves (and they are considerably beneath God), but different sorts of material things as well (and these are all of them obviously beneath man). It is befitting God's justice, therefore, that the damned be tormented by **a plurality** of things. These are the things you wanted, God is saying in effect, and so you shall have them. You wanted **all** of them, and so you shall have **all** of them. And you wanted them so as to have them **forever;** and so, you shall have them **forever.**

The damned will be tormented, and forever, **not only** by corporeal fire itself, **but also** by combustible materials aglow with that fire, e.g., sulfur (brimstone); by storming winds, too;[13] by **the most intense cold** of which water is capable, as an instrument of God's justice, and not only by **the most intense heat** of which fire is capable, in that same role;[14] by the "worm" of a remorseful, gnawing conscience, distressed by past misdeeds;[15] by a weeping without tears, which nonetheless causes an unbearable agitation and aching of the head and the eyes;[16] by as little light, and as much darkness, as is necessary to make seeing an experience of unsurpassable anguish; and generally by conditions most adapted to bringing about the utmost unhappiness of the damned.[17] Unlike the souls in purgatory who are there, in purgatory, primarily for cleansing, though for punishment as well; the damned in hell are there, in hell, for **punishment,** and for punishment **alone.**

---

13   *S.T., Suppl.,* q. 97, a. 1, sed contra.
14   *S.T., Suppl.,* q. 97, a. 1, sed contra, and ad 3.
15   *S.T., Suppl.,* q. 97, a. 2, c.
16   *S.T., Suppl.,* q. 97, a. 2, a. 3, c.
17   *S.T., Suppl.,* q. 97, a. 4, c.

The eternity of hell

If God is infinitely **loving** and infinitely **merciful,** then why, one might ask, is the punishment of the damned, both demons and men, an **eternal** punishment? Is it because God is also infinitely **just?** And does His **justice** somehow override, set aside, annul His **love** and His **mercy?**

Eternal punishment for sin can**not** be **just** -- one might offer as a first objection -- since sin, even mortal sin, can never be other than **temporal.** Imagine a man who does nothing from morning till night but commit mortal sins, and that he does this every day for a million years. What is even a **million** years in comparison to **forever,** to **eternity?** And where is the wicked man who lives for a million years?[18] More to the point, where is the wicked man who lives **forever?** Wouldn't he have to sin **forever** to be **justly** punished **forever?** And if there were such a man, how could he possibly be punished forever? Doesn't the punishment of hell come **after death?** And how can one die if one lives forever?

Aquinas' response to this objection, i.e., to the objection that the punishment should not exceed the misdeed (or fault or sin), is that punishment does **not** have to be equal to the misdeed **as regards how long** it should last; as is the case even with human laws.[19] He explains. There are two questions about punishment: 1) **how severe** should it be?, and 2) **how long** should it last? Now, the **severity** of the punishment should be determined or measured by, should correspond to, the **severity** of the misdeed, so that the more grievous the misdeed or sin the more grievous the punishment. But, the **duration** of the punishment need **not** correspond to the **duration** of the misdeed. For example, an act of adulterous sex, or an act of murder, which takes only a very short time, is not punished with a punishment which lasts correspondingly for but a few moments, even according to human laws. It is rather the case that the duration of the punishment takes into account, and is determined by, the disposition or condition of the sinner. Now, sometimes a person commits an offense

---

18   *S.T., Suppl.,* q. 99, a. 1, obj. 1.
19   *S.T., Suppl.,* q. 99, a. 1, ad 1

repeatedly (e.g., a three time loser, or more), and so is of a disposition toward misdeeds which renders him deserving of being **cut off entirely** from the company of his fellow citizens, by a lifetime in prison perhaps, perhaps even by death. But sometimes, the disposition of the offender (e.g., a first time offender, with a prior life which was exemplary and unblemished) is such that it does **not** render him deserving of being **cut off entirely** from the company of others. In such a case, in order that he might return to, and become a fitting member of the community, his punishment is made longer or shorter, according to what is best suited for his amendment, and for preparing him to live in the community in a becoming and peaceful and fruitful way. This is the way it is with respect to **human** justice in an **earthly** community. -- Similarly with respect to **divine** justice in the **heavenly** community. Mortal sin renders the offender deserving of being **cut off entirely** from the community of those who see God face to face. To be cut off **entirely** means to be cut off for as long as that community will last, and the heavenly community will last forever. Venial sin, on the other hand, does **not** render the offender deserving of being **cut off entirely** from the community of the blessed. And so the punishment of such a one will be longer or shorter (in purgatory, of course, and not in hell), according to how much time is required to cleanse him from the way in which he clings to sin (venial), or sin to him, and thus make him fit to see God face to face with all the others in the heavenly community.[20]

There are other reasons, too, given by certain saintly ones, continues Aquinas, for maintaining that some people are **justly** condemned to **everlasting** punishment, even though their sin took only **a short time** to commit. A first reason is that these people have sinned against an **eternal** good -- by knowingly preferring a **temporal** satisfaction to **eternal** life. A second reason is that in this short life they **never ceased** to desire sin, and die without ceasing to desire it, i.e., remain fixed or obstinate in that desire; and so in the next life they should **never cease** to be punished. A third reason is that these people, when they sinned, sinned with **a willingness to remain in sin forever,** and so should be punished for that willingness with a

---

[20] S.T., Suppl., q. 99, a. 1, c., a princ. ad medium.

punishment which lasts **forever.** Still another reason is that mortal sin (unlike venial sin) really offends God, and deeply, and so deprives us of His friendship; and God is **infinite.** And so, a **just** punishment should be **infinite.** It cannot be infinite **in intensity,** for no creature can sustain an **infinitely intense** quality. Thus, the punishment must be infinite **at least in its duration.** Lastly, the guilt of mortal sin cannot be removed without grace. But men cannot receive grace after death. To die in mortal sin is, therefore, to die with a guilt which will last forever. Everlasting guilt deserves everlasting punishment. Briefly, a mortal sin, though it takes but **a brief time to commit,** is a **knowing** act of **eternal** rejection of the **eternal** love of the **eternal** God. Such a rejection requires, **and justly,** a correspondingly **eternal** punishment.[21] It is clear, therefore, that though mortal sin is temporal in one respect, it is also eternal in another. It is because of the latter that it deserves eternal punishment.

One might observe, as a second objection, that a punishment can be just **only** if it is given **in order to correct.** That is, correction should be **at least part** of the reason for a **just** punishment, whatever other accompanying reason(s) there might be -- like inflicting pain, or imposing limits on various sorts of freedom. Isn't it clear that the **eternal** punishment of the wicked cannot possibly lead to **their** correction; that punishment, to be corrective, must come to an end, so that, having come to an end, it can be followed by its corrective effects on those who have been correctively punished? Isn't it also clear that the eternal punishment of hell cannot lead to the correction of **others** (i.e., other than those in hell), since there will be no others, after the resurrection of the body, to whom correction can be applied. After the resurrection of the body, purgatory will have come to an end, and everybody will be either in heaven, where correction is not needed, or in hell, where correction is not possible.[22]

Aquinas' response to this objection begins by pointing out that, in an **earthly** community, the punishments inflicted on those who are **not** deserving of being **cut off entirely** from the company of their fellow citizens

---

[21] *S.T., Suppl.,* q. 99, a. 1, c., a medio ad finem.
[22] *S.T., Suppl.,* q. 99, a. 1, obj. 3.

are intended for **their** correction, i.e., to prepare them for a return to the community as members who can show some concern for others. But the punishments of those who **are** deserving of being **cut off entirely** are **not** intended for **their** correction, though these punishments may be intended for the correction (a kind of deterring correction) of **others,** i.e., those who have remained in that community as concerned and contributing members. Similarly, the punishments of **those in purgatory** are intended for **their** correction, since they are **not** deserving of being **cut off entirely** from the community of the blessed in heaven, though their wills need to be corrected, i.e., turned away from their attachment to venial sin, which will enable them to enter the community of those who see God face to face. But the **eternal** punishments of the damned are **not** intended for **their** correction, since the damned **are** deserving of being **cut off entirely** from the **heavenly** community.   These punishments are intended, rather, for the deterring correction of those who are still in their earthly lives; for punishments can produce their corrective effects **not only** in those on whom they are actually being inflicted, **but also** in those to whom their having been decreed, as to be imposed on evil doers, has been made known.   And so, the damnation of the wicked is for the correction of those who are now in the Church.[23]

The immutability (obstinacy) of the wills of the damned

Why is it, one wants to ask, that the wills of the damned remain obstinate (immutable) in evil?   That they do, indeed that they must, remain obstinate in evil is clear, since their punishment in hell is **eternal. Eternal** punishment woud **not** be **just,** if the wills of the damned could turn away from their attachment to evil.

Aquinas argues that the nature of **perfect happiness,** which consists in man's seeing God face to face, would be contradicted if man, after achieving it, could turn to what is opposed to it. For then, **fear** of losing happiness would not be wholly excluded, and so desire would not be completely satisfied,[24] and

---

23   *S.T., Suppl.,*   q. 99, a. 1, ad 3.
24   *Compendium Theologiae,* cap. 166, in fine.

perfect happiness would not be perfect happiness. The soul which sees God in His essence has its will firmly fixed on God, and can never turn to what is opposed to Him, because God, who is goodness itself, is not lacking in any good that may be sought elsewhere. And so the soul which sees God's essence must rest fully content with possessing that essence; and desires all other things in appropriate subordination to God.[25]

Can it be said, by a kind of parallel argument, that the nature of damnation, which consists primarily in being deprived of the Beatific Vision, would be contradicted if man, after having been damned, could turn to what is opposed to damnation, i.e., to good, to God? For then, the **hope** of escaping from damnation would not be wholly excluded, and so damnation would not be damnation. Wouldn't the wills of the damned, therefore, have to remain obstinate (immutable) in their attachment to evil, just as the wills of the blessed remain confirmed in their attachment to good? The damned soul does not see God face to face so as to be fully content with possessing God, and can**not** therefore desire other things in appropriate subordination to God. Can it be said that it desires some other thing (or things) **as though** this thing were God Himself (mistakenly, to be sure), **as though** this thing were goodness itself, and so, as not lacking any good which might be sought elsewhere? Can it be said, thus, that its will is firmly fixed, as on its ultimate end, on something other than God, **as though** (but mistakenly) that thing were God Himself? And that this is why it remains immutable (obstinate) in its attachment to evil?

There are **other** reasons for the claim that the wills of damned souls must remain immutable (obstinate) in evil. **A first other reason.** The will of **any** human soul, argues Aquinas, becomes unchangeable as soon as the soul is separated from the body at death. That is, its will can no longer be changed, whether from adhering to good, or from adhering to evil. And this is so because during life, when its will could be changed, the soul was in a state resembling combat in war, in which it could have resisted evil, and with all its strength and determination, to avoid being conquered thereby; and/or

---

[25]   *Compendium Theologiae*, cap. 166, a princ. ad medium.

could have tried with equally great determination to free itself from evil. But, as soon as the soul is separated from the body at death, it is no longer in its prior war-like state. It is then in a quite different state, a state of receiving its reward for having adhered to good (when it could have adhered to evil), or its punishment for having adhered to evil (when it could have adhered to good). And so, it is no longer in a position in which it can change with respect to that to which it might adhere. The soul persists, therefore, in its adherence to good, or in its adherence to evil, whichever was the case as it was separated from the body at death.[26]

A second other reason. The blessedness which consists in the vision of God is **eternal;** so, too, the punishment which is due to mortal sin. But a soul can**not** be **eternally** blessed, if its will is not firmly set, and on the right end. Now, it would be possible for it to cease to be so set, if there were any possibility of its being diverted from its end. But, there cannot be any such possibility; for that would make impossible any enjoyment at all, let alone **eternal** enjoyment, of its right end, i.e., the vision of God. It is necessary, therefore, that its will be firmly set, and on the right end, **and forever,** so that it can never be **turned away from** that end, and thereupon be **turned toward** evil.[27] -- Similarly, a soul cannot be **eternally** wretched, unless its will is firmly set on evil, **and forever,** so that it can**not** be **turned away from** its adherence thereto, and thereupon be **turned toward** good.

A third other reason. Mortal sin is deserving of **eternal** punishment. Now the punishment of a damned soul could **not** be **eternal,** and at the same time **just or fair,** if such a soul could change its will so as to turn to what is good. For then, it would be possible for a soul with a good will to be condemned to eternal punishment. The will of a damned soul, therefore, cannot be changed so as to turn to what is good.[28]

A fourth other reason. The grace of God is necessary to move the will from sin to good. Now just as the souls of the good are **admitted into** full or

---

26   C.G., IV, cap. 92, in princ.
27   C.G., IV, cap. 92, paulum post princ.
28   C.G., IV, cap. 93, in princ.

total participation in God's goodness and grace, so too are the souls of the damned fully or totally **excluded from** God's goodness and grace. And so, they cannot move their wills from sin to good.[29]

A fifth other reason. Just as those who are good, while still living in the flesh, make **God** the end of all that they do and desire, so too those who are evil, while still in the flesh, make **something other than** God, the end of all that they do and desire. But, the souls of the good, on separation from the body at death, continue to adhere unchangeably to the end which they chose for themselves while still in the body -- **and just because they are good.** The souls of the wicked, therefore, will adhere unchangeably, after death, to the end which they selected for themselves, while still in the body -- **and just because they are wicked.** And so, just as the wills of those who were good in this life cannot be made wicked after death, so too the wills of those who were wicked in this life cannot be made good after death.[30]

The main point here, in considering the obstinacy of the wills of the damned with respect to evil, seems to be the following. A mortal sin is a **knowing** act of **eternal** rejection of the **eternal** God; a knowing act of preferring oneself, and/or something other than God (which are only **finitely** good, and **temporal**) to God Himself (who is **infinitely** good, and **eternal),** **coupled with the decision to cling to this preference forever.** To commit a mortal sin, therefore, though it might take but a brief time, is to do something which is **eternal** as well as temporal, to make a choice with an **eternal** dimension. It is to say: "God, I do not need you. I do not want you. I want no part of you -- not now, **not ever."** To commit a mortal sin, therefore, is to sin **with a willingness to remain in such sin forever, with a willingnesss to commit such sin over and over, endlessly.** It seems to be the case, therefore, that the souls of the damned remain obstinate in evil **simply because** they have **chosen** to remain obstinate in evil. -- Such a choice, such a willingness, must be respected by God, it is said by some, because God has endowed us with free will. But, say others, it is not very likely, let alone possible, that someone would make such a decision, a decision which is so obviously

---

29   *C.G.,* IV, cap. 93, ad finem.
30   *C.G.,* IV, cap. 93, in fine.

beyond all reason, so obviously beyond all sanity. Besides, God's love for us
is not so weak that He would allow us to make such a decision. But, again, is
there something wrong with the Divine Psychologist argument (see above
pp. 206-207)?

Heaven

What exactly is heaven, as Aquinas sees it?   Heaven is a place of reward in
which those who are both saved and blessed, unlike those who are saved **but
not yet blessed** (i.e., those in purgatory), enjoy ultimate happiness, perfect and
endless happiness. They see and love God face to face, and forever, without
any possibiliy, even the slightest, of loss, or even of diminishment.   There is
no pain, nor any fear of the remotest possibility of pain, whether the pain of
loss, or the pain of sense.   Pure, unending, unchangeable, perfectly possessed
happiness, which can never be lost, **both** because the wills of the blessed are
immutably fixed on God, **and** because God is imperishable.

Is there a heaven?

When one asks, Is there a hell?, one seems to get **two** opposed answers,
both based on scriptural grounds.   One can argue, as noted above (pp. 201-
202), that there cannot be a hell; or, if there is, that there cannot be anyone in
it.   For, God is our father, as Jesus Himself tells us.   And God's being our
father gives rise to the Divine Psychologist argument. --   But, one can also
argue that there **is** a hell.   For Jesus Himself says that there is, explicitly and
repeatedly.   And most emphatically and dramatically (see above pp. 202-203).

The question, Is there a heaven?, by way of contrast, gets but **one** answer,
namely, there **is** a heaven -- explicitly and repeatedly.   The words of Jesus
affirm the existence of **heaven** just as emphatically and dramatically as they
affirm the existence of **hell.**   And there are no complications arising from any
opposing arguments which could be seen as paralleling the Divine
Psychologist argument **against** the existence of **hell.** To the rich young man,

who had asked Jesus what he must do to inherit eternal life, in addition to keeping the ten commandments, He replied, "You are lacking in one thing. Go, sell what you have, and give to the poor, and you will have treasure in **heaven**; then, come follow me."[31]   During the sermon on the mount, at the end of the beatitudes, Jesus utters these encouraging words, "Blessed are you when they insult you and persecute you and utter every kind of evil against you, and falsely, because of me. Rejoice and be glad, for your reward will be great in **heaven**."[32] *Hebrews*, 11: 16, speaks of the ancients, Abel, Enoch, Noah, Abraham, Sarah, all of whom died in faith, and all of whom desired a better homeland, a **heavenly** one, which God has prepared for them. And there are words other than the word "heaven" used in the New Testament to refer to that place, for example, the place of "eternal life," the place of "glory," "my Father's house," where we shall be "with Christ," where we shall see God "face to face."

Heaven and happiness

Everybody, whether religious believer or not, agrees that **happiness** is what we all want, that it is the ultimate end for which we all strive, that happiness is that for the sake of which we do all that we do, and that there is nothing beyond happiness for the sake of which we might want happiness itself.   And religious believers, most though perhaps not all of them, agree that **perfect happiness** can be attained only in heaven.

But what exactly is happiness?   And what exactly is perfect happiness? In what does happiness consist?   In wealth, in honors, in fame or glory, in power, in some good of the body, in pleasure, in some good of the soul, in some created good?   In the uncreated good which is God Himself?

---

31   *St. Mark*, 10: 21.
32   *St. Matthew*, 5: 12.

Happiness

Happiness is man's **ultimate** end, or goal. Now, an end can be taken to be either **the thing itself** which we desire to attain, or the **attainment and enjoyment** of the thing desired. In the first way, **infinite goodness** is man's ultimate end; for **only** infinite goodness, i.e., something so good that it is impossible that there be something better, can **fully** satisfy man's will. And an end which does not fully satisfy cannot be the ultimate end. In the second way, man's ultimate end is the **attainment and enjoyment** of this fully satisfying end. Putting the two together, one can say, therefore, that to be happy is **to enjoy** (enjoying is **something we do**), having attained it, **that which is infinitely good** (the thing itself enjoyed).[33]

To be happy is **to do something**, emphasizes Aquinas; **to enjoy** is to perform some sort of operation or action. Now, there are two kinds of action. One kind begins in the agent and proceeds to something outward, e.g., to sculpt or to paint. Happiness cannot be this kind of action, since this kind is a perfection **of the outward object;** and happiness is, by way of difference, a perfection **of the agent**. The second kind not only begins in the agent, but also **remains in** the agent, i.e., is an **immanent** action, e.g., to feel, to understand, to will. Clearly, happiness is this kind of action, since this kind is a perfection **of the agent**. Happiness, therefore, is the **immanent action** of enjoying **what is infinitely good**.[34]

But, happiness does not consist in an act of seeing with the eye, or hearing with the ear, or in any other act of sensation, even though such acts are **immanent** actions. For irrational animals have sensitive operations in common with us, yet they do not have happiness in common with us. In addition, **what is infinitely good,** which is the thing attained when we achieve happiness, cannot be a **sensible** good. Nothing sensible can be infinitely good.

---

33   *S.T.,* I-II, q. 3, a. 1, c.
34   *S.T.,* I-II, q. 3, a. 2; especially obj. 3 and ad 3.

Nonetheless, acts of sensation can and do belong to happiness, in a certain way. To explain, observes Aquinas, an operation can be connected with happiness in three ways: 1) as something which belongs to it essentially, or 2) as something which precedes and accompanies it, or 3) as something which follows and accompanies it. Clearly, acts of sensation cannot belong to happiness essentially, for man's happiness consists essentially in being united to what is infinitely good, i.e., to God, the uncreated good; and acts of sensation cannot achieve such a uniting. They can, however, belong to happiness as something which precedes and accompanies. That is, they can be a part of the **imperfect** happiness which we can have **in this life,** since the operations of our intellect require previous and accompanying sensory activity. Acts of sensation can also belong to happiness as something which follows and accompanies. And this is what happens in the **perfect** happiness which will be ours **after this life** in heaven. For, after the resurrection of the body, the body and all the bodily senses will receive a certain overflow of happiness from the happiness of the soul (as noted above on pp. 156-161, especially pp. 160-161),[35] and thereby be perfected in their operations. But the operation itself by which man's mind is united to **what is infinitely good,** i.e., to God, depends in no way on the senses. And so, in **perfect** happiness the **entire** man is perfected, the lower part of his nature being perfected by a kind of overflow from the higher.[36]

In man's higher nature, we find both intellect and will, and the operation of both is needed for happiness; but each in a different way. The **essence** of happiness consists in an act of the intellect, by which **what is infinitely good** is attained and made present to us. This is followed by an act of the will, which rests in, thereby delighting in, that end when attained by the intellect. The **act of resting and delighting in** is a **proper accident** following on the **act of**

---

[35]   The discussion above centered on certain **qualities** of the resurrected **bodies** of the blessed, those who are enjoying **eternal happiness,** i.e., impassibility, subtlety, agility, and clarity, which are felicitous, happiness-causing , effects bestowed on these bodies by a kind of **perfecting** overflow from the happiness of the glorified souls. The glorified body is **completely and perfectly** in the overflowing power of the glorified soul; perfectly dominated by it, embraced by it, loved by it; and thereby rendered a **happy** body.

[36]   *S.T.,* I-II, q. 3, a. 3, c.; and ad 3.

attaining and making present; just as risible is a proper accident of man following on rational, which belongs to man's essence.[37]

Now, it is clear that one cannot delight in something good, unless he has it in his possession, either really, or in hope, or in memory.   Thus, possession must precede delight.   Possession is one kind of act; delight is quite another kind.   Possession makes present; delight rests in and enjoys what has been made present.   Yet, both go together.   That is, whenever one is there, the other must also be there; one as the cause, the other as the effect.   Possession is the cause, delight is the effect.   The relations here parallel the relations between any essence and its proper accidents.[38]   For example, if a figure is a plane figure bounded by three straight lines (the essence of triangle), it is also, and necessarily, a plane figure with any of its exterior angles equal to the sum of the opposite interior angles (proper accident).   And, if a figure is a plane figure with any of its exterior angles equal to the sum of the opposite interior angles (proper accident), it is also, and nesessarily, a plane figure bounded by three straight lines (esence).   The essence is the cause; the proper accident, a ncesssarily following effect.   If the one, then also the other.   To be happy is to possess (by intellect) the ultimate good, and thereupon (by the will) to delight in it.   And the other way around, to be happy is to delight in the ultimate good, which one has come to possess.

The **essence** of happiness, as noted above (p. 220), consists in an act of the intellect, by which **what is infinitely good** is attained and made present to us. Clearly, this is an act of the **speculative or theoretical** intellect, and not of the practical intellect.   For, first of all, the practical intellect, in attaining and making something present to us, does that by being, in some way, the **productive** cause of that thing.   But, **what is infinitely good,** i.e., God, is not something which can be produced, even by infinite power, let alone by the **finite** power of man's intellect.   To explain a bit.   Man's happiness is an operation.   It must, therefore, be man's highest operation, i.e., the operation of his highest power with respect to its highest object.   Man's highest power is the intellect, whose highest object is God's essence.   But God'e essence cannot

---

[37]   *S.T.,* I-II, q. 3, a. 4, c.
[38]   *S.T.,* I-II, q. 2, a. 6, c.

be known in a practical way, not even by God Himself. For God's essence is not something producible. Man's happiness, therefore, consists in the speculative apprehension, i.e., in the contemplation, of the essence of God.[39] Secondly, contemplation, the act of the speculative intellect, is sought for its own sake, and not for the sake of something in some way beyond it; whereas the act of the practical intellect is sought not for its own sake, but for the sake of something else, i.e., some action ordained to some further end. Man's **last** end, therefore, cannot consist in an act of the practical intellect; for then it would be a last end which is not a last end.[40]

Though happiness consists in an act of the **speculative** intellect, it cannot be the case that happiness, i.e., **perfect** happiness, consists **essentially** in the considerations of the speculative **sciences,** i.e., in knowing what can be known by the speculative sciences. For, what can be known by a speculative science does not extend beyond the scope of the principles of that science; since **the whole** of the science is contained in the power of its principles. Now, the first principles of the speculative sciences are received through the senses. And this is why what we know in the speculative sciences cannot extend further than the knowledge of sensible things can take us.   But man cannot be fully perfected if his knowledge is limited in this way. For, beyond sensible things there are the separate substances, i.e., the angels and God. And though the angels and God can be known **in some way** through our knowledge of sensible things, they can be known only **as the causes** of these sensible things, and not **as they are in themselves,** i.e., not as to **what** they are. Perfect happiness consists essentially in knowing the intellect's appropriate objects as they are in **themselves.** It follows, therefore, that man's happiness cannot consist in knowing what can be known in the speculative sciences.[41]

But, this does not mean that man's happiness consists in contemplating the angels, i.e., in knowing **them** as they are **in themselves.** For the proper formal object of the intellect is truth **in its fullness.** Now the angels have **truth** only by participation (not in its fullness), since they, like all created

---

39   *S.T.*, I-II, q. 3, a. 5, c., in princ.
40   *S.T.*, I-II, q. 3, a. 5, c., in medio.
41   *S.T.*, I-II, q. 3, a. 6 c.

things, have **being** only by participation (not in its fullness). The contemplation of whatever has truth by particpation cannot perfect the intellect with its ultimate or final perfection. Only that which is truth **by its essence** can do that. And such a thing can be only that which is being **by its essence.** Nonetheless, it is certainly the case that there would be a certain sort of **imperfect** happiness in contemplating the angels; and, though imperfect, this happiness would be more perfect than the happiness achieved by knowing **all that can be known** in the speculative sciences.[42]

It should be easy, now, to see that man's final and perfect happiness consists in nothing other than the vision of the Divine Essence. Two things must be considered, observes Aquinas, to make this clear. The first is that man cannot be perfectly happy so long as something remains for him to desire and seek; the second, that the perfection of any power is determined by the nature of its object. Since the object of the intellecct is the truth about **what things are,** i.e., about the **essence** of things; it is clear that the intellect attains perfection to the extent that, in knowing a thing, it knows the **essence** of that thing. If, then, the intellect knows the essence of something which is known to be **an effect,** and cannot thereby come to know the **essence** of the **cause,** but only **that there must be a cause;** there remains the desire to come to know the **essence** of that cause. This desire initiates an inquiry which will not cease until there is **full** knowledge of the **essence** of that cause.

Thus, when the human intellect, having come to know the essence of some created thing, knows about God **only** that **He exists (as the cause** of that created thing), the intellect has not yet reached its full perfection, since there remains in it a natural desire to come to know God with respect to **what God is,** and not simply as the cause of the created thing. And so, it is not yet perfectly happy. But, once it has come to know what God is, it is perfectly happy, because it then knows an essence which neither is, nor can be, the effect of any prior cause. To know **what God is,** is to know something beyond which there neither is, nor can be, anything else. To know **what God is,** is to be in possession of what is infinitely, unsurpassably, good. Man's will,

---

42   *S.T.,* I-II, q. 3, a. 7, c.

therefore, comes to rest in it, and delights in it. And there is no desire for anything further. There **is** nothing further. There can**not** be anything further.[43]

It should be clear, therefore, that man's ultimate happiness does not, cannot, consist in wealth, or in honors received from men, or in fame, or in the glory given by men, or in power. Neither can it consist in any bodily good, or in some good of the soul, or in having friends, or in any created good. Man's ultimate happiness consists in God, and God alone.[44] To be sure, the above mentioned goods are in various ways connected to man's happiness, but **only** to the **imperfect** sort of happiness which man can have **in this life.**

No eye has seen

It is difficult, indeed impossible, **to understand** exactly what the happiness of heaven is, let alone **to imagine** what it is. Imagining it is impossible, because it is not something at the level of sensation. Understanding it, too, is impossible, because of the lowliness and weakness of the human intellect, even though it is by our intellect that we will attain the object of our happiness, i.e., the essence of God. We can describe it in various ways, and at great length (something of the length to which human description of it can go, appears just above, on pp. 216-220). But these descriptions, however lengthy, however detailed, and from however many points of view, can never convey exactly what it is that the blessed in heaven experience.

We can say that the happiness of heaven is perfect life with the Most Holy Trinity, a sharing in the life and the love of the Persons of the Blessed Trinity, a sharing in it with the Virgin Mary, with the angels, with the saints, a sharing which completely fills the deepest longings of the hearts of men.

---

[43] *S.T.*, I-II, q. 3, a. 8, c.

[44] For specific and detailed arguments with respect to wealth, honors, fame, etc., see *S.T.*, I-II, q. 2, all eight articles. Questions 3 and 4, too, present many details with respect to **other things** which one might want to consider in their connection with happiness.

The happiness of heaven, we can say, is to be absorbed into God, but without losing one's individual identity, indeed finding thereby one's true identity. The happiness of heaven, we can say, is to be incorporated into the blessed community of all who have believed in Christ and have faithfully done His will. Whatever we say about it, however, leaves it still something beyond all human understanding and description. And this is why the Scriptures speak of it in various images,[45] which tell us as much as we are capable of understanding about it (which is very little, indeed). These images are nothing but **distant hints** about what the happiness of heaven **is like,** and **never** about what **it actually is.** Some of these images: life, light, glory, peace, a wedding feast, a banquet, eating bread and drinking wine, enjoying God's company and conversation, the kingdom, reigning with Christ, the Father's house, our mansions, paradise, the heavenly Jerusalem, friendship, seeing God face to face, the joy of a just married bride and groom. This is why, no doubt, St. Paul (*I Cor.*, 2: 9-10) wrote **this** about the happiness of heaven, i.e., that "no eye has seen, nor ear heard, nor the heart of man conceived, what God has prepared for those who love Him."[46]

---

[45] As always, and in all things, we humans can **understand** only by depending in various ways on **images.** All our intellectual activity is body-bound, first of all to the senses, and thereupon to the imagination. Though intellectual activity is **not performed** by the senses or by the imagination, it cannot proceed without depending on them. They make present to consciousness the **individuals** whose common or shared features the intellect discerns, and through which it understands.

[46] *Catechism of the Catholic Church,* paragraphs 1024-1029.

INDEX

of Christ 113-114

Spiration 79, 82-84, 85

St. Paul 33, 35, 38-41, 50

St. Peter 33, 35, 37-38, 43-44, 46-48
as Barjonas 43, 47
as Rock (Petrus) 44, 47

Substance
Conversion in the Eucharist
167-184
Substance and God 78

Suffering 119-138
and Purgatory 201-204
Argument from Evil 133-139
See also *Pain*
Suffering of God 120-132
Achievements of God's
Suffering 122-124
Suffering of Man 133-139

Tacitus, Publius Cornelius 142

Theology 19, 22

Trinity 71-87
as Four Relations 76-80
as Two Processions 72-76
Five Notions 84-87
Not known by Natural
Reason 71-72
Three Persons 80-84

Truth
Philosophical 26-27
Revealed 30, 35,
Theological 28-29
Understanding 51

Veritas Divina (Divine Truth)
13-14

Virgin Mary 168, 171, 225

Virtue
and Religion 53-59

Wine
See *Eucharist*

Wisdom
the Man of Wisdom 29-32

Words
of Consecration 185-194